TE

3-

D0680455

Two Fronts, One War

Two Fronts, One War
This edition published in 2014 by Frontline Books,
an imprint of Pen & Sword Books Ltd,
47 Church Street, Barnsley, S. Yorkshire, S70 2AS
www.frontline-books.com

Copyright © Charles Sasser, 2014

The right of Charles Sasser to be identified as the author of this work
has been asserted by him in accordance with the
Copyright, Designs and Patents Act 1988.

ISBN: 978-1-84832-727-6

All rights reserved. No part of this publication may be reproduced, stored in
or introduced into a retrieval system, or transmitted, in any form, or by any
means (electronic, mechanical, photocopying, recording or otherwise)
without the prior written permission of the publisher. Any person who does
any unauthorized act in relation to this publication may be liable
to criminal prosecution and civil claims for damages.

CIP data records for this title are available from the British Library

For more information on our books, please visit
www.frontline-books.com, email info@frontline-books.com
or write to us at the above address.

Printed and bound by CPI Group (UK) Ltd, Croydon CR0 4YY

Typeset in 11.2/13.8 point Adobe Jenson Pro

Two Fronts, One War

Dramatic Eyewitness Accounts of Major Events
in the European and Pacific Theaters of Operations
on Land, Sea and Air in WWII

Charles W. Sasser

Foreword by

Michael Stephenson

Frontline Books
London

Contents

Plates and Maps

Plates

Maps

Foreword

THEY ARE DEAD NOW, SO MANY OF THEM—most of them. The story-tellers, the myth-makers, those who made history magical, those who could light the fuse to the whole wondrous pyrotechnical past. Those who had lived the story of the Second World War.

Among them were my parents and uncles and aunts and their friends, all of whom had served—and if not served, experienced—the single most momentous event of the last century (perhaps of any century so far in human history). To try and underline somehow its immensity by trotting out the statistics in lives lost and the other metrics of human suffering, is to indulge in a kind of *Guinness Book of World Records* display that diminishes, vulgarizes in a way, the enormity of that experience. Josef Stalin, a thug and mass-murderer of remarkable talent, said that the death of one person was a tragedy; the death of millions merely a statistic. He knew what he was talking about, having contributed to both ends of the equation.

I was born in 1946 and so my childhood was filled with stories of the war. Both my parents had been in the (British) forces. My mother lied about her age (she was seventeen) in order to enlist in the Auxiliary Territorial Service, then the women's branch of the British Army. My father fought in France and was evacuated at the time of Dunkirk, went to Africa and fought with Montgomery, and finally ended his service in Italy. An American uncle, spoken of as someone exotic and handsome, had been killed flying as a waist gunner in a B-17G of the 338th Bomb Group over Posen in April 1944. Another uncle had been captured by the Japanese when Singapore fell and had spent years enjoying the very tender mercies of his captors (he returned home at war's end weighing in at 80 pounds). Another uncle had had his eardrums blown out as a paratrooper, the deafness forever exiling him to another world. They told stories and stories were told about them. This was not the anorexic tweeting of 140 characters but long homeric sessions in front of a roaring fire, quite often invigorated with a glass (or two) of Scotch, and always fired up with the luminousness of their memories and the generosity of sharing with me—all ears and wide eyes—the extraordinary odyssey they had lived through.

I'm not saying it was necessarily the most accurate history in the world. At times it could be a bit Technicolor, shall we say. But perhaps that wasn't the point. We are dealing here with how a heroic mythology is passed on from one generation to the next. And the intention was to convey the victory that was found in the suffering and the struggle as vibrantly and powerfully as possible, because it is a narrative designed to inspire. It was also, by the way, intended to point out the differences between good and evil as emphatically as they knew how. I went on to study and sometimes question the history they mythologized (to their considerable irritation) but I guess that's what happens, generation after generation.

Now I look back and remember those versions of history, unencumbered by irony or moral relativism. There was a directness, an honesty, that I now find deeply moving. They certainly did not have a sophisticated understanding of the Big Picture (after all, do we?) but they believed that there could be justice and compassion in the world. That sacrifice, hardship, loss, grief—often scouring and terrible—was the price demanded if we were to live not in a perfect world, but in an immeasurably better one than that envisaged by the steely-eyed visionaries of the Third Reich or Imperial Japan.

They believed that thuggery, brutality, and contempt for human life and dignity, no matter how seemingly all-powerful and brilliantly packaged, could be beaten by decent people. I think of those narcissistic SS officers or the preposterous Il Duce poncing about in their ridiculously ballooning riding breeches and polished high boots, like something out of an *opera buffa* (except irredeemably vicious and not at all funny). And I think of my father and my father-in-law and my uncles in their baggy khakis and clunky old boots, so anti-chic, so laughably uncool. And how they, in their ill-fitting uniforms, kicked the Fascist fashionistas from here to the gallows and the grave.

Charles W. "Chuck" Sasser is heir to that inspirational story-telling tradition. He brings things back—old and precious things—and revivifies them with powerful narrative energy. He rehydrates history with an eye for vibrant detail and an ear for the true voice of those who were there. The histories he tells have been drawn from the men and women who lived the war: soldiers who fought in Europe and the Pacific, as well as flyers and seamen, nurses and medics, from every phase and every theater in which the Allies fought. He has interviewed many for the first time and has taken their stories in order to retell them with all the well-honed skill that comes with writing over forty fiction and non-fiction books. The result is pungent and punchy, sometimes profane and often profound, foursquare and forthright: a book informed by a great deal of research and a reverence for its material.

Two Fronts, One War reflects the sturdy and straightforward moral world of those who are celebrated and memorialized here. But this is not to patronize them, for they were capable of powerful expression. My deafened paratrooper uncle dealt with his exile by writing poetry. He was not an educated man, nor an easy one, but he needed to express his passionate life. Chuck Sasser recounts the finding of a photograph that had once belonged to a Marine, in all probability killed on Iwo Jima. Part of the tragic detritus of the battlefield, it is from his woman (wife, girlfriend, we don't know), and on the back was written, "Every moment has its unbelievable moment." It is a profound expression of complex simplicity. So much remembered and anticipated joy is distilled into that one line, and so much heartbreak was waiting for the woman who wrote it.

Two Fronts, One War is certainly not muddied by irony or moral relativism. It is filled with action, heroism, endurance and thrilling derring-do. It is full-on and unapologetic. The good guys say things like "screw the whole lot of you kraut eaters," or "*Banzai* that, asshole," prior to sending their foes as directly to hell as an M1 Garand could facilitate. This perhaps will offend those of a tender post-modern sensibility. The rest of us will cheer, because the good guys won and the bad guys didn't. End of story.

Michael Stephenson

Michael Stephenson is a former editor of the Military Book Club and is the author of *The Last Full Measure: How Soldiers Die in Battle* and *Patriot Battles: How the War of Independence was Fought.*

For the Greatest Generation

Introduction

IF WE DISCARD THE ARGUMENT that the Second World War was actually an extension of the First World War and the revolutions and civil wars of the early twentieth century, then the first European victim of the Second World War was likely an unknown common criminal from one of Adolf Hitler's concentration camps. On the evening of 31 August 1939, Hitler's SS dragged him from his cell, forced him to don a Polish soldier's uniform, shot him, and dumped his body near the radio station in the German frontier town of Gleiwitz as evidence of a "Polish attack" that justified the German invasion of Poland.

What followed was the most destructive conflict in world history. Cities, nations and continents were razed. Millions of people (estimates vary from 60 to 100 million) perished in the 2,433 days from the German invasion of Poland in September 1939 until VE-Day in May 1945 and Japan's official surrender on 2 September 1945. "Body counts," so enormous as to be humanly uncountable, testify to the detached and impersonal nature of the war. The largest numbers of those slain, whether combatants or civilians, died anonymously, unknown except to those few who might have been waiting for them at home.

Often in our historical preoccupation with numbers and statistics, with grand strategies and the sweep of armies, with the goings-on of generals, politicians and dictators, we neglect to realize that war involves real human beings with individual dreams, ambitions and lives. War, as combat veterans understand, is the story of individuals caught up in and painted against a broader tapestry of overwhelming events.

Two Fronts, One War strives to look at the fronts of the Second World War from a dual viewpoint. First, the "Big Picture" lays the larger historical foundation: war in Europe or war in Asia and the Pacific; the invasions of North Africa, Italy and France; aerial, armor, and sea campaigns . . .

What might be called the fronts of the "Small Picture" zooms down to soldiers, airmen, Marines, and sailors whose blood-and-guts, mud-and-shit energy collectively and individually propelled the war: of bomber pilots shot down over enemy territory; dogfaces fighting to gain a toehold on Normandy; men struggling for survival on the Bataan Death March; tankers pushing through Germany; airmen who flew B-29s over Japan's mainland . . .

The Big Picture is about strategies and tactics, decisions and blunders, big defeats and glorious victories. The Little Picture is about incredible feats of heroism and self-sacrifice, devotion to duty, courage, fear, loyalty, and even of great wartime romances . . .

I interviewed more than two dozen U.S. Second World War veterans for the stories in this work, both from the European fronts and from the fronts of Asia-Pacific in order to provide a complete view of a single war with two main fronts. Most of these stories have never been published before they were related to the author. Together, they provide a true and dramatic account of what the war was really like, from the Big Picture and from the Small Picture, of a horrifyingly cruel period of history that changed the world for ever.

Charles W. Sasser

Chapter 1

Japanese Victories

IN THE HALF-LIGHT OF DAWN on Sunday, 7th December 1941, 396 Japanese bombers, torpedo bombers, dive bombers, and fighters penetrated a light cloud haze 250 miles north of Hawaii and set course for Pearl Harbor. The bomber leader, Commander Mitsuo Fuchida, tuned in on the American FM radio station at Honolulu and switched on his direction finder. The station was playing Big Band dance music, interrupted by a weather report that predicted breaks in the clouds and greater visibility by sunup.

The United States was less than two hours away from war.

Japan had had imperial fancies at least since its annexing of Taiwan in 1895 and Korea in 1910. The catastrophic Great Depression that began in 1929 swept the world and provided an excuse for Japan to embark on a military expansion in Asia that would provide it with much-needed natural resources like oil, iron, tin, rubber, and other commodities and allow it to establish a "Greater East Asia Co-Prosperity Sphere" to make the island nation both self-sufficient and a power to be reckoned with.

As Japan's armies spread out into China and bumped up hard against Russia, Emperor Hirohito's generals and admirals began to look south to the rich oil-fields and minerals in the old empires of the British, French, Dutch, and Americans in southeast Asia and the Pacific islands. Relations with the United States deteriorated as Japan's great naval power threatened American domination of the Pacific.

In September 1940, Japan signed the Tripartite Pact with Germany and Italy, which confirmed between the three of them that Europe lay within the sphere of a New World Order to be constructed by Hitler and Mussolini while Japan was left free to spread its own influence in eastern Asia. All three countries pledged to come to each other's aid in the event one was attacked by an outside party not already engaged in the war.

All through 1941, even though Germany had already conquered Poland, Norway, France, the Balkans, and other nations, most Americans felt that the war across the Atlantic affected no vital American interest. In addition to not being prepared psychologically for war, the nation was also not equipped militarily or industrially. Only something major or catastrophic could entice the American public to support anything other than "helping friends," and only then under conditions short of war.

Japan's leaders concluded that war across thousands of miles of Pacific Ocean would be almost impossible for their political enemies to conduct. Britain was barely hanging on against Hitler in Europe and Africa, and could resist but little in Asia. The Dutch were already beaten. General Hideki Tojo, Japan's prime minister from mid-October 1941, argued that America didn't have the will to fight. Besides, it would take months before the Americans were able to float a navy capable of taking on the great Imperial Fleet. By that time, Japan would have carved out its Pacific empire and reinforced its walls.

Admiral Isoroku Yamamoto, commander of the Japanese Combined Fleet, was wary about tugging on the eagle's tail feathers. He knew America's economic potential well, having attended Harvard University and served later in Washington as Japanese naval attaché. Only by a devastating surprise attack, he argued, could Japan hope to kick the United States out of the equation.

"In the first twelve months of war with the United States and Britain, I will run wild and win victory after victory," he predicted. "After that . . . I have no expectations of success."

Tojo agreed it would have to be a surprise attack, starting with Pearl Harbor. Simultaneous with the treacherous attack against Pearl Harbor, Japanese forces would ambush Siam to score a base of operations against Malaya, Burma, and Singapore; would seize the American islands of Guam and Wake and the British Gilbert Islands to block American sea routes to the Philippines; and, finally, would capture Hong Kong and invade the Philippines.

The plan all depended on the destruction of the American fleet with one mighty blow.

In retrospect, President Franklin Roosevelt and his military commanders, advisors, and intelligence experts should have whiffed the stench of conspiracy in the air. There were certainly sufficient clues to warn them of Japanese intentions. Instead, no effective preparations for defense had been made in Hawaii. Neither Washington nor military commanders at Pearl Harbor were aware of the Japanese task force that set sail under Vice Admiral Chuichi Nagumo on 18th November 1941 for the 1,000-mile trek to the Kuriles and, continuing from there, another 4,000 miles to a jumping-off point north of Hawaii.

The task force consisted of six aircraft carriers with 396 warplanes, two battleships, two heavy cruisers, one light cruiser, eight destroyers, three tankers, and a supply ship. The only U.S. reconnaissance planes in the area on 7th

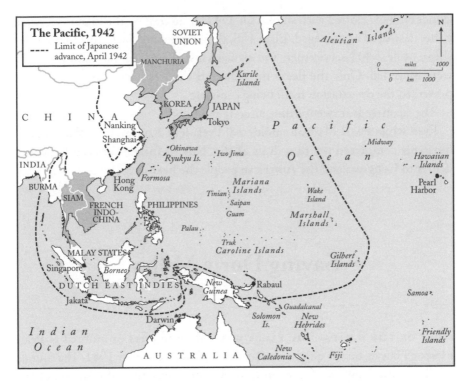

The Pacific, 1942
- - - - Limit of Japanese advance, April 1942

December were patrolling far to the southwest towards the Marshall Islands.

An hour and a half after the Japanese air armada lifted off from Admiral Nagumo's carriers, Commander Fuchida spotted the northern tip of Oahu. He reported ten American battleships, a heavy cruiser, ten light cruisers, and several destroyers tied up in port like ducks on a pond.

At 0749, Fuchida transmitted a pre-arranged radio message: "*Tora! Tora! Tora!*" ("Tiger! Tiger! Tiger!"). This code told Nagumo that surprise had been achieved and that the attack was a go.

The first wave of 183 Japanese warplanes buzzed in like giant bees, unleashing flame and black smoke that immediately enveloped most of the harbor. Battlewagon U.S.S. *Oklahoma* was the first to roll over and sink, trapping more than 400 sailors to die deep within its hull. Battleship *Arizona* blew up in a massive explosion, killing more than 1,000 men.

Parts of Fuchida's force peeled off to strike the U.S. Army Air Force bases at Hickam Field, Wheeler Field, and the Naval Air Station at Ford Island. A U.S. Army Catholic chaplain preparing for an open-air Sunday Mass seized a nearby machinegun and, resting it on his altar, was the first man at Hickam Field to fight back.

The second wave of aircraft zoomed in at 0850 hours to mop up. By 0945, the enemy had disappeared as quickly as they appeared. The sky was clear of clouds but now clotted with smoke. Of 394 U.S. aircraft on the island, 347 were either destroyed or damaged. Eight U.S. ships were sunk, including four battleships, while 2,403 servicemen and civilians lost their lives and another 1,143 were wounded. Only the fleet's three aircraft carriers having been out to sea prevented the devastation from being complete.

The Japanese lost twenty-nine aircraft and pilots.

Even while Pearl Harbor smoldered, President Roosevelt in Washington hurriedly completed the first draft of the "Day of Infamy" speech he would deliver to Congress and the American people the next day.

* * *

Saving Dorie Miller

MOST OF THE U.S. PACIFIC FLEET was tied up to piers or moored at Pearl Harbor, Hawaii, on the quiet, warm evening of 6th December 1941. The sounds of "Battleship Row" were soothing and familiar over the calm waters of the harbor—the gentle flapping of halyards and lines, the slow rise and fall of warships against their docks, an occasional "All Hands" announced from a PA system, laughter and shouts from the docks as sailors in dress whites took off for a night on the town in Honolulu.

Quartermaster Striker Arles Cole, 17, and his buddy, a 21-year-old mess attendant with the unlikely name of Doris "Dorie" Miller, left the battlewagon U.S.S. *West Virginia* (BB-48) and went ashore for liberty, joking and scuttlebutting like all young seamen excited about a few hours' freedom in a "foreign" port. Miller had met a "wahini" who had a girlfriend. Enough said.

"You smell like a Hong Kong whorehouse," the cook chided his young friend.

"What does that smell like?"

Miller laughed. "You."

Miller should have known. He was an "old salt" who had sailed the seas since 1939 when he enlisted in the U.S. Navy as a mess attendant. Few other ratings were available at the time for black men. He had pulled a tour aboard the battleship U.S.S. *Nevada* before transferring to the West Virginia.

At five-nine and 235 pounds, a hundred pounds heavier than Cole, he was dubbed "the Raging Bull" when he played high school football in Waco, Texas. He had since acquired notoriety as "the Fighting Cook," the fleet's heavyweight boxing champ.

Cole, skinny and white, reported to Pearl Harbor for duty in August 1941. He had grown up poor during the Great Depression on a hardscrabble farm in the community of Starrvilla near the little country town of Porum in eastern Oklahoma, a land and time John Steinbeck wrote about in *The Grapes of Wrath*. Starrvilla was named after the famous lady outlaw Belle Starr, whose family still lived in the vicinity.

The Great Depression-era bandit, Pretty Boy Floyd—or "Purty Boy" to the country folk—had continued the Oklahoma "Owlhoot" tradition by supposedly "robbing from the rich to give to the poor." Every old barn or shed in eastern Oklahoma carried with it a story of how Pretty Boy once hid in it to elude "the law." When "the law" finally gunned him down, people came in wagons and old trucks from all over the country to attend his funeral up in Sequoyah County.

Like many Americans, Arles's folks were immigrants, his mother's people from Ireland and his dad's from England. The Irish Nicholsons, his mother's folks, traveled by covered wagon into Indian Territory from near Springfield, Arkansas, in 1896. Lucy Nicholson was born at a camp just inside Indian Territory.

Albert Cole, whose parents migrated from England and found their way to the Indian Nation, was born that same year. Both families settled on log cabin farms near Porum. Albert Cole and Lucy Nicholson married in 1914 when they were both seventeen.

Albert shipped overseas in 1918 to fight in the First World War. Arles was named after an ancient town in southern France where his dad's outfit staged preparatory to moving up into combat.

Rural Americans in the 1930s received their news by battery-powered radios, since few country households had electricity. Newscasts blared constantly about how the United States was next if the Germans continued their quest for power. In bursts of patriotism, young men from all over the nation were enlisting in the armed forces. Arles's older brother ran off and enlisted in the Army in early 1940. Arles joined the Navy on 31st December 1940, only days after his seventeenth birthday, hitchhiking ninety miles to the recruiting station in Tulsa to sign up.

It was late that fateful night when Cole and Miller returned to *West Virginia* after an evening running the strip of cheap bars and "gyp joints" that lined the beaches. It was actually Sunday morning, 7th December. Dorie Miller's "wahini" arrangement hadn't worked out, so the two swabs settled for the saloons and strip joints. No one in town paid much attention to "legal age" when it came to U.S. sailors with money to burn.

Miller straggled below to rack out in crew quarters. Cole crashed in the pilot's house located in the superstructure above the main deck, which was his normal duty station. Still wearing liberty whites, he looked out over the harbor where ships' mooring lights dotted the darkness. He dozed off in the captain's chair.

Neither of the young seamen foresaw the Rising Sun lurking over the horizon. Events were about to transpire that would change their lives for ever.

Cloudy gray dawn seeping through the pilot's house windows awoke Cole. Stiff from the chair, he yawned, stretched, and poured himself a cup of black coffee from the pot always kept hot by the quartermaster watch.

"You look like hell, Cole," the Chief quartermaster said. "No more liberty for you, boy, until you're old enough to change your own diapers."

Cole grinned sheepishly and stepped outside on the open deck to sip his coffee. The water was almost flat and, reflecting the broken cloud cover, as gray as the warships in the half-light. He was standing there, leaning on the rail and contemplating going below for a shower and clean dungarees before chow, when loudspeakers on *West Virginia* and every other ship in port suddenly began clamoring in unison. Amplified voices thundered and crashed from ship to ship, jolting sailors out of their racks before they were fully awake. Cole's coffee cup dropped from numbed fingers.

"General Quarters! General Quarters! All hands! This is not a drill. Repeat! This is not a drill."

Cole heard it first—a high-pitched buzzing that seemed to come from all over. Like hornets in the nest he and his brother poked out of a tree one day down by the creek. Buzzing became a loud drone, and then the sky seemed to shriek.

Clouds appeared to split open to reveal swarms of apparently hostile aircraft. Rays of pale sunshine illuminated the huge red suns on their fuselages as they screamed in low. Bombers and fighters and all sizes in between. Hundreds of them.

Bombs began exploding, geysering water and metal and fuel and blood. Flickering machinegun fire ripped into sleeping ships. A column of water from a near miss erupted alongside *West Virginia* and sprayed into the ship's tall superstructure, drenching Cole. The bay, flat and calm moments before, now churned from the assault.

The reverberating growling of aircraft engines and the jolting thunder of explosions caused mass chaos. *West Virginia* rolled and seemed to hunch against the impact of bombs and torpedoes. Fires broke out. Black smoke wreathed through damaged warships, oozed among twisted and tangled dockside cranes, and crept into structures riddled with bullet holes and explosions.

West Virginia shuddered mightily as what was later determined to be a torpedo from a Japanese midget submarine penetrated its hull below the waterline, almost knocking Arles Cole off his feet. Sucking smoke into his lungs, coughing, eyes tearing, he fled the pilot's house and fought his way through the turmoil down to the main deck and then to the nearest hatch where he plunged into the bowels of the vessel. His designated battle station lay four decks below with the chip's command element in the alternate control nerve center.

He experienced raw terror for the first time in his young life. Bile burnt the back of his throat and his tongue stuck to the roof of his mouth. All around him, running sailors, jarred out of their bunks, many wearing only their skivvies, jammed smoky passageways and ladders as they stampeded to their own GQ battle stations. He glimpsed sailors bleeding or with their hair singed. He heard yelling and screaming. Smoke from burning fuel oil and explosions clotted his nostrils and cut his vision.

Frightened, disoriented, dazed by the suddenness of the attack, it was all he could do to maintain footing. The big battlewagon convulsed with each impact of bomb or torpedo, knocking Cole off balance and slamming him repeatedly off bulkheads and into other sailors. It was like the ship was battling a hurricane at sea. By the time he reached the third deck below, the ship was listing hard to port, taking on water from the torpedo hit suffered at the beginning.

He made his way unsteadily along the center passageway that ran nearly the full length of the warship. Traffic had thinned to only a stray crewmember here and there. The deck was so slanted that he had to walk with his hands pressed against bulkheads in a near-pushup posture. A few more degrees of list and he would actually be *walking* on the bulkheads. The sound and feeling below decks was like being trapped in a tin can being shaken in the fist of a giant.

"She's going down!" a fleeting shadow screamed as it appeared out of the smoke and then disappeared.

Cole willed himself not to panic. Training dictated that he report to his battle station as quickly as possible. On a warship, every man's life depended on fellow seamen all doing their jobs.

What the young QM striker couldn't know from his limited perspective was the extent of the damage already inflicted not only upon his ship but also upon the rest of the hapless fleet. U.S.S. *Oklahoma* had snapped its mooring lines and rolled completely over to stab its masts into the bottom of the bay, drowning many of its crew. The *Arizona* was also sinking after bombs exploding in its main magazine cooked off ammunition that blew out the battleship's fantail. Several cruisers and destroyers were coughing up billows of smoke and riding low in the water.

Below decks on *West Virginia*, lights dimmed and blinked on and off as generators became waterlogged and began to shut down. Seawater gushed through ragged holes torn into the vessel's hull. Passageways were flooding. Oily saltwater swished around Cole's ankles, rapidly rising to his knees as he took a ladder deeper to the fourth level below where the alternate control center was located.

Every instinct raged at him to run for his life.

The lights flickered one last gasp, then quit, plunging the depths of the wounded ship into darkness more complete than anything Cole had ever known. Cold water lapping up around his waist froze his insides. The thud of falling bombs and exploding torpedoes shook the vessel with savage persistence and sloshed around the water trapped inside with him.

He had never felt so alone. He cried out against the blackness, but there was no answer. Finally, his survival instincts took over and he sought a way out of the trap he had entered. He began making his way to starboard and away from the heaviest portside flooding, crossing amidships on slanted footing, feeling his way hand by hand in the darkness while water continued to rise.

He found his escape routes blocked; all the watertight doors were dogged, according to drill. Anyone caught below decks was imprisoned in a dark, watery hell. As his desperation grew, his thoughts turned to home.

His mother always concluded her letters to him with, "Arles, your dad and I are praying for you."

If he ever needed prayer, it was now.

He was beginning to think all was lost when, suddenly, the ship bucked underneath him as a bomb slammed into the main deck above, followed by subsequent convulsions as the heavy unexploded missile pierced down through other decks. A single, amazing beam of light shafted down into the darkness following the bomb's progress, creating a smoky, cathedral-like effect.

The miracle was that the bomb failed to explode when it splashed mightily into the passageway only a few steps from where the terrified sailor cowered. The impact knocked him off his feet. He came up spluttering and froze, staring, waiting to die in a brilliant cone of light when the bomb went off.

It took him another moment or so, standing there waist-deep in water, the shaft of sunlight beaming down on him, before he realized the bomb really was a dud.

A petty officer named Bill White, one of several crawling around inside the *West Virginia* searching for survivors, appeared in the bomb opening in the slant above Cole's head. Spotting Cole, he called out, "This way. There's a way out."

With his help, Cole crawled up and out through the bomb opening and into the drier passageway above. White directed the Oklahoman sailor toward an escape route while he turned down another passageway to look for other survivors.

The sinking ship was beginning to level out as water flooding through the fractured hull distributed itself more evenly in the interior. The darkness was not so complete now. Watertight doors in the upper levels had not been dogged and some of them were open.

As Cole crept his perilous way toward topside and the roar and clamor of the ongoing Japanese attack, he came across a body blocking his exit at the base of a gangway. Light pouring down through the hatch above flushed into the face of his buddy, Dorie Miller. He looked dead.

Grief-stricken, Cole dropped to his knees. After the first shock of discovery, he realized the black cook was only knocked unconscious. Cole shook him, but the cook remained unresponsive. They couldn't stay here. The ship was sinking.

Arles's dad always said you could do lots of things you didn't think you could do when you knew you had to do them. Cole remembered how a skinny little runt back in Porum had lifted a 1940 Chevrolet off his brother-in-law in a spurt of raw adrenaline and determination after a car jack collapsed the vehicle on him.

Papa had better be right.

The little QM striker hoisted Miller's weight across his shoulders in a feat of strength that might have been impossible under less stressful circumstances. Thus burdened, staggering under the load, he labored topside to the main deck. Japanese warplanes skimming above the masts of stricken ships were still strafing and bombing when, exhausted from the effort, Cole gently deposited his big buddy at a casualty collection point where medical corpsmen were triaging a large number of wounded and injured crewmen.

"Thanks, Papa."

Follow-up

Later, Arles Cole learned how Miller had been collecting dirty laundry from the officers' quarters when the GQ alarm went off. An exploding torpedo knocked him off his feet, causing him to strike his head against the steel gangway as he was bolting topside to his battle station in one of the antiaircraft battery magazines.

As Miller revived after Cole carried him topside, a lieutenant running by recruited him to help rescue Captain Mervyn Bannion from the ship's bridge where he still held command in spite of serious wounds. The two men dodged through machinegun fire and explosions to reach their captain, who still refused to leave. In fact, he remained at the helm to direct his sinking ship's depleted defenses until he bled to death.

Although Dorie Miller was only a cook and had had no formal training in operating a machinegun, his battle station in an ammo magazine had allowed him to watch how antiaircraft machineguns were fired. After leaving Captain Bannion on the bridge, he came across an unattended Browning 50-caliber AA position. Enraged at the Japanese sneak attack, he latched on to the trigger of the 50-cal and opened up. He remained at the gun and kept up a blistering fire that was later credited with bringing down at least two enemy planes, fighting his way into history to become the first black serviceman to win the Navy Cross for gallantry under fire. The fleet's heavyweight boxing champ had turned champion gunner. Admiral Chester W. Nimitz, Commander-in-Chief Pacific Fleet, personally presented the medal to him aboard the aircraft carrier U.S.S. *Enterprise* on 27th May 1942.

Miller went on to become an American icon celebrated in fiction and literature as among the nation's "100 Greatest African-Americans." His likeness could be seen on U.S. recruiting posters for the rest of the war. He went on a public war bonds tour. CBS radio portrayed his courage in the series *They Live Forever*. Elven Havard portrayed him in the 1970 film *Tora! Tora! Tora!* Cuba Gooding Jr. played him in *Pearl Harbor*. Dozens of books and scores of magazines and newspaper articles have since extolled Miller's bravery on that morning at Pearl Harbor.

None of them, however, told the rest of the story—of how, in one of those strange quirks that sometimes color history, Dorie Miller would surely have perished and not gone on to glory but for Arles Cole, the skinny kid from Oklahoma.

Promoted to Petty Officer Third Class, Dorie Miller returned to the fleet in May 1943 as a cook aboard the escort carrier U.S.S. *Liscome Bay* (CVE-56). On 24th November 1943, a few days after the battle for Tarawa, a Japanese torpedo sank the *Liscome Bay*. Only 242 crewmembers out of a complement of 644 survived. Doris "Dorie" Miller was not one of them.

Quartermaster Arles Cole, also promoted to Petty Officer Third, heard about the *Liscome Bay* and the death of his now-famous friend while undergoing additional navigation training Stateside. For most of the rest of the war, he served aboard the newly commissioned Fletcher-class destroyer U.S.S. *Prichett* (DD-561). *Prichett* participated in some of the fiercest island-hopping battles of the war—Saipan, Tinian, Guam, the Philippines, Eniwetok, Iwo Jima, and Okinawa.

When kamikazes sank the U.S.S. *Callaghan* on 28th July 1945, killing forty-seven sailors, *Prichett* stood by abeam to protect the disabled destroyer and rescue survivors. Another suicide plane flew the gauntlet of defensive fire and crashed into the water six feet off *Prichett*'s port side, causing heavy damage to the ship's hull, killing two sailors and wounding a third.

Crippled, *Prichett* set sail for shipyards on the west coast of the United States. Less than a month later, while *Prichett* remained in dry dock, B-29 bombers from Tinian dropped atomic bombs on Hiroshima and Nagasaki to end the Second World War.

Arles Cole returned to Oklahoma after the war. He lives in Tulsa.

* * *

Taking the Philippines

THE ATTACK ON PEARL HARBOR is often and mistakenly looked upon as a singular event. In fact, it was part of the opening of a wide front by which the Japanese Empire aspired to extend its influence and possessions. Within a period of less than two hours, Japanese forces struck Siam, Malaya, and Hawaii, taking Hong Kong under their sights four hours later. Landings on Malaya occurred a few minutes before the first bombers arrived over Hawaii.

Through December 1941 and the first months of 1942, the Japanese overran the British Solomon Islands, Bali, Timor, Dutch East Indies, Hong Kong, Malaya, the Philippines, U.S. bases at Guam and Wake Island, and bombed northern Australia. Within four months, a vast area of what had been part of the Far East empires of the European powers, an expanse stretching across more than 6,000 miles, was under Japanese rule.

The only major U.S. presence in the western Pacific was in the Philippine Islands, which the United States had acquired following the Spanish-American War of 1898. The island group lay directly in the path to the oil and other raw materials the Japanese intended to capture and exploit in Malaya and the East Indies.

The Philippines enjoyed semi-autonomous status under President Manuel Quezón. General Douglas MacArthur commanded the Philippine Army and was overall commander of American forces in-country. Early in the morning of 8th December 1941 (about six hours after the start of the Pearl Harbor attack, but the next day by Philippine time), specially trained Japanese pilots flying from Formosa caught most of MacArthur's aircraft on the ground at Clark Field on the main island of Luzon, destroying eighteen B-17 bombers, fifty-six fighters, and a miscellaneous assortment of other aircraft.

General Louis Brereton, commander of the U.S. Army Air Force (U.S.A.A.F.) in the Far East, immediately withdrew his remaining airplanes to Australia and Java. Admiral Thomas Hart, commander of the U.S. Asiatic

Fleet, also took off for safe waters when he realized that the withdrawal or loss of the air forces left his ships vulnerable to almost certain destruction. MacArthur's army of about 30,000 Americans and 48,000 Filipinos would have to go it alone.

It soon became apparent that Washington was not terribly interested in the Philippines. President Roosevelt was not going to expend resources in defense of territory that the U.S. Navy and Army Air Force had already written off. It also soon became clear as the war unfolded that defeating the Japanese took second priority to overcoming Hitler's forces in Europe. The war in the Pacific would remain overshadowed by the more accessible and understandable campaigns in Europe.

Unable to obtain reinforcements and resupply, MacArthur was destined to eventual defeat.

Japanese troops began landing in small bodies on 10 December. On 22 December, 20,000 Japanese landed at Lingayen Bay on the west coast, about 150 miles from Manila. Two days later, another 7,000 came ashore at Lamon

Bay, this time on the east coast and about 100 miles from Manila. The two columns advanced in a pincer movement to take the Philippine capital.

MacArthur declared Manila an open city to prevent its destruction and withdrew to the Bataan Peninsula, where he hoped to hold out until relief arrived. He assured his sub-commanders that "help is on the way from the United States. Thousands of troops and hundreds of planes are being dispatched."

He didn't even believe it himself. Roosevelt admitted privately that the U.S. had no resources to send, especially since Germany and Italy had also declared war on America and would make demands on what limited stock America possessed.

The Japanese promptly blockaded the Philippines as the battle and siege of Bataan dragged through the end of December and into January, February, and March. Rations were severely reduced. Casualties mounted. Dense jungles made defense difficult. Malaria and dengue fever ravaged troops already weakened by dysentery and starvation. Uniforms rotted. Skin on soldiers' feet, hands and bodies sloughed off in smelly patches. Still, the "Battling Bastards of Bataan," as they called themselves, fought on.

> We're the battling bastards of Bataan:
> No mama, no papa, no Uncle Sam,
> No aunts, no uncles, no nephews, no nieces,
> No rifles, no planes or artillery pieces.
> And nobody gives a damn.

MacArthur signaled Washington that "all maneuvering possibilities" were gone and that "I intend to fight it out to complete destruction."

Roosevelt had other ideas. On 23rd February 1942, he ordered MacArthur to turn his command over to Major General Jonathan "Skinny" Wainwright and flee the Philippines; he would be needed later to regenerate an army in the Pacific. MacArthur at first refused, but then relented. He, his wife, and child left by PT boat under cover of darkness. On Mindanao, they caught a Royal Australian Air Force plane to Darwin, Australia. It was in Australia that he made his famous "I shall return" speech.

While the Japanese reinforced with 21,000 more men, starvation and disease decimated Wainwright's command to the point that only about one quarter of those remaining on Bataan were able to fight. The American-Filipino defensive line collapsed on 3rd April. On 9th April, troops on Bataan under Major General Edward King Jr. surrendered. General Wainwright and the units with him on the tiny island of Corregidor just off the coast held out for another month before they surrendered on 6th May. Wainwright survived the war in captivity.

Rather than capitulate to the expected savagery of the Japanese, some Filipinos and a few Americans escaped into the mountains to become guerrilla fighters. For those who could not escape, surrender became the first step into a long nightmare of captivity.

Mass cruelty and brutish behavior was the rule rather than the exception for the Japanese soldiers of that era. Allied armed forces personnel in the region, as well as civilians for that matter, knew to expect no mercy if they were captured by Tojo's Imperial hordes.

On Christmas Day 1941, Japanese troops had stormed the British field hospital on Hong Kong Island. Undefended, the hospital was occupied only by unarmed doctors, orderlies, female nurses, and wounded soldiers. Japanese infantry rounded up the nurses and gang-raped them repeatedly, then executed most of the medical staff and patients, using bayonets in order, presumably, to save ammunition.

The same thing happened on 14th February when the Japanese invaded Singapore and rampaged through Alexandra Hospital.

Japanese commanders expected to take some 25,000 reasonably healthy American and Filipino prisoners on Bataan. Instead, there were more than twice that number, most of whom were sick and starving. Walking skeletons. About 2,000 either died or were executed immediately before the sixty-five-mile "Bataan Death March" began.

In one bloody two-hour orgy, Japanese soldiers bayoneted and beheaded 350 Filipino soldiers. Guards forced captives to bury their comrades alive, even as victims feebly struggled to get out of their graves.

The long, slogging trek to POW camps north of Manila in the vicinity of Cabanatuan took five days for men in better condition, twelve days for those less fit. They were herded like dying cattle in temperatures that soared into the nineties Fahrenheit. Men who stumbled and fell were executed where they lay. Those too weak to continue walking were clubbed or bayoneted to death.

More than 600 Americans and at least 5,000 Filipinos perished on the march. Survivors arrived, noted an American doctor who made it through, "on the marrow of their bones." Another 1,000 Americans and 16,000 Filipinos would die of starvation, disease, and brutality in the POW camps.

* * *

The March

SERGEANT JAMES GAUTIER JR. knew help from the U.S. wasn't coming. These were desperate times. You could see it in the faces. They were gaunt and bearded, eyes hollow, greasy hair infested with lice. All the horses and mules had already been slaughtered and eaten.

Gautier, from Louisiana, was an aircraft mechanic with the U.S. Army Air Force's 27th Bombardment Group when the Japanese began bombing the Philippines. Once the enemy established beachheads on Luzon, lieutenants and sergeants herded all the support personnel like Gautier onto the parade ground at Fort William McKinley a few miles outside Manila and issued each a Springfield rifle, 90 rounds of ammo, a box of Nabisco hardtack crackers, and a can of corned beef.

"Congratulations. You are now in the 17th Provisional Infantry Battalion. You're infantry now. By God, act like it. Go out and shoot some Japs."

After the Japanese landed thousands of additional troops at Lingayen Gulf General MacArthur ordered "Plan Orange" to be implemented, giving the signal for the Americans and Filipinos under his command to fight a delaying action as they squeezed even tighter onto the Bataan Peninsula and waited for help that was never coming. By March, they had been pushed back into the jungles about as far as they could be pushed. The next step was into the ocean—or death.

Enemy bombing and shelling took a steady toll, but that was nothing compared to losses from lack of food and medicine. Gautier lost over thirty pounds. He, like other soldiers, spent as much time scouring for food as he did fighting Nips or hiding from exploding shells.

The MLR (main line of resistance) kept to the edge of the jungle. From positions there, Gautier's platoon looked out over a nearby agricultural area that grew rice, sugar cane, peanuts, and other truck crops. Like raiding monkeys, Gautier, Cecil Berry, Jesse Knowles, Grady Inzer, and some of the other bolder GIs crawled out of their holes and sneaked out into the fields. They tied sheaves of rice and sugar cane to their backs and crawled back.

Some guys in the platoon built a crude wooden press to extract juice from the cane, which was then boiled down to syrup and poured over rice flour hotcakes. Seawater produced salt. Occasionally someone killed a water buffalo for a real feast.

As soon as the Japs realized what was going on, they torched the sugar-cane fields and killed all the water buffalo in the vicinity. That left edible wild roots and plants, monkeys, lizards . . . A bamboo rat could be turned into a passable meal. Hair, bones, *everything* was eaten.

Soon, there was nothing left but insects—and then there were no insects.

The Japanese never let up. They knew the Americans and Filipinos were about done for. In between air raids and shelling by big 240-mm guns, whose approaching shells sounded like railroad boxcars hurled through the air, enemy aircraft "bombed" with propaganda leaflets.

TICKET TO ARMISTICE
USE THIS TICKET TO SAVE YOUR LIFE
YOU WILL BE KINDLY TREATED
Follow These Instructions:

1. Come toward our lines waving a white flag.
2. Strap your gun over your left shoulder muzzle down and pointed behind you.
3. Show this ticket to the sentry.
4. Any number of you may surrender with this one ticket.

Japanese Army Headquarters
Sing your way to peace
Pray for peace

None of the Americans took up the offer. Jesse Knowles snorted. "Peace, my ass! They'll shoot us down like dogs."

Men died or were wounded in unusual ways.

One morning, Gautier and Knowles returned from a listening/observation post out ahead of the MLR and heard that someone in the platoon had scrounged some rice for hotcakes. They were approaching the "kitchen," a small open fire, when someone yelled "Air raid!"

Men scattered like a flock of startled birds. Gautier scrambled one direction, Knowles the other. A bunch of guys jumped into a gaping shell crater that was half-full of muddy rainwater. Hillhouse's ass stuck up out of the hole since he was on a pile of other GIs. He howled in pain and terror when a bomb exploded nearby and a piece of shrapnel ripped off part of one cheek.

A string of exploding shells chased Knowles down a trail through the jungle. He figured he was a goner when pain seared through the back of his neck and knocked him flat on his face. Afterwards, medics at the aid station removed a small chip of hot shrapnel that had stuck to his skin, leaving only a blister.

"Better sign up with us Baptists right now, Cajun," he chided Gautier. "I'd be dead by now if I was a Methodist like you."

On another day, Cecil Berry and Gautier were eating, if ingesting such sparse fare could be termed eating, when a staff sergeant they didn't know sat down on the ground between them. They looked up when they heard a big 240-mm "boxcar" ripping across the sky. By this time, they could predict with some accuracy where the shell would land by the sound it made coming in. This one was not going to be near. They kept eating, too weak and weary really to give a damn.

The shell hit in some guava trees about a hundred yards away, too distant to cause any damage. Or so they thought. Without a word, without so much as a sigh, the staff sergeant sitting between Gautier and Berry toppled over. A single fragment from the big shell had pierced the back of his head, killing him instantly.

Death was going to find you when your number came up, soldiers said, ready or not.

By the first week of April 1942, General MacArthur had bugged out of the Philippines and "Skinny" Wainwright assumed command. Everyone knew it was about over when one of the Filipino outfits pulled out and disappeared into the mountains during the night of 6th April. At daybreak, Gautier, Knowles, and Inzer watched Jap landing barges full of troops chug across the bay to land on the beach below the deserted village called Orion. Japanese as thick as red ants swarmed the burned-up rice paddies down below the high ground left undefended by the deserting Filipinos.

Officers ran up and down the MLR. They looked scared to death.

"Hold the line," they encouraged, "but be prepared to move out. Retreat when the gong rings. We'll have trucks to take you back."

Back where? Into the ocean?

The "gong" was a triangle bell located at the command post. Soldiers numbed by the sight of so many enemy waited for the gong to sound. Finally, Gautier's platoon sergeant sent a runner to the CP to see what the hell was going on. He returned twenty minutes later, out of breath.

"The CP is cleared out," he gasped. "Everybody is gone."

The grim-faced platoon sergeant turned to a group of about fifty stragglers. He simply stared at them for a long time before he took a deep breath to calm his nerves.

"Destroy your machineguns," he said. "Break up into small groups or go by twos and head south. Try to avoid the Japs. Try to save your skins. It's every man for himself."

The Japs were starting to open up with small arms and machineguns.

"I'm heading south," Gautier informed Knowles and Inzer. "You coming?"

Knowles grinned through his desperation. "Aw, Gautier. You just want me with you 'cause you know God takes care of Baptists."

"We'll make a good team. This Methodist is going to work as hard as I can to help the Lord save my butt."

"I'm coming along," Inzer offered. "With you two Bible thumpers, I'll be the safest man on Bataan."

Too late. The Japanese had them surrounded. Thousands of American and Filipino soldiers milled about as word circulated that General King had gone out to surrender to keep his command from being annihilated. Gautier bent the barrel of his rifle around a tree. Most of the other soldiers did likewise. Then he, Knowles, and Inzer gloomily trudged toward a designated assembly point. The war was over for the Battling Bastards of Bataan—but the long nightmare was just beginning.

The Japs weren't fooling around. For them, fighting to the last man or committing suicide were the only honorable alternatives for a defeated soldier; surrender was inconceivable. They held only contempt for those, friendly or enemy, who failed to live up to that standard. Therefore, they felt no obligation to treat them humanely.

Gautier and his friends and the other bedraggled and ragtag Americans and Filipinos were assembled in rough ranks and ordered to sit on the ground. Japanese soldiers wearing loose-fitting uniforms that made them look like wrinkled brown bags surrounded the prisoners with bayonets fixed on their long rifles. Acts of brutality were the only thing that seemed to make them laugh or smile.

Guards went down the ranks demanding money, watches, pens, rings, and anything else of value. To Gautier's horror, he watched a guard chop off the finger of a soldier whose ring wouldn't come off his swollen hand. The soldier's buddies on either side jerked him upright lest the guard not stop with one finger.

Another American had some Japanese souvenir coins in his pocket. A guard yanked him out of formation and stabbed him repeatedly with his bayonet until the prisoner stopped screaming and moving.

Guards stopped in front of Inzer and Gautier. Heart pounding, Gautier handed over his watch, rings, and money. One of the soldiers rifled through Gautier's billfold and discovered a picture of his wife. He took it out, grinning, and held it up.

"Wifu? Wifu?"

"Yes."

The guard tossed it on the ground, dug his heels into it, then stepped over in front of Inzer. Inzer's jaw set and his muscles tensed. Gautier silently prayed that the Jap would not provoke him. Inzer wouldn't take mistreatment without fighting back.

Inzer glared at the Jap and silently handed over his valuables.

Gautier and Inzer soon got separated from Knowles and the rest of their platoon as, with clubs, rifle butts, and bayonets, the Japanese herded thousands of hapless prisoners over to the National Highway and started them moving north. Gautier's combat boots had all but rotted off his feet during the months of fighting and isolation in the jungle. Miraculously, he happened upon a discarded pair of white low-quarter shoes and switched out his worn-out boots for them.

Prisoners going one direction and Japanese vehicles and soldiers going the other clogged the road, kicking up a pall of choking dust from the unpaved highway. Temperatures hovered in the low nineties, with humidity to match. Fighting another bout of malaria, Gautier felt as though his body was on fire.

The prisoners staggered and stumbled past artillery and trucks full of soldiers being brought forward for the assault and siege on the island of Corregidor, where General Wainwright was holding out. Just for sport, Japanese soldiers coming by in trucks whacked prisoners with rifle butts or long bamboo poles. Those unable to get back up were bayoneted and left lying in the road in pools of their own blood.

Men too weak from wounds, sickness, or starvation to keep up were also weeded out. Fresh corpses soon littered the road. Older bodies previously fallen in battle bloated in the merciless sun, split open, and oozed maggots. Gautier experienced severe nausea, but had nothing in his stomach to expel, not even water.

Several men broke ranks to fill their canteens from artesian wells along the route. Guards descended on them, yelling and lashing out with their sticks and rifles. Crazed with thirst, one prisoner eluded them and dashed for the nearest water. A shot cracked. His head busted like a melon and he dropped, one hand reaching to within an inch of the water.

After that, no one in the columns dared stop or break rank without permission from guards. Men with dysentery relieved themselves as they walked, adding to the general overall foulness of the march and the disgust of the Japanese. The stronger tried to help the weak, but all were in such bad shape after more than three months of combat and deprivation that they barely had the strength to help themselves. Men cried tears of rage and frustration when others stumbled and fell and they could do nothing to aid them. Some wept loudly as Japanese soldiers methodically and with pleasure, it seemed, dispatched the fallen.

Whenever the guards called a rest halt and the Japanese rested, prisoners were forced to stand at attention facing the hot sun. This was the "sun treatment." It was worse than marching. Men collapsed. Guards charged in and kicked them back to their feet. Those unable to rise again were shot.

Still, no one was given water.

Gautier wondered how long this would go on, how far they would have to walk. Of course, prisoners were told nothing. After a few miles, suffering seemed to shut down his mind. He and Inzer trudged along together on auto-pilot, both of them exhausted and consumed with malarial fever. Gautier began seeing streams of cool, clear water where they did not exist, food that vanished as he approached, the face of his wife . . . He plodded along in a trance-like state, through the heat and dust, mind fuzzy, feet dragging out step after step.

In order to make them more manageable, prisoners were marched in groups of about 100 with distance between the groups. In the afternoon, they came to a wooden bridge spanning a narrow, stagnant stream that opened into the bay. Green scum scabbed the surface. When the Japs indicated the prisoners could drink, the first water they had had all day, thirst-crazed men stampeded into the creek, staggering and gasping and throwing themselves into the stream.

Gautier thrust his full head underneath the scum and sucked in water. His head began to clear and he felt stronger. He finally came up for breath and looked around. Several feet away, bloated corpses floated on the surface, their nationality indistinguishable due to decay and the hordes of black flies that covered their exposed sections.

It was a sickening spectacle, but Gautier forced himself to drink all he could hold. He had to survive.

They stopped for the night in makeshift compounds enclosed in barbed wire, each holding a thousand or more men packed into an area not big enough for 500.

The next day began with an hour's "sun treatment" and became a replay of the first. There was no water, no food, and noticeably fewer prisoners than the morning before. A glance back down the road explained why. Corpses lay scattered along it like old bags of clothing.

So many prisoners had dropped out by the third day that the groups had to be combined to reach a count of 100. That late afternoon they reached the town of Balanga and still other crude barbed-wire compounds. To the rear of the guard posts at the entrances to the enclosures towered six-feet tall piles of bloody corpses, all tossed on top of each other in a grisly scene of horror. Every time a guard clubbed a debilitated prisoner to the ground, a couple of Jap soldiers grabbed the body by the arms and knees and heaved it to the top of the pile.

A guard took a swing at Gautier with a heavy stick. He ducked and his Frank Buck helmet took the brunt of the blow. His knees sagged, but he lurched on through the gate before his abuser could get another swing at him.

Inzer was gone by the time he picked his way into the mass center of prisoners and collapsed.

"Inzer? Inzer?"

A Japanese at the fence pointed a rifle at him. Gautier's mouth clacked shut and he hunkered down to make himself as small as possible. He stole a look at the pile of bodies, but couldn't tell if Inzer's had become a part of it or not.

A large Jap soldier wearing thick-rimmed eyeglasses paraded around outside the wire displaying an American's head stuck on the end of his bayonet. The gruesome trophy was caked with blood and dust. Sightless eyes bulged and the mouth gaped above ragged skin where the neck had been chopped through. Gautier looked at the head only long enough to ascertain that it hadn't belonged to his friend.

They were fed on the following night, the first nourishment they had had since surrendering. A prisoner stood at the gate to the compound with a tablespoon and a bag of uncooked rice. As each man entered the enclosure, his mouth snapped open and the server shoved in a spoonful of rice. Guards watched to make sure no man received more than his fair portion.

Gautier found a place to sit on the ground and tried to work up enough saliva to soften his rice so he could chew it. He had had nothing to drink all day. Finally, he swallowed the hard grains whole.

At some point during that interminable night, a prisoner crazed with hunger, illness, and thirst awoke from fitful dozing and, hallucinating, began screaming and thrashing about. His buddies tried to calm him. Too late. Machinegun bullets ripped into the crowd, splashing blood and flesh.

Many dead were left inside the wire at daybreak before the "sun treatment" and the start of another torturous day on the road to hell.

For Gautier, as for most prisoners, memories of much of the march were fogged and fragmented. He vaguely recalled a Filipino girl by the side of the road tossing a piece of coconut into the column. It hit the dusty road. Two colonels rushed for the morsel and ended up in a fight over it. The episode was apparently so amusing to the Japanese that they neglected to kill either one.

A little later, a Filipino man hovered next to the road trying to sell canteens of water to the Americans. The prisoners had nothing left to trade except the rags on their backs. Someone grabbed a canteen from the would-be merchant's hands, shoved it inside his shirt, and ducked back into the middle of the formation before the Filipino could identify who snatched it.

That was the way it went for five, maybe six, days. The numbers of survivors dwindled almost hourly. They had walked over sixty miles on a single spoonful of uncooked rice and only enough water to keep them alive by the time the pitiful procession reached the railhead at San Fernando.

At last they were served a meal. At least the rice was cooked and served on small squares of board shingle. Gautier got in line at the compound entrance where other prisoners heaped rice from a kettle onto the shingle. By this time, he had learned to keep his head down and look at no one in order not to inadvertently invite abuse from guards.

A familiar voice greeted him at the rice pot. "Aw, Cajun, but you're a pitiful sight. What have they done to you?"

He looked up into the face of Jesse Knowles, whom he hadn't seen since the beginning. He was so overcome with joy that he could have hugged the grinning scarecrow that Knowles had become. Knowing better, he returned a painful half-grin.

"I might have known you'd find a way to get on the gravy train," he bantered back.

"Shut up and stick that board over here if you want something to eat."

Knowles dipped as much rice on the board as he could get away with.

"Have you seen Inzer?" Gautier asked him.

"Not since we left. Tough as he is, I think he'll make it. I just hope he don't slug some guard and get himself killed."

From San Fernando, prisoners were driven into solid metal boxcars on a narrow-gauge railroad, jammed in so tight that they could barely breathe. A number smothered to death or died from the stifling heat during the four-hour transport, but they could not fall to the floor until after the doors opened at their destination.

Camp O'Donnell lay only nine miles down the road. Gautier and Knowles spotted a square figure emerging from one of the cars ahead of them.

"Inzer?"

A grin crossed the short man's face. Together, Gautier, Inzer and Knowles marched into captivity.

Follow-up

Burial details at Camp O'Donnell worked every day just to keep up with the dying. During heavy rains, corpses floated up out of their graves. At night, stray dogs howled and fought and dug up corpses to eat.

Sergeant James Donovan Gautier Jr. was shipped to Japan in July 1944 to work in the mines. He survived the war and returned to the United States where he eventually reunited with Grady Inzer and Jesse Knowles, who had also survived captivity. Gautier remained in the military as a career soldier before retiring in 1960 and returning to Louisiana.

Chapter 2

Battle for the Aleutians

FOLLOWING INITIAL JAPANESE SUCCESSES IN 1941 and 1942, Admiral Isoroku Yamamoto devised a scheme to snare the U.S. Pacific Fleet in a final major battle that would destroy American sea power, leave Hawaii vulnerable to capture, and thus force the United States to sue for peace. His target— Midway Island, the last U.S. base between Japan and Hawaii.

His strategy was to trick U.S. forces by sending a Japanese diversionary force to capture the two lightly defended Aleutian islands of Attu and Kiska. While that was being accomplished, he would land a Japanese marine force on Midway to lure the main U.S. fleet into his trap.

Seizure of Attu and Kiska, Yamamoto also considered, would cut American Lend-Lease shipments to Russia, isolate most of Alaska and open it for eventual occupation, and deny the Americans an invasion route to Japan by way of the Aleutians and the Kurile Islands.

The Aleutian Islands, more than100 of them, ran from the tip of the Kamchatka Peninsula in Russia to the tip of the Alaska Peninsula. Although the westernmost islands in the chain—Attu and Kiska—are 1,700 miles from Alaska, they are nonetheless American territory.

In May 1942, Admiral Chester Nimitz, Commander-in-Chief Pacific (CINCPAC) sent a dispatch to Rear Admiral Robert A. Theobald, commander of Alaska's Naval Sector: "The Japanese have completed plans for an amphibious operation to secure an advanced base in the Aleutian Islands . . . Japanese Task Force has left Japan with probable objective Aleutian Islands and/or Alaska . . ."

Theobald's naval forces in Alaska and the Army's Alaska Defense Command led by Major General Simon Bolivar Buckner were shoddily prepared for any major actions. Nonetheless, Buckner swore that "if the Japanese come, they may get a foothold. But it will be their children who'll get as far as Anchorage, and their grandchildren who'll make it to the States. And by then they'll be American citizens."

Unknown to Japan, the U.S. had intercepted and decoded Japanese communications. Instead of falling for the Aleutian diversion, Admiral Nimitz

planned to turn the trap against the Japanese at Midway. While the Japanese closed in on Midway with 4 carriers, 6 battleships, 12 cruisers, and 44 destroyers, the Americans set sail to ambush them with 3 carriers, 8 cruisers, and 15 destroyers.

On 4th June 1942, American torpedo bombers and Dauntless dive bombers caught the Japanese by surprise and sank all four Japanese carriers including Vice Admiral Chuichi Nagumo's flagship. The American victory was decisive, won by aircraft from two carrier forces that never even sighted each other.

In the meantime, Attu and Kiska were left virtually undefended. Both islands proved to be easy pickings. On 6th June, an occupation force of 1,200 Japanese Naval Infantry surprised the isolated weather station at Kiska's Reynard Cove and occupied the island. Hours later, another 1,200 Japanese landed unopposed on Attu. An enemy nation had seized and occupied a part of America's homeland for the first time since the War of 1812.

Immediately, the Japanese reinforced and dug in, setting up ack-ack and harbor guns, constructing a submarine base, and bringing in antiaircraft and communications personnel. Although Admiral Nimitz knew his undermanned and underequipped Alaska Force could not yet push the Japanese off the islands, he could not let them sit there, establish themselves, and gain confidence. He ordered General Buckner and Admiral Theobald to put pressure on the invaders and keep them off balance, uncertain, and on the defensive.

For the next ten months, the U.S. tightened its air and sea blockade around the two islands in a slow-momentum "shoe-string" counteroffensive to cut off Japanese resupply and isolate the Rising Sun's remote stronghold. By May 1943, the U.S. had built seaports and air and troop bases on the islands of Adak and Amchitka and increased military strength in the theater to nearly 200,000 men. At the same time, Japan increased its troop strength to 6,000 on each of the two islands.

It was a matter of when, not whether, America would recapture its lost territory.

* * *

Bitter Cold

BY 11TH MAY 1943 it had been nearly a year since the Japanese had attacked and seized American territory—the two small islands of Attu and Kiska at the tip of the Aleutian Islands. Fog seemed to freeze in the dawn air off the coast of Attu as two submarines, *Nautilus* and *Narwhal*, broke through the ice floes like silent surfacing whales. Just as silently, soldiers burst from the steel tubes, gathered in the mist at the rear of the subs and inflated rubber boats.

The subs submerged, water rose, and the rubber boats full of heavily armed combat infantry floated free. With hardly a word, soldiers grabbed paddles and struck out toward their objective. Loaded rafts stretched across the gray surface of the sea, the head and tail invisible to the middle in the fog. The battle to recapture Attu was about to commence.

In the bow of the first rubber raft rode the commander of the 422-man light battalion, Captain William H. Willoughby. His Combined Provisional 7th Scout Company and 7th Reconnaissance Troop was one of the best-prepared and best-equipped American forces in the entire Pacific Theater. A rock-jawed, athletic man in his early thirties, Willoughby was career military and knew how to get things done.

For the past several months he and his Scouts had trained mercilessly for this day, in the field more hours than most infantry or Marines spent in their chow lines during a lifetime. It made little difference what the weather was—snow, freezing rain, blizzard—they were out on the snow and tundra busting their balls.

"You come to this outfit, you train your asses off, or you go back to the Women's Corps," Willoughby warned. "You had better be prepared when we go to run the Japs back where they came from."

One of the best scroungers in the business, Willoughby had conned and cajoled supply officers into handing over insulated boots, Arctic parkas, long-handles, and other gear for his special forces. When that didn't work, he and the other scroungers in the unit stole what the men needed. Nonetheless, he browbeat his men on the need to avoid frostbite and trench foot.

"Conditions can be brutal. I don't care what we're wearing, more of us will fall to weather than to enemy bullets."

His prediction was to be eerily prophetic.

The concept of Operation Land Crab, of which Willoughby's Scouts were the prong, was for U.S. troops first to retake Attu before using it as a springboard against neighboring Kiska. Attu was about forty miles long and seventeen wide. Commanding General Albert E. Brown would split his 7th Infantry Division into three regiment-sized elements. The Northern Force under the command of Colonel Frank L. Culin would land at Holtz Bay, the Southern Force under Colonel Edward P. Earle at Massacre Bay, while the third regiment remained in reserve. Captain Willoughby's Scouts would go ashore at Scarlet Beach on the west shore of the island and press east toward the main Japanese encampment at Chichagof Harbor in the north while it covered the exposed flanks of the main forces.

If all went according to plan, the three forces would link up in Jarmin Pass between Holtz and Massacre Bays and trap the Japanese resistance in Chichagof Valley where they would be vulnerable to naval bombardment, air attacks, and a massed infantry advance.

It took Willoughby's flotilla of rubber boats more than two hours to wend its way through the dark waters. Daylight didn't so much arrive as the darkness sort of thin out. The beach loomed only a few yards away before the lead boat spotted it. Scouts scrambled onto the hard-frozen soil and muskeg and were met—by more darkness and silence.

"This looks like when they went in on King Kong's island," a soldier observed, referring to the movie starring Fay Wray.

"Let's hope King Kong's not waiting for us," his buddy responded.

Captain Willoughby and his lieutenants hiked up to where the hills began and, still finding no signs of the enemy, moved the battalion through blowing snow to a mountain crest from which they could see Holtz Bay below in the distance. From there, they continued east at a snail's pace due to snow and ice and muskeg, a layer of thick, slimy decayed vegetable matter that made walking slippery and treacherous.

In the meantime, Colonel Culin and his Northern Force at Holtz Bay and Colonel Earle's Southern Force at Massacre Bay made their designated landings in heavy seas as the wind kicked up. Waves capsized one landing craft and drowned a dozen soldiers. Fortunately, nothing greeted the invaders ashore except ravens, more fog, and eerie silence.

After making their unopposed landings, troops of the invasion forces, plagued and delayed by terrain, weather, and supply problems, began working their separate ways to their link-up point in Jarmin Pass. As for the Japanese under the command of Colonel Yasuyo Yamasaki, they dug in on hilltops surrounding Chichagof Harbor and Massacre Bay, a strategy that would cost the Americans severe casualties. Delaying forces were sent out to harass the approaching Americans.

At 1800 hours, the fog having been dissipated somewhat by winds off the sea, Willoughby's Scouts heard mortar fire from the direction of Massacre Bay. As darkness overcame them, they set up camp in a gale chilled by temperatures of ten degrees and falling. Miserable, they ate cold rations and huddled in the freezing dark and waited for daylight.

Willoughby suffered his first casualties that night. Although he instructed his officers and NCOs to keep the men moving about, snatching sleep in only brief catnaps to avoid cold injuries, a few avoided detection and stayed in their holes with wet feet. They awoke with frostbite.

There was no turning back, nowhere to turn back to. Injured and wounded could not be left behind. They had to accompany the forward march until the Scouts linked up with other forces.

By daylight of the second morning, all three American elements were engaged with the enemy. Only the Northern Force made any significant progress, having fought its way inland for two miles before it bogged down for the rest of the night.

From that day forward, progress toward Jarmin Pass for all three attacking U.S. elements could be measured in mere feet and yards. Opposing forces slugged it out under the most brutal conditions suffered by troops in any theater of the war. GIs slid down steep, snow-covered slopes on their butts, like "human toboggans," and took cover behind icy rocks and boulders.

By the third day, most of the Americans were critically short of food, ammo and supplies. Navy battleships pounded the enemy-held ridges with their big guns until they ran out of ammunition, after which infantry had to rely on mortars and howitzers for heavy support. Weather restricted air cover, which was intermittent at best.

Embroiled in hot firefights one after the other, Willoughby's Scouts found themselves pinned down for several days as they succeeded in diverting the enemy's attention from Colonel Culin's main Northern Force moving toward Jarmin Pass from Holtz Bay. The bitter weather continued to take its toll. Nearly half of the Scout force came down with frozen feet and frostbite.

While in the stalemate, the battalion surgeon, Captain David Klein, set up an aid station in a ravine behind the lines. It consisted of a cave dug into a snow bank. The wounded and injured lay side by side on shelter halves in the cave, shivering violently even while unconscious. They also went hungry since aircraft tasked to airdrop provisions could not locate them in the fog.

Miraculously, even as cold injuries continued to climb, the Scout battalion held. Willoughby was to note in his makeshift journal later how, "Since we couldn't get any sleep at night, we weren't about to let the enemy sleep. We kept up a din around the clock so that they wouldn't divert any forces away from us against Culin."

Even the enemy grudgingly respected the Scouts' fortitude, as noted by one Japanese officer's entry in his diary: "Enemy strength must be a division."

Since Willoughby could not retreat, his only recourse was to attack and move forward—which he did. One soldier noted how, during the fighting, "dead Japanese, hunks of artillery, pieces of guns, and arms and legs rolled down out of the fog on the mountain."

Gradually, the Americans improved their tactical positions and began to make progress. Captain Willoughby's Scouts pushed across the western mountains while being opposed all the way. Weary and weather-bitten Scouts slithered across the ice, pitching grenades and running from rock to rock. The air pulsed with the chatter of machinegun fire as the Scouts attacked the high ground above Holtz Bay to give Northern Force some relief. They secured the summit above the main Japanese camp at Chichagof and dug in while Japanese with megaphones shouted taunts in English that would become all too familiar to GIs island-hopping across the South Pacific.

"Amelican GIs. You die tonight!"

On 15th May, the Americans received their first major break since the operation began. During the night, the Japanese fell back to a ridge on the opposite side of Holtz Bay, apparently retreating to prevent being squeezed between the Northern Force and Willoughby's Scouts. That left Jarmin Pass in possession of the Americans.

Now unopposed, Willoughby, himself limping and gaunt from the fighting and the pressures of leadership, led his men down out of the mountains into the pass. Only forty were able to walk without pain. In some cases, men literally crawled on their hands and knees to Holtz Bay to link up with Northern Force.

These suffered from terrible sores on their knees and, in some cases, gangrene led to amputations.

Miraculously, only eleven Scouts were killed during four days of mountain fighting. Harsh weather conditions claimed the majority of casualties, most of whom had to be medically evacuated to hospitals and hastily erected aid stations. Willoughby ended up with 165 men out of his original force of 422, and most of these wore bandages.

With the linking up of the three elements in Jarmin Pass, weather-beaten that they were, the Americans formed an unbroken semicircle that, as planned, trapped the enemy against the sea on the northeastern corner of Attu. Finally released to join the fight, the reserve regiment brought the total number of Americans in the battle to almost 16,000.

Ridge by ridge, peak by peak, Americans gradually closed the noose around the enemy. By 24th May, almost two weeks into the battle, most of the remaining Japanese were dug in on the jagged summit of Fish Hook Ridge. They showed no willingness to give up.

Bitter fighting continued for another three days as GIs fought their way up the ridge, inching through rocks in a deadly game of hide and seek. Enemy soldiers hiding in snowdrifts and among iced boulders rolled grenades downhill among the attackers. Each time the weather cleared, even if for only an hour, U.S. planes hammered the Japanese camp at Chichagof Harbor.

"Am suffering from diarrhea and feel dizzy . . ." Japanese Lieutenant Nebu Tatsuguchi confided in his diary. "It felt like the barracks blew up, things shook up and rocks and mud fell all around and fell down; strafing planes hit the next room; my room looks an awful mess from the sand and pebbles that come down from the roof. Consciousness becomes insane. There is no hope of reinforcement. Will die for the cause of Imperial Edict."

By nightfall of 28th May, the eighteenth day of battle, Americans controlled most of Fish Hook Ridge and parts of Buffalo Ridge to the east, on the opposite end of which the Japanese established their final line of defense. With fewer than a thousand soldiers remaining, the Japanese were in dismal straits. Nonetheless, the *bushido* code would not allow them to surrender.

"The remaining ration is only for two days," Lieutenant Tatsuguchi noted in his diary. "Our artillery has been completely destroyed. I wonder if some of the men are still alive. Continuous cases of suicide . . ."

Colonel Yamasaki opted for a final desperate measure to wrest at least a small victory from certain defeat. "We are planning a successful annihilation of the enemy," he assured his soldiers as dusk fell on 28th May.

Lieutenant Tatsuguchi was more realistic: "At 2000 we assembled in front of headquarters," he told his diary. "The last assault is to be carried out. All patients in the hospital are to commit suicide . . . Gave 400 shots of morphine to severely wounded and killed them . . . Finished all patients with grenades . . . Only thirty-three years of life and I am to die here. I have no regret. *Banzai*, my beloved wife . . ."

A few hours later, Colonel Yamasaki led a *banzai* charge through an opening in the American lines left when Baker Company, 32nd Infantry, of the Southern Force, withdrew to the rear for a hot breakfast before launching another attack against the Japanese at daybreak. The only U.S. defenders standing against the Japanese charge were Captain William Willoughby, fifteen other officers, and several "noncombatants"—engineers, medical personnel, and field headquarters staff. Willoughby's remaining Scouts had been pulled back to rest and recuperate.

The commotion awakened Willoughby. Game and as tough as always, the Scout commander rallied the other officers sleeping in the Operations tent. They dashed into a nearby defensive trench. Hordes of Japanese shouting *"Banzai!"* and firing from the hip charged out of the morning darkness.

It was all over in moments. Willoughby and his band of fellow officers were steamrollered. Eleven of the sixteen were killed almost immediately. A machine-gun bullet creased Willoughby's cheek, followed by the explosion of a hand grenade that knocked him unconscious and out of the fight. The remaining four officers were also wounded, but survived.

Further up Engineer Hill, medics, engineers, supply and personnel clerks, chaplains' assistants, and anyone else who could fire a gun, although not a combatant normally, fought fiercely for their lives. Willoughby and his officers had sacrificed themselves to provide crucial time for them to get armed and ready.

With the aid of howitzer batteries firing down from the top of the hill, the defense held and repulsed the waves of frantic Japanese. Some 500 of those remaining, many of them wounded, withdrew into the darkness at the base of Engineer Hill. Soon thereafter, Americans overheard shouting and wailing as the Emperor's men committed mass suicide by pulling the pins of grenades and clasping them against their chests. At daybreak, the bottom of the hill presented a grisly scene of blood and body parts.

Follow-up

Yamasaki's charge was the last Japanese assault on America's homeland. The Battle of Attu ended with only 28 Japanese survivors; 6,950 died. The Japanese also lost 60 airplanes, 6 submarines, 7 destroyers, and 9 cargo and transport ships during the eleven months they occupied the two Aleutian islands.

The U.S. suffered 3,829 casualties during that same period—549 killed in action, 1,148 wounded, and 2,132 disabled by illness, cold injuries, drowning, and other accidents. Although the Attu campaign received scant attention in U.S. newspapers—"No Marines, otherwise it would have been world history," one disgruntled Army veteran complained—it would rank as one of the most costly American battles in the Pacific Theater.

Kiska proved to be a minor postscript after the savage fighting on Attu. An American invasion force found the island deserted. Japanese destroyers had secretly evacuated all its occupation troops under cover of darkness and fog.

"Island hopping" and amphibious landings became standard operating procedure against the many islands that dotted the Pacific from Hawaii to Japan and south toward Australia while the bloody Aleutian campaign at America's own doorstep became only a historical footnote.

Captain William Willoughby, promoted to major and then to colonel, was evacuated Stateside to recover from his wounds. He remained active in the war until it ended.

Chapter 3

South Pacific Ordeal

AFTER THEIR EMPIRE'S STUNNING DEFEAT at the Battle of Midway in June 1942, the Japanese thought to protect their newly acquired holdings in the South Pacific by cutting U.S. communications and supply lines to that region. In May 1942, they occupied Tulagi and then, a little later, Guadalcanal, two islands at the southern tip of the Solomons, a string of islands east of New Guinea. They began building an airfield on Guadalcanal and a small naval base on nearby Tulagi. The side that controlled that airfield would gain an important advantage in dominating the South Pacific.

On 7th August 1942, the 1st Marine Division landed on Guadalcanal in the first significant American ground action of the Pacific War. By the end of the second day, Marines had seized the airstrip, which they renamed Henderson Field, as well as nearby Tulagi. Although Marines had the airfield and a small section of the coast, Japanese forces possessed most of the rest of the island.

No one anticipated that the struggle for a 2,500-square mile plot of jungle, mountain wilderness, and sharp-bladed grass taller than a man would be so long and fierce. It continued on land, at sea, and in the air for the rest of the year.

Almost nightly, Japanese naval gunfire bombarded American airplanes caught on the ground at Henderson Field while Japanese infantry charged out of the jungle to attack weary defenders. As soon as the sun started to come up, however, the Japanese infantry faded back into the wilds and the Emperor's ships fled to avoid retaliation by U.S. long-range bombers. The enemy might own the night, but the Americans regained operational control at daybreak.

Supply lines for both sides depended upon the sea approaches to Guadalcanal. Warships, submarines, and aircraft struck each other without warning and turned the sea lanes into a deadly no-man's land. Unable to employ large, slow transport ships because of the threat of American air, the Japanese made use of high-speed destroyers and cruisers under the cover of darkness to land reinforcements and support in their efforts to retake the airfield. By October, the Japanese had 22,000 men on Guadalcanal to the United States' 23,000. A decisive showdown was at hand.

As the large presence of enemy naval forces posed a serious threat to the American foothold, CINCPAC's Admiral Chester Nimitz deployed his own vessels to block "the Slot" between Guadalcanal and the Japanese base at Rabaul and stop the "Tokyo Express" ships from reaching Guadalcanal.

On the night of Sunday, 11th October, the Japanese Navy sent a major supply and reinforcement convoy steaming through the Slot. It consisted of two seaplane tenders and six destroyers, while a second armada of three heavy cruisers, two destroyers and perhaps several freighters made a run to shell Henderson Field.

Shortly before midnight, U.S. Naval Task Group 64.2 under the command of Rear Admiral Norman Scott raced to intercept and engage the enemy fleet. Scott's Task Group consisting of five destroyers—*Farenholt, McCalla, Buchanan, Laffey,* and *Duncan*—and four cruisers—*San Francisco, Salt Lake City, Helena,* and *Boise*—came upon the enemy warships as they attempted the sea passage between tiny Savo Island and Cape Esperance, the northern tip of Guadalcanal.

* * *

Shark Attack

WAKES TRAILED IN NARROW CONTRAILS of white foam on the sea's gentle surface as Admiral Norman Scott fanned his five destroyers into an anti-submarine screen out ahead of and off the flanks of his four cruisers. The horizon lay like a large crystal dome of fading colors at sunset, empty except for a massive thunderhead building up to the east. The Japanese men-of-war were still 110 miles away.

The Number 2 gun mount on the destroyer U.S.S. *Duncan* was the first 5-incher forward of the bridge. Nine men operated the gun in battle. Boatswain's Mate Third Class Roy Boehm controlled the weapon's elevation-and-depression mechanism and operated the trigger. Admiral Scott's sound of GQ—General Quarters—sent all hands to their battle stations.

From the aft deckhouse, slowly growing louder, rose the voice of someone singing. His voice was as clear as the tones of a church bell. A hush fell over *Duncan*. The ship seemed to go into reverent suspended animation for the length of time it took one young and frightened sailor 3,000 miles from home to sing an old country hymn.

> Amazing Grace, how sweet the sound
> That saved a wretch like me . . .

Nearly two years earlier, in January 1941, Roy Boehm's parents announced during a raging New York City snowstorm that they were getting divorced. The revelation shattered his life. "Which one of us do you want to live with?" his parents asked. He was their only child and still three months away from his seventeenth birthday.

"I'm enlisting in the Navy as soon as I can," he informed them. "If there's a war, I don't want to miss it."

He soon found himself thrown into the mêlée of the Second World War aboard the Livermore-class destroyer *Duncan* in the South Pacific, delivering cargoes of fuel from New Caledonia to Maggot Beach by Henderson Field on Guadalcanal. U.S. aircraft suffered from chronic shortages of gas.

Marines at Henderson Field were getting the hell beat out of them almost nightly. Those who came down to Maggot Beach to help unload supplies looked gaunt and hollow-eyed; they had been limited to a maximum of two meals a day for most of the time since their landing. Sailors tossed food at the Marines like rich men feeding beggar kids.

"Poor damned Joes," murmured Dubiel, a member of Boehm's gun crew. "At least we get a warm rack to sleep in and three hot squares a day. That's luxury living in this war."

He thought about it a moment.

"But they ain't gonna get their island sunk out from under them," he added.

Japanese submarines prowled the waters around Guadalcanal like sharks. But tonight enemy submarines weren't the real threat.

At 2225 hours, 11th October 1942, Cape Esperance on the northern tip of Guadalcanal lay abeam. Admiral Scott formed his nine-vessel squadron for battle and set course directly for Savo Island, visible only as a tiny ink blot on the horizon. Destroyers *Farenholt*, *Duncan*, and *Laffey* led the battle column in that order while *Buchanan* and *McCalla* sailed drag behind the four cruisers *San Francisco*, *Salt Lake City*, *Boise*, and *Helena*. The armada bristled with a total of 19 x 8-inch guns, 30 x 6-inchers, 56 x 5-inchers, 25 torpedo tubes, and 6,000 men.

At 2330 hours, Admiral Scott ordered a reverse course to continue patrolling the "gateway" between Savo and Cape Esperance. Somehow, his orders as to the procedure of the turn were misunderstood. While lead ships *Farenholt*, *Duncan*, and *Laffey* executed the tactical turn in a single column, like a string of railroad cars following the leader, the rest of the ships reversed simultaneously, like reversing the slats of a Venetian blind. The three lead destroyers were cut out of the formation.

It was during this confusion that the Japanese formation bound for Guadalcanal blundered into the American Task Force. Having circled wider than the other ships, *Duncan* was alone heading directly into the paths of the advancing enemy warships. One moment Boehm saw nothing from his gun mount except darkness and the faint sheen of starlight on calm seas. The next moment, ghostly forms took shape. Ships seemed suddenly to leap out of the darkness.

The first ship he saw, less than 2,000 yards away, carried the swept-back stacks of a Japanese heavy cruiser. Behind it sailed a file of vessels appearing one by one out of distant darkness. Not counting the sunken freighter off the coast at Maggot Beach, Boehm had never seen enemy ships at such close range.

"Enemy ships—visible to the naked eye," he called out.

The alarm was already being sent. *Duncan's* steel deck vibrated as her engines kicked to full speed and she veered toward the Japanese warships.

Boehm watched mesmerized as a torpedo from *Duncan* inscribed a phosphorescent wake in a slightly curving line across the black face of the ocean. Before it struck its target, Admiral Scott's other ships opened up with everything they had in a gigantic continuing explosion of bright flashes and flaming meteors. Sheets of flame belched from guns. Star clusters bursting high aloft bathed the desperately maneuvering mixture of friendly and enemy ships in eerie shadows and reflections. It was like being in the heart of a violent electrical storm.

Boehm had the enemy cruiser in the sights of his 5-inch gun. He aimed at the bridge, locked his feet around the base of his high seat, and kept firing while he rode out the recoil. The target was so near that tracers barely arched. Red flame streaked across the water and ate into the enemy vessel.

Duncan's torpedo finally struck the Japanese cruiser in a heavy explosion that rode it out of the water on a red ball of flame. Boehm continued pinging armorpiercing rounds into its deckhouse. The cruiser wasn't going to die easily. Its guns blazed back while *Duncan* maintained pursuit, intent on dogging the Japanese to their grave.

In the middle of the formation, cut off from the American column, *Duncan* found itself trapped between friendly and enemy guns, a lightning rod attracting fire from both sides. Blinding flashes of explosions rippled along its sides where it was being torn apart.

Suddenly, Boehm found himself trapped by a detonation of intense heat and light. Blood spewing from shrapnel wounds on his face half-blinded him. As he fought to ward off panic, he spotted Dubiel lying unconscious on the mount deck, his legs draped into the open powder room. Fire glowed below where Shurney the shell man looked trapped against the bulkhead.

"They're all dead!" Shurney shouted. He looked in shock. "The powder room's about to explode. Get the hell out of here."

He lurched up through the hatchway from the powder room and disappeared.

Still under steam but dying, *Duncan* circled slowly to port. Flame hissed from the bridge. Beyond, the Jap cruiser was also ablaze.

Duncan shuddered so violently in its death throes that Boehm had to crawl on hands and knees to the hatch where Dubiel's legs dangled into the powder room. The heat on the steel deck from the fire below blistered his hands. Flames shooting out from the hatch engulfed Dubiel's legs and feet.

Dubiel moaned. He wasn't dead after all. Shells impacting the destroyer knocked Boehm over Dubiel's unconscious form and slammed his head against the deck. When he regained his senses, flames were shooting out of the ship from every crack, fissure, and loose fitting. *Duncan* was being blown apart, like a chip of wood thrown onto a pond for shotgun practice.

As Boehm dragged Dubiel onto the open deck, a thin crying sound like a trapped kitten might make issued from the starboard 20-mm antiaircraft gun mount. Boehm left Dubiel lying on deck while he checked the AA guy. Dark blood gushed from his mouth and he died with a deep rattle in his chest. Boehm removed the guy's life jacket and put it on Dubiel.

Dubiel, whose legs were charred black, screamed as Boehm dragged him to the ship's port side. Then, thankfully, he lapsed into unconsciousness again.

Undecided about what to do next, Boehm looked around at the turmoil that engulfed him. *Duncan*'s forward stack had been blown off. Flames and smoke enveloped the bridge. Ammunition continued to cook off. Surreal scenes flitted before his eyes: screaming, shouting seamen running madly about like hell's denizens; fiery debris exploding in the air; flames hissing and coiling out of burning ammo magazines like great serpents; faces reflecting red fear from the fires; men abandoning their doomed ship and jumping over the sides into the dark, oily waters . . .

Since Dubiel was still breathing, Boehm, struggling, dragged the comatose sailor to the edge of the ship and heaved him overboard. He hit the water with a flat splash.

"Good luck, buddy."

Duncan with its beautiful polished warship decks and sleek Livermore lines was about to go to its watery grave. The nineteen-year-old boatswain's mate stood momentarily poised between blazing chaos aboard ship and the calm black of the ocean below and beyond. Then he made a racing dive over the side of the ship, trusting momentum to carry him through the licking flames.

The plunge overboard drove him deep into dark, warm waters. Wounded and weakened, he fought to hold on to his senses. If he passed out, he would keep sinking. In the confusion, he had neglected to look for a kapok jacket to keep himself afloat.

The shock of the water cleared his head. He floundered to the surface. Blazes from burning ships, along with flares and gunfire, sparkled the ocean for miles in all directions. Flotsam littered the sea. Something banged into him. He grabbed it. A wooden spar the size of a telephone pole. It had to be from a Japanese ship, since American warships were built entirely of metal. Spluttering water, he bellied up onto the spar.

A bedraggled figure clinging to the other end of the spar cried out in alarm and threat. Boehm reached cautiously for his sheath knife. The Japanese sailor glared at him through the haze of night and battle. Boehm figured the guy would come for him. The Jap probably figured Boehm would go for him. Both remained frozen with indecision for a long moment.

Finally, Boehm eased off the spar on his end. The Jap eased off his end. Each swam away as fast as he could in opposite directions.

Boehm dug deep strokes into the ocean. He wished he could run on water. As luck would have it, he splashed against someone else floating face up in a kapok jacket. Dubiel! Boehm could hardly believe it. The sailor was raving, out of his mind with pain.

"God, God, I wanna go home."

Duncan, still under steam but running amuck, suddenly loomed above them. Boehm grabbed the ranting sailor by the nape of his life jacket. The stricken destroyer's prow glistened as the ship rushed by so near Boehm felt he could reach out and grab it. He held on to Dubiel and his life jacket with a drowning man's grip as the wake caught them and drove them tumbling underwater.

When they surfaced, after what seemed hours, the world had grown quiet and warm and peaceful. The battle appeared to have abruptly ended. The oppressive weight of the tropical night seemed to have flattened the sea. The only vessels within view were burning. A pinprick of match flame marked *Duncan*'s departure as it slowly sank.

"Home . . ." Dubiel pleaded.

The presence of another human being in that vast, dark expanse of water, even though injured and only semiconscious, provided Boehm a great immediate comfort. Dubiel's life jacket would keep them both afloat.

"Boehm . . . We're not going to make it, are we?"

A swell of water lifted them enough that Boehm glimpsed an ink blot against the horizon. It had to be Savo Island.

"We'll make it, buddy," Boehm said.

He began swimming toward the ink blot, towing Dubiel with one hand.

The thirty-minute Battle of Cape Esperance, one of half a dozen major sea battles to occur around Guadalcanal, ended with the sinking of one Jap cruiser, one destroyer, and one freighter. While the American cruisers *Boise* and *Salt Lake City* and the destroyer *Farenholt* were damaged, only *Duncan* was lost. Over 200 seamen from *Duncan* took to the sea to escape the floating inferno.

Although rescue attempts began immediately, many survivors remained in the ocean until late the following day. Wreckage, human dead, and surviving seamen filled the gateway between Savo Island and Guadalcanal. Commingled American and Japanese blood acted as bait chum in the water. Sharks sliced toward the battle site, intent upon feasting on hapless prey.

Dubiel drifted in and out of a coma throughout the long night while Boehm towed him. At some point, Boehm shed his shoes and dungaree shirt and knifed off the legs of his dungaree trousers to make swimming easier. He didn't care if Savo was occupied by friendly or enemy forces. Savo was the only hope for Dubiel and him.

The sun rose so fiercely that Boehm, dazed and dehydrated, thought at first it must be a fire or an explosion. Salt water had caused his face to swell. His eyes felt like they were dipped in acid. He had been swimming for hours dragging Dubiel through the water, gauging direction merely by instinct and occasional glimpses of the little island. He felt drained, verging on total exhaustion.

"Keep going!" It played over and over in his brain like a stuck record.

As the sun climbed upward into a hard, blue sky, Boehm became aware that Dubiel and he were not alone in the bright sea. He felt another presence. He trod water, blinking his eyes rapidly to clear them.

Fins! Cutting the surface like the blades of knives.

Until then, he thought he had passed the point of caring about anything. But seeing the fins, he experienced utter fear, near-mindless horror. Merely sighting sharks was enough to panic the bravest heart. But to be in the water *with* them!

How long had they been nearby without his noticing? Four or five fins circled, cutting nearer and nearer, getting bolder. He reached for his knife. It was gone, lost during the night's long swim.

He had but one choice—continue swimming. He had heard that showing panic induced an immediate attack. Thank God Dubiel was blissfully out of his mind. Boehm steeled himself and crawled slowly through the water, attempting to avoid the appearance of being a potential victim.

The sharks closed in.

The casual, detached way they approached set Boehm's heart to pounding and ignited every nerve ending. Black fins slicing the water, drooping teeth-filled jaws, glinting snake eyes looking them over as impersonally as a trout about to take a live grasshopper.

One of the fish, larger and bolder than the others, darted in for a bite.

A scratching, tingling sensation shot through Boehm's foot. He shouted, kicked at the beast. Drove it off.

His foot was bleeding from the attack. Not ten feet away glistened the dark back of the giant predator.

It circled.

He drove it off again and again. The smaller sharks retreated, leaving the field to the large one. Boehm's head ratcheted on his neck as he attempted to keep watch on the fish and anticipate its next approach. It required every ounce of his strength and resolve simply to remain afloat and hold on to the unconscious Dubiel. Exhaustion, wounds, and debilitating fear were taking a toll.

There was something to be said for unconsciousness. Dubiel had no idea they were about to become some creature's main course.

The shark's fin disappeared beneath the sea. Not seeing it proved more terrifying than seeing it. Boehm spun in the water like a top, searching, darting eyes peering into the clear green water, wincing from the reflected brightness of the sun. He felt like a crippled deer surrounded by wolves.

A dark shape deep, deep below rapidly grew larger, like looking through a camera lens and suddenly zooming to maximum close-up. Screams welled in Boehm's throat, blocking it. Big and powerful, the monster brushed sandpaper rough against the sailor's bare legs.

Dubiel screamed. He must have had some awareness at the last instant as his body erupted out of the water. He twisted violently in the white froth and then he was gone in the attack, wrenched from Boehm's grip, his scream suddenly broken off to live forever in Boehm's nightmares.

It was all over that fast. A smear of red stained the sea, trailing down into the depths. Boehm lost all control. He beat the water frantically with arms and legs as he swam with renewed desperation, knowing deep down that he could never out-swim sharks but determined nonetheless to make them work for their dinner.

Follow-up

For some inexplicable reason, the sharks kept their distance after snatching Dubiel. Boehm was all but delirious by the time a rescue boat of U.S. Marines plucked him out of the swell.

Roy Boehm remained in the U.S. Navy as a career, serving in the Second World War, Korea, and Vietnam. In 1961, he founded and was the first commander of the U.S. Navy SEALs. He retired with the rank of lieutenant commander after thirty years' service and died in Florida in 2009.

Chapter 4

Mediterranean Battles

DURING A FEW SHORT MONTHS following Hitler's invasion of Poland on 1st September 1939, Germany managed to conquer Western Europe and send the British packing back across the English Channel. The fighting then remained largely a European affair until Germany launched Operation Barbarossa against Russia in June 1941 and the Japanese struck Pearl Harbor in December 1941. That let the genie of world war loose. By the time the Second World War ended, a total of fifty-five nations were officially involved in a war that was truly worldwide and the first total war in the history of the planet.

Even before Pearl Harbor, the United States had not kept its hands completely out of the spreading conflict. It supplied industrial support and actual war materiel to Britain during that nation's dark days in the Battle of Britain. Quite a large number of American aviators volunteered to fly with British airmen against German bombers and fighters.

The U.S. also provided convoy escorts against German U-boat "wolf packs" in the North Atlantic and sent out patrols to locate Nazi warships and report them to the British. The first American battle casualties of the war actually occurred seven weeks *before* Pearl Harbor when, on 17th October 1941, a U-boat torpedo damaged the U.S.S. *Kearny* off Iceland while it was on convoy escort duty. Eleven American sailors died.

The tides began to turn against the Axis powers after Pearl Harbor and America's entry into the war. By the summer of 1943, the Germans and Italians had conceded North Africa to the Allies and pulled out with their tails between their legs; U-boats lost their edge in the Atlantic; Russians were kicking the stuffing out of the Germans on the Eastern Front; the U.S. and Britain were bombing German cities; Australia had stopped the Japanese in Papua New Guinea; and American forces were fighting their way up the Solomon Islands.

After fascist forces surrendered in North Africa on 12th May 1943, the Allies looked around for their next domino to tackle and settled on Italy. The plan was to knock Mussolini out of the war while diverting German divisions from the Eastern Front and Occupied France as a prelude to a landing in Northwest

Europe, 1939

Atlantic
Ocean

N O R W A Y

S W E D E N
(neutral)

F I N L A N D

Oslo

Helsinki

Leningrad

North
Sea

ESTONIA

IRELAND
(neutral)

UNITED

LATVIA

S O V I E T   U N I O N

LITHUANIA

DENMARK

Baltic
Sea

KINGDOM

Königsberg

London

Hamburg

Minsk

NETHERLANDS   Berlin

BELGIUM   G E R M A N Y   P O L A N D

Warsaw

Paris

LUX.

Frankfurt   Prague   Kraków

F R A N C E

C Z E C H O S L O V A K I A

Munich

Vienna

SWITZERLAND
(neutral)   AUSTRIA   H U N G A R Y

Budapest

R O M A N I A

Marseille

Belgrade   Bucharest

YUGOSLAVIA

SPAIN
(neutral)

B U L G A R I A

Barcelona   Corsica

Sofia

Rome

I T A L Y

Balaerics   Sardinia

ALBANIA

G R E E C E   TURKEY

M e d i t e r r a n e a n   S e a

Sicily

N

Malta

0   miles   250

0   km   250

Crete

Europe. Until Italy, America's direct military contributions to the fighting in Europe had been relatively modest.

None of the Allies figured on having to fight their way up the entire boot of Italy. The German Commander-in-Chief South, Field Marshal Albert Kesselring, correctly predicted that an Allied landing was a certainty after the fall of North Africa. He had moved sixteen divisions into Italy by the time Britain and America landed on Sicily on 10th July 1943, followed in August and September by seaborne landings in quick succession in Calabria, and at Taranto and Salerno. Although General Dwight Eisenhower, commander of all U.S. forces in the European Theater, announced Italy's capitulation on 8th September 1943, the fighting in the boot was far from finished.

Kesselring's strategy was to hold the Allies as far away from Germany proper as possible using the natural terrain of the Italian Apennines to his advantage. He was confident he could retain Italy and the Balkans almost indefinitely by establishing a series of defensive lines and fighting as long as possible at each one before giving up ground to withdraw to the next for a repeat performance. That the Allies were still fighting in Italy up to VE-Day 1945 attests to how well his scheme worked.

Kesselring's first main position was the so-called Gustav Line that stretched roughly from Minturno near Italy's west coast to Ortona in the east. Monte Cassino, a 1,700-foot peak topped by a medieval Benedictine monastery, dominated the line, overlooking the Liri Valley and Route 6, the main approaches to Rome. The Allies and the Axis slugged it out over this real estate through the winter of 1943–4 until the struggle ended in May 1944. The Allies lost 31,000 men killed, wounded, or missing before the monastery lay in ruins and their multi-national army secured the Gustav Line.

Even so, they were barely halfway up Italy's boot—and Kesselring was waiting at the next line.

* * *

Scalps

THE ARMY DRILL INSTRUCTOR'S PLATE-BRIMMED HAT rested on the bridge of his nose.

"Boy!" he barked. "What's your name?"

"John Fulcher, sir."

"Hellfire, boy, I ain't no 'sir.' I'm a sergeant. I work for a living. You know how to shoot, John Fulcher?"

"I can shoot a acorn outa the top of a ol' oak tree with a .22."

"Can ya now? You an Injun, huh? You ever scalp any white men?"

"Not yet I ain't, Sergeant."

The green recruits of the 36th Division, Texas Army National Guard, fidgeted in the sun and dust of that autumn of 1942 at Camp Bowie, Texas. They were rough-looking farm and ranch boys in faded overalls, cambray work shirts, old hats or caps, and scuffed boots or brogans repaired with baling wire. John Fulcher, twenty-five, was a wiry six-footer with the black hair and coppery skin of a full-blooded Cherokee mother and the lighter-colored eyes of his German-Irish father. He was the first of five brothers to enlist for the war.

The Army's best marksmen often came from the American Southwest, where lanky farm boys in Texas, Oklahoma, New Mexico, and Arizona grew up as wild as the rabbits and deer they pursued. Or they came from the hill country of Alabama, Tennessee, Virginia, and Kentucky. Barefooted with flop hats and wearing dusty runover boots, they were crack shots with their old .22s and .30-.30s long before they ever saw a 1903 Springfield or an M1 Garand.

John Fulcher really *could* shoot an acorn "outa the top of a ol' oak tree." He attended sniper school at Camp Bowie where he learned how scout-snipers operated in six-to-twelve men teams out in no-man's land, sometimes even behind enemy lines. They were the eyes and ears for their battalions and companies.

That was the scouting part. The other part was sniping. Wherever they found enemy patrols or movements, they picked off Germans with well-aimed shots from hiding until the enemy were terrified to go where snipers might be lying in wait.

The Army issued Fulcher and his team new M1D rifles still in their protective Cosmoline wax. The "D" model was an ordinary Garand, except it had a heavy match barrel and a flash suppressor, a set trigger action for a smoother squeeze and discharge, a leather cheek piece, and a telescopic sight.

Then the Army sent them to war.

The 36th Division landed at Salerno with three other Allied divisions on 9th September 1943. Assault soldiers were still packed into transports out to sea when word went around that Italy had surrendered. Everyone assumed that meant the landing was called off. No such luck. The Germans had taken over.

The Allied troops had to fight their way off the landing beaches. Sniper squads waited until after the first waves secured the beachhead before they went ashore. From the rails of transport decks they watched smoke boil up from the battle while the clamor of the fight pounded around them. It was deafening, like sticking your head underneath a giant washtub while about two hundred thousand bullies beat on it with clubs.

Snipers went into action once the long push began up the Italian boot. The Germans set up a series of defensive lines in the mountains, each of which had to be breached before they would move back to the next line. They left elements behind to harass and delay advancing Allies. It was among these that Fulcher and the other sniper teams "established a presence."

A single shot would ring out from a ridge or hilltop. An officer, if possible—someone else in the ranks, if not—dropped like a sack of rotted potatoes. Nazis knew snipers were always out there, but they never knew where they were or when they would strike. That made life hellish for the Germans.

It was slow going through Italy. Cold weather settled in, a wet, bone-chilling cold that came with drizzling rain and sleet. Hitler's troops bogged down. The Allies bogged down at their throats. Dogfaces huddled miserably underneath their ponchos and cursed the war, the weather, and sometimes each other. Snipers didn't have the luxury. They were always out ahead, their job to keep the Germans nervous and worried about which of them might get it next.

Fulcher made sergeant and moved up to sniper squad leader. Promotion was a matter of attrition; the former sergeant caught a round.

Half of the snipers in Fulcher's team were Indians, including two Sioux from the Black Hills. Other GIs often jokingly referred to Fulcher and his men as savages. "The war party's going out scalping," they'd crack. The Germans were so unnerved by American sharpshooters that word had it they executed on the spot any Yank sniper they captured.

One afternoon, Fulcher's six-man patrol was scouting a road through the woods in no-man's land when the point man spotted a German snooping toward them on the same road. The patrol went to cover in roadside bushes. The German hadn't seen them.

Fulcher pointed to one of the Sioux and drew the edge of his hand across his throat. The Indian nodded. Instantly, a hatchet appeared in his hand and he slithered through the brush like a snake until he came to thick undergrowth growing out over the road. The unsuspecting German kept coming, shuffling along in a sort of weary dogtrot, his head bobbing. Fulcher figured him to be an advance scout for an element that would be coming along shortly. He and his Indians had to work fast.

The Sioux waited perfectly still until the German came bobbing along, his jackboots crunching rock and dirt. Fulcher saw the German's face. Put him in GI fatigues and you couldn't have distinguished him from America's tired and shaggy grunts.

The Sioux sprang onto the road behind the soldier and severed the German's spinal cord just below the neck with his hatchet. He ducked a geyser of blood as the body toppled. The corpse was still twitching when the Sioux dragged it into the bushes.

Sure enough, the dead man's buddies in gray-green uniforms came hiking up the road toward the front, seemingly confident that their scout would warn them of any danger. A thought struck Fulcher.

"Scalp the sonofabitch!" he said, pointing at the dead Jerry.

The Sioux knifed a thin line around the dead man's head from the brow and above the ears to the back of the neck, then peeled off the thick cap like peeling an orange. He and the other snipers dragged the warm corpse out next to the road, propped it against a tree, and folded its hands in its lap. From a short distance away, he appeared to have stopped to rest. He looked like he was wearing a red skull cap of the sort Jews wore.

The other Germans rounded a bend in the road and came tramping up. The first one to spot their dead comrade stopped like he had collided with an invisible wall. He swung his rifle to the ready. He looked uncertain. Fulcher imagined him blinking with anxiety. The other Germans jabbered like a flock of starlings in a bare elm tree.

One of them called out the dead man's name. "Heinz! Heinz!"

When he failed to respond, the entire gaggle advanced, their eyes riveted on the grisly spectacle. When they were near, their faces shattered in the sudden terror of realization.

They still wore those expressions when Fulcher and his squad ambushed them, shooting down eight of them in the middle of the road. Two escaped. Fulcher let them go to spread the word.

Whenever the next Germans came along, they would find nine of their comrades scalped and sitting like ducks in a row alongside the road with their hands folded in their laps. Fulcher figured their Teutonic fondness for order would appreciate that.

Dog-tired and footsore, Fulcher's company of the 36th Division wended its way into one of those countless, nameless towns they encountered up Italy's boot. It had been gutted by shellfire. The company's point blazed a pathway around piles of brick and collapsed framework and broken glass. Fulcher's team was holding back with Headquarters toward the rear of the moving formation when a shot echoed ahead in the ruins. All Fulcher saw from his position were the backs of GIs as they ducked behind parts of walls and buildings.

A few minutes later, another shot rang out. And another. A German sniper. Fulcher held his men tight until a runner slid in next to him.

"The commander wants snipers. That bitch of a Kraut done drilled three of us."

Fulcher tapped one of the Sioux as his spotter. The two men slithered forward through the debris until they came to a street intersection filled with wreckage from a recent shelling. A bed with the mattress still on it rested atop a pile of concrete rubble. One of the sniper's victims lay in the intersection. Fulcher decided the German must be hiding further down the street where he could control both the street and the intersection.

"Keep everybody down," he instructed the company commander. "We'll see if we can take care of the bastard."

Fulcher and his spotter worked their way across an alley blind to the sniper's street and eased along a shell-pocked rock wall overgrown with dead ivy. The wall bisected a little knoll in what had once been someone's front yard. They settled down to look things over. A sniper required patience.

"Krauts don't watch Roy Rogers," Fulcher whispered to his partner. "Let's give him a target and see if he shows himself."

The trick always worked for Roy. The spotter crawled down to the end of the ivy wall nearest the street while Fulcher eased the muzzle of his M1 through a crack in the wall clogged with enough vine to camouflage his presence. As he peered through his scope, his spotter placed his helmet on the end of a stick and slowly thrust it into view above the wall and moved it along as though someone were trying to sneak past and wasn't being too careful about it.

He jerked it down and waited a minute or so before resuming the charade. This time the enemy sniper was ready. That German *didn't* watch Roy Rogers or he would have recognized the oldest sagebrush trick of the Old West movies.

A 7.92-mm German bullet drilled the helmet and sent it spinning. Fulcher caught a glimpse of movement through his scope, a thin puff of gun smoke popping from a window about 100 yards down the street. There wasn't much left of the building, but it had enough roof over its remaining window to hold shadows inside.

Fulcher held his fire. It was like when you spooked a squirrel into its hole. Sit down and wait. Sooner or later, curiosity overcame caution and the squirrel stuck its head out again. While a good sniper was a survivor and never shot more than once or twice from the same hide, Fulcher was counting on this guy being careless or lazy.

The day was overcast and it was dark inside the house behind the glassless window. Presently, Fulcher detected movement. He shifted his crosshairs and bided his time.

He picked up the dull gleam of a rifle barrel. Then a faint man-outline materialized as the German peeked out to see what was going on. Just like a squirrel.

Fulcher fired.

An invisible rope seemed to jerk the German's weapon from his hands and hurl it into the street. The German's body flung itself forward across the windowsill where it hung head down, the body in a spasm and draining dark blood. Then it was still.

Fulcher was scalping the dead German when a green boot lieutenant who had just hooked up with the outfit came up to see what was happening.

"Omigod!" he gasped, turning pale like a west Texas sky in the middle of summer. "You barbarian sonofabitch! What do you think you're doing?"

He turned from pale to mesquite gray-green when Fulcher grinned and held up the fresh scalp. It was still dripping.

"Whassa matter, sir? Ain't you never seen no dead Kraut before?"

The lieutenant made it to the corner of the house before he started puking.

"Guess he ain't at that."

Follow-up

John Fulcher survived the war, was discharged and lived in Texas and Oklahoma until his death in the late 1990s.

* * *

Up Front

KNOWN TO FELLOW SOLDIERS as "The Medicine Man," Sergeant Rayson Billey, a full-blood Choctaw Indian from Oklahoma, came ashore with the 45th "Thunderbird" Infantry Division during the Salerno landing on 10th September 1943. Bitter fighting had reduced Billey's Kilo Company to only seventeen GIs out of the original 197 by the time the Allies reached Naples on 1st October. Although an enlisted man, Billey was acting company commander. All the officers had been killed or wounded.

Just before darkness fell, Billey led his depleted band of Thunderbirds through a small village seven miles north of Naples. The village was all but abandoned, having been shelled repeatedly during previous fighting. Communications between units at the front were often iffy, for a number of reasons, among them being that outfits were scattered all over the landscape as they advanced toward Field Marshal Kesselring's next line of defense. Having lost commo, Billey kept with his last orders—keep moving forward. Somewhere out there on the landscape, other units of the 45th were also on the move forward.

Billey didn't realize it, but his seventeen battle-weary men of Company K had moved out ahead of the friendly advance to become the leading element for the entire Allied army.

An old man in the Italian village slumped on the front steps that were all that remained of his home. He looked up and silently pointed north when asked about the Germans. Behind him, huddled on the open foundation of the house, a young woman sat and cried while holding her three young children. Billey's men doled out what few rations they could spare and continued on down the road north and out of the village.

It was a quiet evening that leeched sunlight from the valley while the sun still shone high on the ridges and mountains occupied by the Germans some twenty miles ahead. Purple shadows slowly inched up the sides of the mountains and finally a moonless night settled over Italy. Around 2200 hours, a GI whom Billey had sent ahead as scout slipped back down the road and signaled that danger was close.

"There's a big plateau about a mile ahead," the scout reported. "The airfield on top is swarming with Krauts. If our guys walk up on it, they're mincemeat."

Studying his map, Billey saw that most of the routes north led past the plateau. Approaching units would be spotted miles out from its flat top. If true that it was crawling with Germans, as Billey's scout contended, Allied units could walk into an ambush of considerable size and power.

Sergeant Billey decided personally to lead a scouting party to take another look at the enemy positions. He left twelve men behind to rendezvous with and warn other battalions that should be sweeping through within the next hour or so while he picked out four of his best men to go with him on what would turn out to be one of the single most daring conquests of the Italian campaign.

Billey first had his selected party strip off any equipment that might make noise and give them away. Armed with pistols, knives, machetes, and M1 Garands, wearing only fatigues and soft caps, the little band vanished into the night.

Terrain in the lowlands was mostly flat and covered with scrub vegetation and trees growing along small streams and washouts. In single file, Billey and his patrol used all available cover to avoid being spotted. It was tough going, and slow at times, as they crept through patches of forest, waded streams, and finally ended up crawling on their bellies in order to reach the foot of the mesa unobserved.

It was not a particularly high feature, perhaps a hundred feet rising out of the plains, but it was tall enough to provide a commanding view of the flats stretching out from it on all sides. More significantly, it was a formidable obstacle capable of being defended almost indefinitely against much larger forces. Artillery and warplanes on the airstrip up there were going to take the lives of a lot of GIs unless Billey and his men did something.

Clouds broke for a brief period to allow starlight to wash across the face of the cliff ahead. Billey noticed a drainage area that broke off the top of the plateau and appeared to provide a partly concealed access to the top. It gave him an idea.

"If we can wipe out the sentries up there," he proposed in a whisper as he and his men lay with their heads together behind the cover of a boulder field, "we can open it up for a sneak attack and save a lot of our guys. It's risky. Anyone want to go back, I won't think any the less of you."

Sergeant Billey had earned a reputation for taking risks. During almost a year of fighting in North Africa, Sicily, and now Italy, he had been wounded three times and twice listed as missing in action. Bill Mauldin, the famous 45th Division "Willie and Joe" cartoonist, once heard a rumor that the Medicine Man had been killed. Suffering from battle fatigue, Billey had supposedly died in a one-man charge with a bayonet against an enemy foxhole. The War Department notified Billey's family that he was missing, presumed dead.

The rumor turned out to be false. Billey soon surfaced, alive and well. After wiping out the foxhole, he had found a place to catch a nap. It took him some time to find his way back to his own lines.

In Sicily, an enemy machinegun pumped six holes through his rain slicker. None of the bullets touched him. He killed the machinegunner. Later, when Germans captured him, he escaped by slaying two of his captors with his bare hands.

Escapades such as these were what earned him his "Medicine Man" nickname. The Choctaw Indian had much medicine that seemed to protect him. Tonight, he would need all the medicine he possessed to pull off this mission and return safely with his men to lead an attack force through the hole they hoped to create.

The five Thunderbirds crept upward through the steeply rising washout toward the top of the dark plateau, often pausing to look and listen. As they neared the upper edge, an unmistakable German sentry's silhouette, with his coal-scuttle helmet and rifle slung over one shoulder, appeared against the lighter night sky.

Billey signaled his companions to remain concealed while he drew his machete and stalked up through the wash until he was less than ten feet from the enemy sentry. The soldier stood next to the lip of the cliff and gazed out across the plains. He cupped his hands and the flare of a match washed across a young face that looked tired and sleepy. He lit his cigarette and drew smoke into his lungs for a long breath.

Billey used to his advantage that moment when light from the match destroyed the lookout's night vision. Springing to his feet and vaulting to the lip of the mesa, he was on the sentry before the guy knew what had him. A swing of his sharpened machete almost decapitated the German. The Choctaw caught the body before it fell and went into death spasms that might alert other sentries. He waited until the twitching stopped before he laid the dead man on the ground.

He wondered how many more sentries he and his men would have to kill tonight.

Eliminating the one soldier provided an opening by which the five Thunderbirds gained access into the picket line on the plateau's southern face. From there on, it was a matter of locating sentries one by one and putting them out of their misery and out of the war. It was almost too easy; obviously the Germans never expected the enemy to walk into their high redoubts like ghosts.

A couple they stalked and did in with knives or machetes. Others succumbed to subterfuge and deceit, as when Billey donned a dead German's distinctive helmet and rifle and casually approached his next victim. Unaware of impending disaster, expecting the approaching shadow to be a buddy coming over to jaw or share a cigarette, the German didn't know what was going on until it was too late.

Within an hour, Sergeant Billey and his team slaughtered eighteen Nazi sentries and thereby destroyed the plateau's early warning system. Battalions guided by the K Company men Billey left behind surreptitiously scaled the unguarded escarpment and caught the Nazi airfield by total surprise, killing or capturing over 200 enemy pilots, artillerymen, and soldiers, and seizing a total of 60 German tanks, 22 Messerschmitt Bf-109 fighter planes, 18 88-mm artillery pieces, and scores of personal weapons, grenades, ammunition, and explosives.

Not one American was killed in the operation.

Follow-up

Army cartoonist Bill Mauldin was with the headquarters detachment that followed after the assault. He personally encouraged commanders to recommend Billey for the Medal of Honor. Billey eventually received a Bronze Star with "V" for valor for his exploit.

For some men who went to war, everything that followed for the rest of their lives was anticlimactic. It was that way for Sergeant Rayson Billey until he died in 1989. He often went out wearing an old military blouse and an Aussie campaign bush hat bedecked with a few of the military ribbons he was awarded: two Bronze Stars, three Purple Hearts, the French Croix de Guerre . . .

Bill Mauldin, who later won fame for his "Willie and Joe" cartoons and his classic WWII book *Up Front*, recalled Billey as "a tough, seasoned old soldier. And a decent man, a man who killed because it was what he had to do, not because he wanted to . . . He taught me about the Army and how to get along in the infantry."

Billey had been Mauldin's self-defense instructor during Basic Training. The two men became close friends.

Born and reared in New Mexico, Mauldin enlisted in the Army in 1940 and was assigned to the 45th Infantry Division in-training at Fort Sill, Oklahoma. The 45th was an Army National Guard outfit composed of soldiers from Oklahoma, Colorado, Arizona, and New Mexico. Mauldin worked for the division newspaper and, having shipped overseas with the 45th in 1942, began the cartoon series featuring the unshaved, mud-splattered soldiers Willie and Joe who slogged through Italy and other parts of Europe. He transferred to *Stars and Stripes* in 1944.

Mauldin acknowledged that his cartoon character Willie with the "Indian nose" was patterned after Rayson Billey. Billey, the cartoonist said, was "the bravest man I've ever known."

Bill Mauldin died in 2003.

Chapter 5

The Bombing of Germany

EXCEPT WHEN THE WEATHER WAS TOO FOUL TO FLY, the skies over East Anglia, Yorkshire, and other locations in eastern Britain were full of bombers leaving for, or returning from, raids against the German war machine. British Halifaxes, Lancasters, and Stirlings, and American B-17s and B-24s often limped back with smoke streaming from their engines and pieces of their fuselages shot away by enemy fire. Returning-home crashes averaged about four a day. Civilian cars passing the air bases were sometimes struck by crashing bombers ploughing through fields and hedges and across roads.

By 1943, some 4 percent of eastern England's land was covered by more than 200 major airbases. Bombers flew around the clock, the British Bomber Command conducting night raids while the U.S. 8th Army Air Force took its turn during daylight hours in precision-bombing high-value targets. Their aim was the "progressive destruction and dislocation of the German military, industrial and economic system, and the undermining of the morale of the German people to a point where their capacity for armed resistance is fatally weakened."

Germany had initiated the indiscriminate killing of enormous numbers of civilians with its attacks on British cities during the Battle of Britain. Britain and the United States also soon blurred the traditional lines between proper military objectives and civilian targets. Civilians became targets of incendiary bombs dropped into residential areas of cities. "Dehousing of the German work force," was how Winston Churchill put it.

"When those Germans start putting those fires out," observed one U.S. airman after a raid on the port of Emden, "they won't have enough water left to make a good pot of tea."

The armor-plated B-17 Flying Fortress was America's primary bomber in Europe, having arrived in England to join the 8th U.S.A.A.F. in July 1942. The four-engine B-17 with its crew of ten—two pilots, a bombardier, a navigator, a radio operator, and five gunners—bristled with machineguns designed to fight off the enemy's aerial attacks. The "Fort," as it was commonly called, dropped more bombs than any other aircraft of the Second World War. Of the million-and-a-half tons of bombs dumped on Germany and its occupied territories by U.S. aircraft, nearly half were dropped by B-17s. Hundreds of Forts were also lost over Axis-dominated Europe. During a single week in October 1943, the 8th U.S.A.A.F. lost 148 bombers and 1,500 crew members.

On the day of a bombing sortie, jittery airmen downed breakfast and headed for the briefing room where operations officers locked all doors and revealed the mission map on a blackboard. Ops officers described the weather outlook, targets, approaches, and expected enemy ground and air defenses. Afterwards, the aviators synchronized their watches and made their way to the flight line with all their gear.

After taking their positions in the air, the formations roared out across the English Channel where they rendezvoused with their fighter escorts. After that, pilots and air crews each wearing about sixty pounds of gear spent up to ten miserable hours crammed inside the long steel tubes.

Each man wore a parachute, a steel-reinforced vest to protect him from flak splinters, a bulky insulated flight suit to keep him warm in frigid altitudes above 20,000 feet, helmet, personal weapons, flotation devices, a survival kit, an oxygen mask, without which he might develop altitude sickness and die of lung collapse or fluid overloading, and assorted other pieces of equipment.

The flight was a combination of discomfort and grinding tedium. The simplest task, even changing positions, required concentrated effort. Radio operators listened to static hour after hour through their earphones. Pilots and co-pilots struggled to hold their planes in combat formation that allowed them to fend off enemy fighter attacks. Bombardier-navigators pored over their charts and maps. Gunners scanned for Luftwaffe fighters even as unprotected liquids like water and milk froze solid in the rarified air and exposed skin stuck to metal surfaces.

On occasions 30 percent of planes and crews that set out on a mission failed to return. One airman described the English Channel as "the shortest stretch of water in the world when you're going out—the longest when you're coming back."

* * *

The Encounter

A WAR SUN ROSE RED AND INFLAMED over the North Sea as First Lieutenant Charlie Brown, twenty-one, lined up *Ye Old Pub* with the other B-17 Forts on the taxiway of the 8th U.S.A.A.F. base at Kimbolton, England, on 20th December 1943. More than 400 Flying Fortresses of the 379th Bomber Group took off at thirty-second intervals, circled off the coast as they formed up, and then swept out over the North Sea toward Germany. Their target: the Focke-Wulf aircraft factories in Bremen.

Pilots called the Flying Fortress a "damned good plane" celebrated for its ability to absorb battle damage and keep on flying. On more than one occasion, a B-17 had lost engines or had pieces shot off, had even been left behind as lost, and still managed to straggle safely back to its base in England.

Today, Lieutenant Brown and his crew were going to find out just how durable the plane could be.

As usual, the first leg of the flight was long and uneventful. Things only got really interesting once the bombers neared Germany. There was minimum chatter on the radios. Lieutenant Brown relaxed in the left seat to conserve his energy for the raid. Rather, he relaxed as much as a man could weighted down with flight gear and on his way to a party where the hosts tried to kill the guests.

Ye Old Pub occupied a position toward the center of one of the tail elements. The big birds flying in formation reminded Brown of Canadian geese migrating. They seemed to fill the sky as far ahead as the eye could reach, fading in and out of clouds, then suddenly emerging to reflect sunlight. P-38 fighters flying escort patrolled the formation's flanks, ready to engage when German fighters swarmed the bombers like bees whose hive has been violated.

Through breaks in the cloud cover, Brown watched the curvature of the earth pass far below. Bremen lay inland from the North Sea. The bombers would start their bomb runs after they crossed over Germany's coastline.

As usual, the Luftwaffe's Messerschmitt Bf 109 fighters were waiting to bounce them almost as soon as they passed into German territory. Bf 109s were world-class one-seaters, long-nosed, painted gray-green with big Maltese Crosses festooning their fuselages, fast, maneuverable, and armed with machine-guns and cannon. More than a match for American P-38s. They suddenly appeared, shoaling up from bases whose radar provided advance warning of approaching enemy aircraft. Radios in the B-17 formations began crackling with sightings of "bogies."

While heavily armed for defense, B-17s were not built for maneuverability. They were bomb platforms, which meant a pilot's responsibility, no matter what was going on around him, was to concentrate on not colliding with other bombers while keeping on a steady and level course to the target. Flying a bomber through the hell of an air battle required nerves of steel.

Enemy fighters buzzing like giant wasps blew through the B-17 formations, their guns blazing, bullets piercing metal with loud ticking sounds. Lieutenant Brown gripped the control yoke white-knuckled and concentrated on nothing but keeping his plane in the air and on course. His gunners had the duty to protect the ship. *Ye Old Pub* vibrated from the fury of 50-caliber guns opening up on fast-moving attackers appearing and disappearing in the mêlée.

Bombers always went down in a fight. Off to his right, Brown saw a B-17 suddenly spin out of control, oily black smoke trailing from its engines as it began a slow-motion death spiral toward earth. P-38s dived to protect it from an enemy *coup de grâce* before the crew had a chance to bail out.

"Get out! Get out!" It was almost a prayer from one of Brown's gunners.

The Germans had other targets and pulled off the dying one. A distant gnat emerging from cloud cover rapidly morphed into an attacking shark that filled Brown's windshield dead ahead. The Messerschmitt's guns sparkled with streams of tracers that spider-webbed Brown's windshield. Instinctively, he ducked as the Bf 109 pulled up and zoomed over his head. That was when he realized the jolt he felt was a bullet slapping into his shoulder. He glanced over and saw the look of shock on the face of his co-pilot, a second lieutenant on his first mission.

"All right, I'm all right," Brown groaned.

He pulled aside his flight jacket to check his shoulder and found that, while painful, the flesh wound was not life threatening. He pressed a bandage against the bloody hole and returned to the business of flying.

Things, however, were worse than he imagined. Through the intercom came information that the tail gunner and one of his waist gunners were hurt. On top of everything else, Number 2 engine began to sputter. Fuel and oil misted from it out into the slipstream. Brown feathered the prop immediately to prevent fire. That cut his power by at least one-quarter and dropped *Ye Old Pub* behind in the formation.

Losing an engine near the beginning of a mission was cause enough to abort. But not this near the target. Brown trimmed his tabs to compensate for the drag from the dead engine and pressed on. His bombardier crawled forward into the nose bubble ready to take over as the bombers adjusted course to pass over the enemy aircraft factories.

As soon as the Bf 109s pulled off, 88-mm antiaircraft guns on the ground took up the assault. Puffs of gray and black smoke with red cores dotted the air throughout the formations. Planes went down like crippled geese. Flak fragments rattled against *Ye Old Pub's* skin. Brown heard someone praying over the intercom. His hands froze to the controls, his mouth so dry his tongue felt like a cucumber.

He saw Bremen ahead and turned control of the plane over to the bombardier and his Norden bombsight.

The bombardier began his countdown. "One minute . . . Forty-five seconds . . . thirty . . . fifteen . . . Bombs away!"

The Focke-Wulf factories were cradled between railroad tracks and a low range of hills smeared with city suburbs. Black smoke roiled skyward, rising, rising, as wave after wave of B-17s dropped their loads on the factories and other nearby targets in the city. Fire embered red at the core of the smoke.

Antiaircraft fire continued as thick and ugly as ever. No sooner had *Ye Old Pub* dropped its bombs than it shuddered violently from a direct hit. The bombardier screamed in agony as the Plexiglas nose shattered and flame lashed up to sear the plane's already-webbed windshield.

Brown fought to prevent his ship from falling off into a slow death spiral. He knew they were in bad shape by the sluggish controls and the aircraft's unresponsiveness. He was so busy keeping the plane in the air that he had no time to check on the condition of his crew.

He turned off the target and headed back to England, lagging further and further behind his formation. Hordes of enemy fighters were waiting to renew their attack as soon as the 88s let up. Machinegun and cannon fire riddled crippled B-17s, knocking many of them out of the air. Bf 109s swarmed over the bombers like flies on the carcass of a dead cow.

Eight of the nine members of Brown's crew were hit by now; only the co-pilot was unscathed. The tail gunner was dead and the second waist gunner had his leg shot off and was dying. Messerschmitts blasted off the bomber's rudder, knocked out a second engine, and destroyed the plane's oxygen supply. At 25,000 feet, with the ship's nose shot away, temperatures inside the plane plummeted to twenty degrees below zero. Guns froze. Worse yet, the crew began to pass out due to lack of oxygen.

Gasping for air, his vision blurring, Brown blacked out and fell forward against the yoke. The co-pilot was already unconscious. The plane tipped over on one wing and slowly spiraled toward the ground. German fighters scored it as a sure kill and raced off to pick on other stragglers.

By some miracle, Lieutenant Brown regained consciousness during the plane's long four-mile plunge toward earth. Although wounded and still groggy from oxygen deprivation, he pulled up the wreck when it was only 200 feet away from crashing. He began to nurse it in what he thought to be the direction of the North Sea for the long crossing back to England.

By all appearances, with its nose shot off, fuselage riddled with bullet holes, two engines feathered and still smoking, the plane shouldn't still have been in the air. Furthermore, it was all alone in enemy skies and, like a sick straggler cut from a herd, a ripe target even for a German on the ground with a rifle.

Lost and with his instruments malfunctioning, Brown was actually flying in the opposite direction from where he wanted to go. The bomber soon attracted the attention of an enemy airfield as it roared over at low altitude. A Bf 109 scrambled into the air to finish off the badly damaged bomber and its half-dead crew.

Perhaps the Messerschmitt pilot was curious about why the plane did not defend itself and how a plane with so much damage could still fly. Instead of administering a final death blow, he flew up alongside *Ye Old Pub* to take a close look. Holes and big rents in the bomber's fuselage allowed him to see crewmen inside trying to help each other.

He made a second pass. Still groggy, Brown glanced over and was shocked to find the German fighter keeping pace with him a wing's length away. The two pilots looked each other over. Finally, making his decision, the German signaled for Brown to lower his landing gear and return to the German airfield.

Brown was still too dazed to understand. Besides, his landing gear was destroyed. He continued on his course, fully expecting the Bf 109 to take final action.

The Messerschmitt made a third pass and pulled up alongside the stricken bomber. Somehow, the enemy pilot seemed to understand that the B-17's crew had no idea where they were going and that they were too beat to respond to his signals.

Rather than shoot down the helpless Americans, the German flyer at last convinced Brown to turn about 180 degrees and follow him. And thus it was that a Nazi fighter pilot escorted a crippled American bomber out to the North Sea. He flew alongside for a minute to make sure Brown was on course to England. Then he saluted, dipped one wing, and circled back toward Germany, having extended an extraordinary gesture of chivalry from one airman to another.

Follow-up

Charlie Brown and six members of his crew of nine survived the war. He flew a total of twenty-six bomber missions and remained in the U.S. Air Force to retire as a lieutenant colonel. For forty years after the war, he attempted to locate the Luftwaffe pilot who had given his life back to him. Fewer than 1,300 German pilots of the 30,000 who fought in the Second World War lived until the war ended.

In 1988, a newspaper in Oregon ran Brown's story of the incident. A German fighter-pilots' magazine picked it up. In 1989, the pilot of the Bf 109, Franz Steigler, and Charlie Brown were reunited. Steigler had ended the war with twenty-eight confirmed aerial victories, one less than he would have had if he had chosen to shoot down Brown's B-17 over Germany that fateful 20th December 1943.

* * *

Paying the Price

BETWEEN 1940 AND 1945, the skies over German-occupied Holland witnessed some of the fiercest aerial combat in the history of aviation. Thousands of Allied bomber formations—Americans by day, British by night—crisscrossed the eighty miles of Dutch territory between the English Channel and the German border to strike targets in Berlin, Hamburg, and the Ruhr.

The Germans concentrated massive numbers of antiaircraft guns and Luftwaffe fighters in the Netherlands to intercept attacking bombers. By war's end, the Dutch estimated that 7,000 aircraft had crashed in Holland or were otherwise destroyed there. Of these, 3,300 were British, 2,500 German, and 1,200 American. An estimated 1,000 of these plunged into the Zuider Zee, a deep inland sea about 120 miles long and fifty wide. Some crews of the doomed WWII aircraft bailed out into the sea or ditched there successfully and survived. Most, however, were never seen again.

* * *

Survivor

COLD, DARK AND DISMAL, 11th January 1944 began like the previous fifty-one days Staff Sergeant Jack Lantz had known in England. Weather forecasters at the Ridgewell U.S.A.A.F. base were predicting breaks in Central Europe's cloud cover for the first time in days, but flight engineer Lantz had his doubts as he rigged up in fleece-lined flying gear and, carrying his flight bag, cut across the ramp to B-17 serial number 42-37719, 533rd Bomber Squadron, 381st Bomber Group, 8th U.S. Army Air Force. The right waist gunner, Sergeant Raymon Beus from Utah, and tail gunner Sergeant George A. Whitney from Massachusetts joined him. Beus studied the sky.

"Too much weather," he predicted. "We'll be scrubbed."

"It'll keep the Jerries grounded," Lantz said. "That's a good thing."

"There are good things in this war?" Whitney interjected sarcastically.

Weather or no weather, the mission was a go. More than 600 B-17 Flying Fortresses and B-24 Liberators set out to bomb aircraft factories in Halberstadt and Oschersleben. Lantz's crew of ten was relatively new to the war. Even the pilots. All were teenagers or in their early twenties. Lantz was nineteen. This was his fourth combat mission.

Instead of the weather breaking, it deteriorated. Bombers late on takeoff aborted due to poor visibility. Those already in the air continued. Only 238 aircraft reached their targets, the others turning back due to weather and mechanical malfunction.

Fifteen were shot down, the losses beginning in heavy flak at the Dutch border. Shrapnel severed oil lines to Number 3 engine of Lantz's B-17. Blowing oil slicked the wing and coated the horizontal stabilizer. Pilot Lieutenant Donald Nason feathered the prop.

That was just the start of the Fort's problems. Apparently, flak had done more damage than initially estimated. Number 4 lost power. Number 2 began popping and misfiring. Rapidly losing power and lift, the plane fell out of formation. Nason had no choice but to turn back. But a bomber alone in enemy airspace was easy prey.

"What's our position?" he asked Lieutenant C. D. Fiery, the bombardier-navigator.

"We're over water," Fiery responded.

The B-17, still losing power, dropped through the ceiling of dark and ominous clouds. Almost immediately, a squadron of German fighters appeared in the distance against the weather-smudged horizon. Nason needed to get back into the clouds to evade them. That required muscle.

"Restart Number Three," he instructed the co-pilot, Lieutenant Joe Byser.

Lantz overheard the order through his earphones. His duty as flight engineer was to maintain and oversee the mechanical health of the ship. Oil still gushing out of Number 3 alarmed him. One spark and the plane went up in flames. He keyed his mike to warn the pilot—but too late. The co-pilot was Johnny on the spot. The prop of Number 3 rotated out of feather.

Flames instantly consumed the engine and lashed back in the slipstream over the wing. With Numbers 2 and 4 also leaking fuel, the plane was only minutes away from being consumed in a sudden fireball. Frantic intercom communications erupted as the rest of the crew recognized what was happening.

Fire like that left the crew only one recourse. As plane commander, Lieutenant Nason made the decision. "Bail out! Bail out now!"

He would remain at the controls and be the last man out—or he would go down with the ship.

With nervous, fumbling fingers, Lantz hurriedly disconnected his oxygen line, heated flight suit, and intercom and started aft to the Joe Hole, a door in the deck of the airplane through which the crew might escape by parachute during an emergency. The ship was already beginning to fill with smoke and to yaw and buck, making walking difficult.

Radio operator Ralph Lab was at the Joe and desperately stomping on the door to get it open. His eyes were white-rimmed and seemed to bug out of his face in terror.

"I pulled the hinge pins but the bastard is stuck," he shouted at Lantz.

Lantz took a turn stomping on the door. It refused to give. Lab backed off and got a run at it, leaping into the air and landing on the door with both feet.

The door gave. It and Lab vanished instantly, sucked out into the air.

Wind howled. Nothing was visible below except shreds of clouds whipping past. Sergeant Paul Stonich, the ball turret gunner, and Ray Beus stumbled toward the opening as the plane yawed heavily into its burning engine. One after the other, without a word, the two airmen stepped through the portal and vanished.

Although terrified, Lantz hesitated to follow them. Lieutenant Nason might still try a dive to whip out the blaze and save the airplane. Bouncing from side to side, he fought his way to the right waist station and plugged into the intercom. No one answered him.

The plane felt as though it were about to go into a flat spin, one of the most difficult attitudes from which to recover. Finally figuring it was time to get out while the getting was good, Lantz returned to the Joe Hole. By then, the plane was indeed spinning toward earth. The air stream was so strong that it blew Lantz back inside when he tried to hurl himself out.

Growing more desperate by the moment, he flattened himself on the cold metal deck and tried to pull himself through the hole hand over hand. That didn't work either. He hadn't the strength to overcome the pressure created by the B-17's spin. While other options ran crazily through his head, the slipstream somehow caught his exposed left shoulder and suddenly wrenched him tumbling through the opening.

While in the air, he glimpsed a piece of cowling flash by, missing him by inches. Apparently, there had been another layer of clouds below, for they closed around him, shutting out the sun and blocking vision. He pulled his ripcord. The parachute popped open and clawed air, yanking him up short.

Then everything went startlingly quiet. Moments later, he emerged below the ceiling and noticed several other parachutes dropping out of the mist around him. They were too far off to hail them.

Below lay the Zuider Zee, a large body of water surrounded by land and cities. Black smoke smoldered and bubbled in the water where the plane had apparently plummeted into the inland sea while Lantz was still inside clouds. Scattered debris floated on the water in the vicinity of where Lantz calculated he was about to land.

Off to his right he spotted distant sailing boats. Nearer were two larger fishing boats. He yelled at the boats as soon as he was lower and preparing to splash down, thinking sound would carry farther in the air than after he hit the drink.

The speed of his descent plunged him deep into the frigid sea. Shocked and disoriented by the sudden temperature change, he seemed to take forever to surface and rid himself of his parachute before it dragged him under and drowned him, Mae West or not.

Exhausted from the effort, spluttering water and panting, he looked around and saw nothing except more water. His legs and arms were already numb and almost useless because of the cold. He was incapable of speech other than incoherent babbling when one of the fishing boats appeared and pulled up alongside. Two fishermen threw him a thick, knotted rope and pulled him up on deck and carried him below to a wood-burning stove.

They removed his soaked clothing, rubbed and slapped circulation back into his tortured body, and dressed him in dry trousers and a blanket. The Dutch Harbor Patrol arrived shortly thereafter. One of the policemen spoke some English.

"We are force to turn you to the Germans," he said regretfully. "They know a plane come down. If we do not give you to them, they will . . ."

He left the sentence unfinished, but the meaning was clear.

A Wasserschutzspolizei (Water Police) boat carrying Gestapo and SS men garbed in black foul-weather gear sped out to take charge of the American prisoner. One of the SS men yelled furiously at Lantz, threatening him. Not understanding, Lantz tried to ignore him and the fear that his raving ignited. The German boat commander scowled.

"This war, young man, I'm afraid is over for you," he said in passable English.

Follow-up

Jack Lantz was the only survivor of the crash. The bodies of Lieutenants Donald A. Nason, Joseph J. Byser, Athan Anagos, C. D. Fiery, and Staff Sergeant Luster T. Harrah washed ashore and were buried. The following crewmembers are still missing: Sergeant Raymon C. Beus; Sergeant Ralph L. Lab; Sergeant George A. Whitney; and Sergeant Paul W. Stonich.

Lantz spent the rest of the war as a prisoner initially at Stalag Luft VI outside Heydekrug in East Prussia near the Baltic Sea and later at Stalag XIB in Germany. When the British 7th Armoured Division, the "Desert Rats" of North Africa fame, liberated him on 16th April 1945, only weeks before the end of the war in Europe, he weighed only 117 pounds distributed on his six-foot-two frame.

Lantz returned to Tulsa, Oklahoma, after the war where he became a successful businessman and where he still lives.

Chapter 6

Prisoners of War

FOR MOST OF HUMAN HISTORY, combatants on the losing side of battle expected either to be executed or taken into slavery. Little distinction was made between fighters and civilians, except that women and children were less likely to be slain. Women were commonly kept as sex slaves. The earliest known camp specifically built to hold prisoners of war was established at Norman Cross, England, in 1797 to house captives from the French Revolutionary and Napoleonic wars.

Efforts to prevent the inhumane treatment of prisoners of war (POW) started with the Brussels Conference of 1874. The movement to improve POW treatment continued with the 1907 Hague Convention and with the Third Geneva Convention of 1929 that made it internationally illegal to torture and mistreat POW. However, not all nations were signatories to the Geneva Convention, and even those that were varied considerably in the care they took to follow the law.

Imperial Japan became notorious in the Second World War for its mistreatment of those it captured. Germany and Italy generally treated POW from the United States, Britain, France, and other Western countries with some regard to Geneva guidelines. However, Germany failed to apply the same standards to Russian POW, as well as to other Slavs or Jews of whatever nationality, whom they often tortured, used as slave labor, or executed. The Soviet Union reciprocated.

Nearly 58 percent of Russian POW held by the Germans died in captivity of various causes, significantly by torture and execution. Almost 36 percent of Germans seized by the Russians died in a comparable manner.

It is unclear exactly how many combatants of all sides ended up in some form of detention, but it certainly exceeded the 8 million of the First World War. Approximately 135,000 British fighters and 96,000 American servicemen were taken and held by the Germans during the war. While most guests of the Stalags believed the Germans mostly did the best they could, others accused them of brutality and forced labor.

The German Army simply found itself overwhelmed with prisoners they could not reasonably look after. First of all, prisoners had to be moved away from the front to detention camps behind lines. That meant prisoners often had to march hundreds of miles since transport commanders rebelled against hauling them, claiming the POWs infested their vehicles with lice. Many died on the way because rations were barely enough to keep them alive.

Conditions in the Stalags were primitive. The camps were squalid, food meager. A typical meal consisted of a slice of black bread and a bowl of watery potato soup. Medical support was even less readily available. Diseases like typhus (spread by lice) took a terrible toll.

"The German plan was to keep us alive," one American POW said, "yet weakened enough that we wouldn't attempt to escape."

"The only difference between Stalags and concentration camps was that we weren't gassed or shot in the former," recalled another. "I do not recall a single act of compassion or mercy on the part of the Germans."

* * *

The Diary

DURING HIS TENURE AS A GUEST OF THE THIRD REICH, Staff Sergeant Jack Lantz, captured after his bomber went down in the Zuider Zee in January 1944, met a Brit in the Stalags whom the Jerries had captured in 1940. "Peter," which is all Lantz remembered of his fellow POW, kept a diary about his lengthy captivity. Somehow, Sergeant Lantz ended up with the last parts of Peter's diary:

> At Gross Tychow, July 1944, we were marched to the coast and then transported in the hold of a boat to Anklam. POWs were then handcuffed together and marched up to the camp. During this short period, guards moved aside and out of the forests came the Kriegs Marines [sic] with fixed bayonets. I always remember there was a German captain on a bicycle who was yelling, "These are the people who bombed your women and children. Now is the time for your revenge." The Kriegs Marines commenced prodding prisoners with bayonets. Those who couldn't keep up the pace dropped by the wayside bringing down the prisoner he was chained to who now had to endure repeated prods with bayonets. At end of the road a place was squared off, ironically staffed by German doctors, to look at wounds inflicted by their own troops. One prisoner of war had at least sixty wounds

and his blood-stained vest was kept to show the Red Cross.

At Gross Tychow, this was a place.

Camp leader came in with a message to tell us we were going to be evacuated on 6 February [1945] due to Russian advance. Go by foot. Tommy and Slim were in hospital at time.

First day, marched from Stalag Luft 4, housed in a village. Destination unknown. Walked for another few days and passed through Anklam. During evening we slept in corn loft. We were very hungry and cold.

February 19, set out from Brest at 9:30 and have long march. We passed sign post that read: "Berlin, 190 kilometres." Arrived at place called Gerlitz or Gorlitz at dusk.

Lots of blisters and were trying to get sacking to tie around feet.

Arrived at Brugen on 23 February and were billeted in barn. Commenced raining very hard, stomach trouble, blisters. Damp and dismal.

1 March. Still in Bregow [Brugen], due to prisoners with dysentery and pneumonia. Gale blowing.

March 4. Received a bread ration.

American was taken to New Brandenburg with pneumonia.

8 March. John, one of medics, and myself left for Luplow to look for a place to set up a small room to treat POWs.

12 March. Borrowed some cooking utensils from one of the German fraus. Now encountering lots of refugees fleeing from the Russian advance. They say that the Russians are 15 kilometres away. Doc spent two hours with one of the refugees, but he died. Vic went into New Brandenburg to try and locate Red Cross parcels which were supposed to be on a train destined for POW camps.

March 13–14. Got hold of some barley for sick, made up a mixture with milk from a farm. Found large unused chicken house which was rigged up as a place for hospital. Very bitter night. Then moved into one of the horse stalls, which was warmer, but I don't think horses appreciated company. Chicken laid an egg in one of the feeding troughs. Became quite a treat. Managed to persuade German captain to take me into town to try and get some medical supplies. Issued a slice of bread on this particular day, but ration of meat didn't look very appetizing.

German, a captain, said possibility of move in a cattle truck.

17 March. Left Luplow for a place called Kleet. At 1400 we left in train cattle cars, very crowded.

18 March. Arrived at place called Butznow at 0600. Remained in cattle cars all day and during this period we had two air raid alarms. Also hear heavy anti-aircraft fire and heavy thuds.

Arrived at a place called Magentow and departed at 1235 for Hamburg, arriving in Hamburg at 1600. Shunted onto a railway siding in Hamburg and left there overnight. Guards said, "This will give you a taste of what it's like to be bombed by your own bombers."

All night saw flashes through the cracks in the cattle cars and the ground was shaking violently. Shrapnel kept peppering down on the roof of the train.

21 March. Arrived at Fallingbostel, Stalag XIB, north of Hanover. Prisoners were deloused before entering camp. Conditions were pretty terrible. Some spuds and some very gritty bread and a small ration of syrup, about a tablespoon a week.

26 March. First issue of Red Cross parcels. Plenty of air raids by this time, sound of aircraft at night, most of night.

Food—one slice of bread. Acorn coffee. German officer spoke of further cuts in food.

Air raids every day. B-17s overhead and very big raids in the direction of Hamburg. Flak lit up the sky at night and we could see the big red glow from where bombs had dropped.

5 April. All feeling very weak.

10 April (1945). Only few guards left. Guards had handed over their rifles and had taken to wearing white coats and white hats . . .

Follow-up

Jack Lantz was liberated on 16th April 1945 from Stalag 11B at Fallingbostel. He never learned what happened to "Peter," although he tried unsuccessfully to locate him after the war and return his diary. He assumed Peter survived the war.

Chapter 7

Mediterranean Air Force

IN A NEW YEAR 1944 MESSAGE, General Henry "Hap" Arnold, Chief of Staff, U.S.A.A.F., summarized the goal of the Allied air buildup and the carpet bombing of Germany and its satellites: "Destroy the Enemy air force wherever you find them, in the air, on the ground, and in the factories." Germany's Luftwaffe had to be annihilated if the Allies were to make their landing in Europe before the year was out. Otherwise, troops landing on the beachheads would be picked off before they could establish a toehold on Fortress Europe.

To aid in this goal, the U.S. 15th Air Force came on-line in the Foggia area of southeastern Italy. The Allies had captured Foggia and its important airfield complex in September 1943 in the wake of the ground advance up Italy's boot, thereby increasing access to targets in the Balkans, Greece, the Danube basin, southern Germany, and Silesia that were otherwise out of range of the 8th U.S.A.A.F. in Britain.

Throughout 1944, 15th AF bombers struck German-held bastions deep within the Reich's southern approaches, targeting submarine bases at Toulon, rail yards at Budapest and Bucharest, and especially the oil fields at Ploesti in Romania that provided a third of the fuel needed by the Luftwaffe. During a series of twenty missions from April to August 1944, U.S. flyers from Foggia all but shut down Ploesti's oil fields.

The 15th paid a bloody price for its success: 223 of its planes were shot down.

* * *

When Your Number Is Up

AS A B-17 FLIGHT NAVIGATOR, Lieutenant Haig Koobatian accepted that the sun rose in the east, that rain was wet, and that his number might well come up before he reached fifty missions, after which he was eligible for transfer off combat duty. A chart in the Ready Room at the Foggia Airbase in Italy listed the names of all flyers. Names were crossed through when an airman completed his fifty missions—or when his number came up and he failed to return from one.

Flying a metal tube filled with high octane fuel and explosives while people tried to shoot it down did not portend a long and fruitful life. There were too many ways to get your number marked off.

Although the most obvious perils were enemy fighter planes and antiaircraft fire, airmen could also die from innumerable other causes—crashes brought about by mechanical problems, carelessness, such as getting out of formation and being hit by bombs dropped from airplanes above; fog and unexpected storms; navigational mistakes that resulted in a plane's wandering around over enemy territory until it ran out of gas or hostile fire brought it down; trying to take off overloaded; psychological hazards like watching your buddies not come back day after day until you reached the point of mental breakdown, sometimes with disastrous results ... Almost a third of bomber crewmen had their numbers come up before fifty.

It was a nerve-wracking way to fight a war.

A typical mission meant rolling out of your bunk at 0330 hours in order to have time to eat breakfast, get your gear ready, and take off at 0530 before the sun came up. A Flying Fortress carried fuel for about ten hours in the air, depending upon such factors as bomb load, wind speed and direction, altitude, temperature, and necessary evasive movements. From Italy, a bomber squadron could reach and return from: Berlin in 8.5 hours; Bleckhammer, Poland, in 8 hours; Munich or Vienna in 7; the Ploesti oil fields in Romania in 8 . . . Targets were railroads and depots, oil fields and refineries, communications centers and airfields, troop concentrations, or whatever else might come up in the normal course of war.

Flying a mission involved hours of freezing drudgery followed by harrowing minutes over the target. Altitudes of 20,000 feet or more in unheated, un-pressurized cabins meant oxygen masks and battery-heated, fleece-lined flight suits and boots. Along the way, crews munched on cold cheese sandwiches and drank milk if it hadn't frozen in temperatures of forty degrees below.

Lieutenant Koobatian, a 22-year-old with crew-cut brown hair and a thoughtful grin, arrived at Foggia in March 1944 and was almost immediately inducted into the numbers game. He and another navigator, a lanky Texas captain named Edwards, were assigned a tent together and began making it habitable against a Mediterranean climate known for hot, dry summers and wet, miserable winters and springs. They were constructing a floor for their tent using old bomb crates to keep off the soggy ground when the squadron navigator of 419th Squadron, 301st Bomber Group, stuck his head through the flap opening. Rain was falling steadily, pounding on the tent and running in underneath the edges.

"Lieutenant Koobooten—?"

"That's *Koobatian*, sir."

"Whatever. Get your gear together. The weather is supposed to clear. We need one more navigator—and you may as well start today."

Normally, a Fort's crew stayed together. However, individuals could be pulled off other crews to fill in when necessary.

Koobatian, a green one-bar fresh out of training who dared not speak up for himself, threw down everything and was ready to comply. On the other hand, Captain Edwards had been around awhile.

"Sir, Koobatian just got here," Edwards drawled in his Texas twang. "It's rainy and muddy and we're trying to get our house squared away. There are plenty of other navigators who have been here long enough to get set up. Why don't you take one of them this time?"

The squadron navigator stood in mud just inside the front door of the tent. He looked around at the mess. He nodded his head. It was logic he couldn't argue with. He ducked back into the rain.

About three hours later, Koobatian heard the engine roar of the formation returning after having conducted a bombing mission against a rocky island off the coast where the German Navy might be trying to set up a base. He and Edwards were finishing unpacking and storing their personal gear when a terrific explosion on the runway shook the ground. They rushed outside to see a ball of fire rising into the air after one of the bombers crashed on landing.

All ten members of the crew died in the conflagration. Koobatian later learned that he would have been the navigator on the ill-fated flight but for Captain Edwards's intercession. A replacement had been assigned in Koobatian's place—and lost his life because of it.

"I guess your number wasn't up," Edwards marveled.

Koobatian began to feel that *Somebody* must be looking out for him. His plane returned unscathed from missions in which nearly every other aircraft landed riddled with bullet holes and flak damage. He became a good luck totem. Other crewmen tapped him on the shoulder for luck and wanted to fly with him.

Late on an April afternoon in 1944, loudspeakers mounted around tent city at Foggia announced the posting of the next day's battle orders in the Ready Room. Lieutenant Koobatian and his crew ambled over to check their fate. His squadron, the 419th, was assigned to bomb an aircraft engine plant in southern Germany. Koobatian was designated lead navigator for the twenty-three-bomber formation. His bombardier slapped him on the back.

"We don't feel right if you're not with us, Haig," he said. "Nobody gets hurt when you're in a plane."

Flying Fortresses taking off from the steel-mesh airstrip in the next morning's pre-dawn made the black sky throb with their mighty engines. The first planes in the air circled the field and waited until every aircraft reached altitude and formed up before they headed for Germany. They flew in a staggered combat box in which each B-17 covered others with its 50-caliber Browning machine-guns mounted in the nose, tail, dorsal, waist, and belly positions.

As navigator, Koobatian twisted himself into the cramped nose bubble where he had a good view of the ground and reference points. The sun rose in a glorious spectrum of color, turning the earth into a shining ball and trans-forming engine vapor trails into iridescent patterns etched against deep blue. The view took his breath away, what with his being encased in clear glass except for his back. It gave him the feeling of floating in space, a detached observer of earth and its puny inhabitants. God Himself must enjoy such a view.

Most of the crew had little to do for the next three hours. Koobatian took care of his navigator duties with charts and pencils, checking off landmarks and making sure the squadron remained on course. Pilot Harold Van Lowen and co-pilot John Gilbert shared the flying. The rest of the crew kicked back to wait.

The atmosphere changed once the bombers reached enemy airspace. Tension increased. Anxious eyes scanned the sky for intercepting fighters. First sightings of the enemy always chilled Koobatian's blood. He was busy with his calculations when an excited voice burst across the radio net: "Bogies, one o'clock high!"

Welcoming committees of Focke-Wulfs and Messerschmitts arrived to engage the bombers' air cover fighters and make their high-speed strafing runs at the formation, zipping down seemingly out of nowhere, whipping through like sharks loosed into a school of yellowtail. The trouble with a seat in the nose cone was that while it provided an unparalleled view of God's creation, it also thrust the observer into the same unobstructed view of hell.

As German fighters slashed through, guns flickering, the bombers replied with their formidable 50-cals. The nose gunner in the bubble with Koobatian slung red tracers. The B-17 seemed to shudder with the recoil.

Off to the right flank, the crew of a stricken Fort began bailing out of every shattered orifice. These were men that Koobatian knew. Buddies. He could almost see their eyes as they tumbled into the frozen air and streaked toward earth. Their abandoned B-17 tipped onto one smoking wing and plunged after them.

Enemy fighters slashed, ripped, and tore, inflicting what damage they could before the bombers reached their destination. Once the fighters withdrew, ground-based antiaircraft batteries took over. Individual storm clouds of black smoke jagged with orange blasts of lightning filled the sky. B-17s had to enter the tempest and survive it in order to reach their targets.

Airmen in a high pitch of excitement and fear yelled and screamed warnings and entreaties, prayers and death rattles over the radio as, flying through deafening thunder and blazing balls of light, they were buffeted and rattled about in their metal coffins. Shrapnel fragments piercing aircraft skin made distinctive ticking sounds and sometimes left gaping holes. Oil leaking from damaged engines misted in the air and clotted on the windshields of trailing aircraft.

One Flying Fortress detonated into blue wind-whipped flames. Another bomber, trailing thick black smoke from both starboard engines, was suddenly consumed by fire. Crewmembers abandoned ship, leaping into space. Flaming human figures burned through the air like roman candles at an Independence Day fireworks show. Koobatian couldn't hear them screaming, but he knew they were.

Stuck out there in his box seat, alternately praying and trembling from fear, Koobatian could do nothing except stare in mesmerized horror. Great gaps appeared in the bomber formation as plane after plane succumbed to the most devastating AA barrage Koobatian had ever encountered. At this rate, none of them would make it to the target.

While *Somebody* might be looking out for him, it seemed that *Somebody* was looking the other way this morning. Maybe today was the day his number came up.

Koobatian resigned himself to his fate. Time sequences lost all meaning. Everything was present with no past, no future, merely a vast existing vacuum of now. He wondered how anyone could keep his wits when the world was going mad.

"We can't make it!" a pilot shrieked over the air, his voice strained and terrified. "We'll never get to the target. There are no planes left."

Perhaps what Lieutenant Koobatian experienced next was some form of higher consciousness, a result of extreme fright when a man's eyes focus outside his normal sphere and he sees things the average person does not see. All he knew was that he *saw* what he saw. He experienced it—and no one could tell him he didn't. Whatever happened, he believed it saved his life and the lives of his fellow crewmen.

A fire suddenly appeared, suspended in the sky ahead. Like an enormous bonfire that discharged wonderful sparks leaping through the air. It was not flak. The fire grew until it seemed to fill up the universe, warm and glowing and not terrifying at all. From Koobatian's perspective, it appeared an all-encompassing heavenly light, the eternal assurance of God's presence.

His fear inexplicably drained away as the assurance crossed his mind that everything was going to be all right, that that *Somebody* who looked out for him had pulled a protective shield around his bomber.

The mission commander ordered through the radio net: "Turn back! We can't make it through. Turn back!"

Pilot Van Lowen shouted at Koobatian through the plane's intercom. "Reverse one-eighty. Give me directions home!"

Only six B-17s of the original twenty-three that set out on the mission returned. The others were either shot down or forced to make emergency landings. Surviving airmen stared at Koobatian as though he must have been hallucinating when he told them what he saw. Nonetheless, they conceded that their numbers had not come up. Not this time.

Follow-up

Haig Koobatian finished the war in Italy and returned home after VE-Day. He lives in California where he has devoted his life to exploring his personal spirituality. "It may sound crazy," he wrote in a letter, "but all one has to do is to read stories of men in action, under severe mental strain, to realize there are some unanswered questions over which we should brood, questions about the validity of some of our conventional thinking."

Chapter 8

Invading Europe

IT HAD BEEN CLEAR TO THE NAZIS since 1942 that their enemy would land on mainland Europe sooner or later. In preparation for that eventuality, Hitler ordered the construction of the Atlantic Wall, a line of massive coastal fortifications stretching from Norway to the Spanish border. A work force of more than 100,000 laborers, many of them captured prisoners, used 2 million tons of steel and 20 million tons of reinforced concrete to build what Hitler viewed as an impregnable bulwark against the enemy's landing anywhere along 1,700 miles of European coast.

In addition, the Germans planted 4 million antipersonnel and antitank mines, constructed reefs of underwater obstacles that would rip the bottoms out of landing craft along likely landing beaches, flooded low-lying areas behind the coasts, drove sharpened stakes in the ground, and stretched barbed wire across open fields against paratrooper and glider landings behind the beachheads.

Although the Germans had twenty-four regular field divisions stationed in France by the spring of 1944, including ten panzer divisions, Field Marshal Erwin Rommel thought their use and deployment unsatisfactory when Hitler assigned him to inspect the Wall.

"If we are not at the throats of the enemy immediately he lands," he warned, "there will be no restoring the situation, in view of his vastly superior air force. If we are not able to repulse the Allies in the first forty-eight hours . . . then the invasion will have succeeded . . . It is absolutely necessary that we push the British and the Americans back from the beaches. Afterwards, it will be too late. The first twenty-four hours of the invasion will be decisive. It will be the longest day."

While Germans prepared to defend, Americans and British prepared to attack. Since surprise was vital, the Allies launched Operation Fortitude to mislead Germany into believing the Allies would land in France in the Pas-de-Calais region, across the narrowest part of the English Channel, when in fact the real target was Normandy. Bomber raids were distributed into the Calais region to make Hitler think a landing area was being "softened" for invasion.

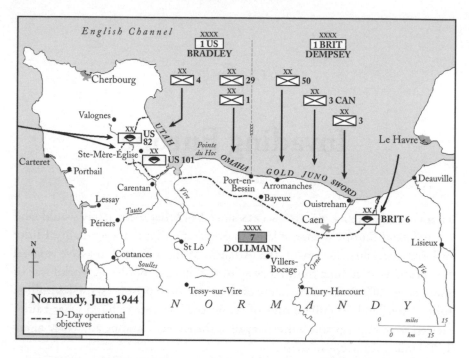

The fields of Suffolk, Essex, and Kent also appeared to indicate a Pas-de-Calais landing. They blossomed with huge "invasion" encampments crammed with rubber blow-up tanks and airfields clustered with mock-up transport planes made from plywood. This phantom army even had a commander. General George Patton frequently "visited" the various units of his "command" to fool Nazi spies.

By the end of May 1944, Britain had become what General Dwight D. "Ike" Eisenhower, Supreme Commander Allied Expeditionary Force, called "the greatest operating military base of all times." The American buildup shipped in 50,000 tanks and armored vehicles, 450,000 trucks, 450,000 tons of ammunition, and 1.5 million troops. Counting Canadians, Free French, and Free Poles, the invasion force fielded some 3 million men, all waiting for the signal to begin.

Four years earlier, the Royal Navy, aided by miscellaneous civilian watercraft, had rescued the British Expeditionary Force from the beaches of Dunkirk. Since then, other expeditionary forces had successfully landed in North Africa, Sicily, Salerno, and Anzio, but none compared in power or purpose to the vast armada that now prepared to set sail for France. More than 7,000 ships, including 1,213 warships, had assembled to haul a first wave of 287,000 men across the English Channel and protect them on their way.

All they needed was the order to go.

Operation Overlord, the overall code-name for D-Day when the Allies would make their landing in France, had been initially set for early May, but had been postponed several times for various reasons. Now it was set for 5th June. While May in England had been a gorgeous month of sunshine and fair weather, the first week of June brought in squalls and lashing rain. In crowded harbors from Falmouth to Harwich to Weymouth Bay, more than 100,000 troops were packed on ships waiting. Some of them had been aboard since 1 June, their nerves seared and their stomachs rebelling from seasickness. Another 150,000 or so waited to climb aboard.

Another postponement was almost out of the question. Troops had already been briefed and the gigantic machine set in motion. It could not be slammed in reverse without serious risks of disorganization and loss of security.

Hard rains drummed late into the night of Sunday, 4th June 1944, when General Eisenhower called a meeting of his staff and key subordinates at his headquarters in Bushy Park by the Thames. Military meteorologists were predicting a possible break in the weather after midnight. Turning to British General Bernard Montgomery, Eisenhower asked, "Do you see any reason for not going on Tuesday?"

If the invasion force did not set out for France tomorrow, 5th June, for the landing on Tuesday, 6th June, it would have to wait for at least another two weeks for favorable tides and moonlight.

Montgomery replied, "I would say—Go."

After further discussion, Eisenhower finally concluded, "Well, boys, there it is. I don't see how we can possibly do anything else. I'm quite positive we must give the order. The only question is whether we should meet again in the morning."

All agreed that the final order should wait until after meteorologists reported on the weather at 0415.

Although it was still booming rain when the conference adjourned, the weather seemed to be clearing by the time commanders reassembled for the final and irrevocable decision. Meteorologists predicted the weather might clear sufficiently for the operation to launch on 6th June. That was enough for Eisenhower.

"Okay. We'll go."

Winds still kicked up waves four to six feet high on the morning of 5th June 1944. Clouds remained low and threatening as troops still waiting on land began loading aboard transports. General Eisenhower sent a message to be read to all troops prior to battle:

> Soldiers, Sailors, and Airmen of The Allied Expeditionary Force!
> You are about to embark upon the Great Crusade, toward which we have striven these many months. The eyes of the world are upon you. The hopes

and prayers of liberty-loving people everywhere march with you . . . The tide has turned. The free men of the world are marching together to Victory!

* * *

Pray and Pass the Ammunition

On 4th June 1944, the Sunday before D-Day, U.S.A.A.F. chaplain George R. Barber, thirty, and a Catholic colleague called Roberts held church services on eleven different ships in Weymouth Harbor aboard which soldiers of the landing forces awaited orders for the crossing to France. The two chaplains rode a little motor launch from ship to ship, bracing themselves against squalls of wind-driven rain so brisk that the raindrops stung their faces. Whitecaps choked the air with salt spray and all but capsized the little boat on several occasions.

Clambering aboard the ships, soaked to their skins, the chaplains shucked off their rain slickers and boots and conducted services under whatever cover was available. Never had church services been so well attended. It seemed there really were no atheists in foxholes—or aboard ships that would land their congregations near enemy-held foxholes within the next few days.

Six feet tall with piercing blue eyes, his dark hair cut close to his scalp, Chaplain Barber might easily have been mistaken for a regular soldier but for the gold crosses on his collar.

"Jesus will be with you—and I'll be right there with you as well," he assured young GIs, who looked anxious, anticipating what would certainly be a day they remembered. If they survived it.

The chaplains continued their rounds until after nightfall and exhaustion overcame them. They handed out hundreds of little pocket Bibles.

"Remember your mothers, your fathers, your brothers and sisters," Reverend Barber preached. "They all love you. They are praying for you too. We're on God's side and He's on our side and we're going to win."

"Chaplain, you don't have to go on this crossing," spoke up one young soldier. "Why are you doing it?"

"God will show me my duty. Let us pray . . ."

A lanky 44-year-old man with a war correspondent's patch on his shoulder attended one of Chaplain Barber's sermons. He had big ears and a wide grin that stretched all the way across his face. He was a reporter for the Scripps-Howard newspaper chain and would win a Pulitzer for his war coverage.

"Chaplain," said Ernie Pyle, "I guess I'll be seeing you on the beach. Keep your powder dry."

"God is my sword and my shield."

"Then keep your shield up, Padre."

On the morning of 5th June, the invasion fleet streamed out into the stormy English Channel. Wind in fierce gusts buffeted transports, landing craft, battleships, cruisers, torpedo boats . . . thousands of them. The largest invasion force ever assembled.

Swarms of fighter planes wove a protective screen above the armada while on its flanks British and American warships patrolled in their ceaseless search for U-boats. Flotillas of minesweepers led the way to clear the waters of German mines.

Chaplain Barber gripped the rail of his constantly pitching transport and marveled at the power about to be unleashed on the Germans. Salt spray whipped into his face. The constant thrumming of ship and aircraft engines throbbed deep into his marrow. Never in history had mankind witnessed such a spectacle.

As D-Day dawned, soldiers aboard transports anchored twelve miles off Omaha Beach saw with the naked eye the wide strip of beach that, at low tide, stretched from the sea breakers for over 1,000 feet, the length of three football fields, to the dark jutting cliffs that harbored German defenses. Although the cliffs could not be easily seen in back of the seawall because of the dim light, Chaplain Barber knew they bristled with pillboxes, bunkers, trenches arranged for interlocking fire, bulwarks, parapets, machinegun emplacements, strongholds for artillery and coastal guns . . .

The coastline appeared impenetrable beneath scattered wisps of cirrus blowing over the Channel while the major cloudbank escorted rain deeper inland across Normandy. Omaha Beach, where the chaplain would land, seemed to glow between Nazi-built obstacles of wood, steel, and wire that cast shadows of harsh lines and intricate patterns on the sand. Foaming breakers at near low tide followed the gentle curve of the beach, lapping at one another in twisting ranks, one after the other.

If Overlord went as planned, eight divisions of infantry and paratroops would land in Normandy early on 6th June 1944, D-Day, three from the air and five from the sea. The U.S. 82nd and 101st Airborne Divisions would parachute in along the east coast of the Cotentin Peninsula to secure the western flank of the beachheads, while the British 6th Airborne jumped in east of the River Orne to block German reinforcements. Seaborne invaders would storm ashore on five separate beaches code-named Utah, Omaha, Gold, Juno, and Sword along a sixty-two-mile stretch of shoreline.

These beaches would become killing grounds starting at dawn. The higher flats, gullies, and ridges from the waterline on into Normandy would erupt in a volcano-like explosion from the tons of bombs and shells hurled at them.

Chaplain Barber slept little the night before the landings. The tossing of the ship in the waves kept him awake. At least that was what he told himself. He kept getting up and climbing topside to gaze through the dark toward France. He noticed other soldiers on the decks around him, silently smoking cigarettes, waiting. Ernie Pyle walked over.

"It's always worse just before it starts," he said.

Barber nodded. "Can't sleep?"

"Huh-uh. You either?"

Since commanders thought it would be a good thing for their men to have a substantial breakfast before the action began, Navy cooks prepared eggs-to-order, hash browns, sausages and bacon, steaks . . . The works. "A last meal for the condemned," some joked with dark humor.

The assault began with massive Allied air raids behind the German defensive wall. Bombs whistled through the clouds. Thousands of them fell like deadly rain while the throbbing of massive engines from unseen bombers vibrated the ground and sea. Bombs erupted in the deep, ear-shattering thunder of worlds being rent. Dense walls of smoke tumbled and tossed in the wind, billowing up from the rear of the German perimeter that divided the coastal fortifications from Vierville-sur-Mer.

Thousands of ships dotted the sea for as far as the eye could see. It seemed a man could skip from ship to ship all the way across the English Channel and never get his feet wet.

Battleships belched fire and smoke from their enormous 14-inch guns with shock waves that threatened to swamp smaller craft in their vicinity. Volleys of rockets flashed overhead in a brilliant fireworks display, boring holes through air and smoke. Unlike the aircraft bombing, which had been cautiously conducted toward the enemy's rear for fear of hitting incoming Allied troops, the Allied navies laid steel directly on target over the heads of inbound landing craft. The main ferocity of the shelling concentrated on German defenses above the bluffs overlooking the beaches. The morning's first sunshine tinged great clouds of smoke and vapor an earthlike yellow while the shadows were a sorry blue.

Breakfast for the troops might not have been such a good idea after all. Many of the men became seasick and were vomiting from their greasy meals as waves of landing craft bucking in the swell plowed toward the beach like a hatch of baby turtles. Along with the LCPs (Landing Craft, Personnel) and LCTs (Landing Craft, Tank) came the surf, just rolling and rolling, accelerating over tidal runnels to wash up on the sand and splash against antitank and anti-personnel obstructions constructed in the water and at its edge.

The earsplitting naval barrage went silent when the first wave of landing craft reached sand. Suddenly, it was eerily quiet except for the steady plopping of enemy mortar rounds landing in the water. Higgins boats bucked up and down in the heavy surf as doors opened to lower steel offloading ramps. GIs laden with weapons and combat kit poured out into the breakers in long lines, rifles held above their heads.

Chaplain Barber, who remained on his transport and would not land until later in the afternoon, found himself with a box seat to watch the Allied invasion of Fortress Europe. Binoculars provided him a close-up view. He caught his breath in terrified awe, dumbstruck, when German officers finally ordered their men to commence firing. All he could think of was that this was becoming a bloodbath, a disaster.

Enemy machineguns and mortars opened up while snipers hiding in trenches began their gory work. Men dropped all along the beach as they exited landing craft. Here and there, men plunged out of sight in the tidal runnels. Even wearing inflatable Mae Wests, they had to fight desperately to get back to the surface with their packs and assault jackets filled with ammunition. Some made it to the shallows and crawled up on the beach. Others drowned.

GIs swam, waded, crawled, or slithered onto the sand where there was no cover, no place to hide from the murderous fire. The slaughter was fast and merciless. The air crackled with bullets. Corpses lay strewn across the sand and bumped against each other in the shallow water near the beach. Bodies without legs and arms and heads lay among mangled human parts. The sea ran pink with blood.

Burned-out landing craft and immobilized vehicles, some still flaming, studded the beach. In the surf the tide rose around a waterproof tank that had lost its floatation. A dead man hung from its turret. Heads of other dead men bobbed in the water near it. Of twenty-nine flotation tanks offloaded from transports when the assault began, twenty-seven foundered in deep water, drowning many of their crews. Only two tanks made it to the beach.

Ashore, an officer waved for his men to follow him. An exploding Nebelwerfer round sliced him neatly in two at the waist with a shovel-blade-sized piece of shrapnel. Tracer fire from a concrete pillbox stitched the hard beach with bullets. A GI knelt to fire into a draw opening. His head exploded in a pink cloud. A snarling machinegun wounded another soldier in the stomach and legs. He finally reached a portion of the seawall before he died.

The seawall afforded exposed GIs their best hope for survival. Barbed wire curled above it, beyond which rose bluffs veined with trenches linking German infantry, snipers, rocket launchers, and mortar and machinegun crews. One of the few surviving officers, Colonel George A. Taylor, rallied small groups of survivors and led them to the seawall.

"Two kinds of people are staying on this beach," he yelled. "The dead and those who are going to die. Let's get the hell out of here."

Very few invaders from the first wave reached the seawall. The invasion all along Omaha stalled with the remaining American soldiers pinned down. Some men tried to dig foxholes in the wet-packed sand. Others slithered forward, using corpses and German obstacles for cover. Still others played dead in hopes German shooters would overlook them. The tide creeping in drowned wounded men who hadn't the strength to crawl out of its reach.

After having cut the first wave to ribbons, Germans began shooting the bodies, exploding heads and torsos, riddling wounded men with their arms out-stretched pleading for mercy.

Chaplain Barber, unable to watch any longer, dropped his binoculars. He knelt on the deck of his transport and began to pray.

Chaplains did not carry weapons. Barber loaded a small backpack with Bibles when he went ashore with one of the later waves at about 1400 hours that after-noon. He prayed with the men aboard the LCP as it chugged in toward the blood-soaked sands. He prayed for his country and for success in the ongoing battle.

A Higgins boat near his hit a mine as the landing craft weaved through floating carcasses and debris toward a landing. It blew up in a horrendous burst of flames, killing all aboard. Blood, body parts, and entrails flew through the air.

By this time, the Germans were too busy fighting off invaders who had finally reached the seawall and were starting to climb the cliffs to concentrate on sub-sequent waves of landing craft. The chaplain plunged into the surf with the other GIs when the assault ramp dropped. He noticed pocket Bibles he and other chaplains had handed out at Sunday services floating in the water or washed up on the sand with the bodies of dead soldiers.

The beach was a bloody mess, the aftermath of slaughter. Wounded men ignored the furnace sound of the battle and attempted to help men in worse shape than they. Soldiers screamed when they died. Others sighed. Still others simply relaxed as the life spirit left them.

Chaplain Barber's heart ached from grief and pity and anguish as, oblivious to the danger he faced, he dashed among the broken, weeping men and tried to comfort them as they drew their last breaths. "God is going to see us through. God loves you. If you have to make the ultimate sacrifice, God will help you. He's prepared a place for you in His Kingdom."

Only four chaplains made the Omaha landings: George Barber, a Navy chaplain named Hollingsworth, and a couple of other Army padres. They made themselves useful by teaming with combat medics in patching up the wounded and dragging them to the relative cover of the seawall.

Always under fire, Barber darted from place to place responding to wounded men who cried out for help and mercy. Here ministering to a soldier who was dying, there bandaging a mangled arm or leg, everywhere tarrying with little knots of terrified GIs to lead them in prayer before they again rose to take on the enemy blazing down at them from the heights.

Truly, it was the chaplain's longest day. Never had he ministered to a flock under such horrendous and perilous conditions.

Finally exhausted and realizing he had a long night ahead of him, Barber dug a foxhole for himself behind the seawall at the base of the bluffs while tracers weaved intricate patterns in the gathering nightfall. At least he could get his head down in the hole and stay away from bullets when he wasn't needed.

By 0330 on 7th June, the tide of battle was shifting. Americans had wiped out enough of the enemy that they could scale the cliffs and carry the fight directly into German trenches. Shooting became less intense. Chaplain Barber climbed out of his hole and helped evacuate casualties.

Bloodstained and filthy, weary to the bone, Barber finally collapsed in his foxhole and opened a can of Spam. While he ate, the sun rose and painted the surf foam pink because of all the blood. Clumps of bodies still littered the beach like bags of old clothing. Ernie Pyle dropped into the foxhole with the chaplain. Like chaplains, the correspondent was unarmed, carrying only his camera, a portable typewriter, and a canvas bag full of papers.

"I figured I'd see you here somewhere, padre," he greeted Barber.

"You all right, Ernie?"

They shared the tin of Spam, taking a few minutes' respite in the midst of turmoil. Afterwards, Chaplain Barber sighed and turned to look up at the cliffs towering above his head where fighting still raged. He picked up his Bible.

"Time to get back to work," he said.

Follow-up

George Barber served a second combat tour as a chaplain during the Korean War. He retired from the U.S. Air Force with the rank of colonel before returning to California to reestablish his home and ministry. He died in 2004.

* * *

Airborne Assault

ALL WITHIN LESS THAN THREE YEARS, the United States raised, organized, trained, and equipped five parachute infantry (airborne) divisions for use as a powerful combat force in the war. Since current airborne-capable aircraft proved inadequate, the Army Air Force turned to civil designs to find its transport planes. Thus appeared the C-47 Douglas Dakota, a low-wing, twin-engine airliner converted to military needs. It was capable of hauling eighteen parachutists and their gear. A massive production program provided hundreds of them for the D-Day invasion of France.

Operation Overlord called for initially landing eight divisions in Normandy, three of them from the air. The U.S. 82nd "All American" Division and the 101st "Screaming Eagles" would spearhead the invasion by dropping jumpers behind the beachheads along the east coast of the Cotentin peninsula while the British 6th Airborne dropped east of the River Orne. Their missions were to secure the invasion's flanks by controlling roads leading to the beachheads, diverting German troops, disrupting the enemy's lines of communication, and capturing essential bridges over rivers to allow the Allies to break out once they landed.

On the evening of 5th June 1944, 1,400 transport aircraft, mostly Dakotas, and 3,500 gliders, carrying a total of 20,000 men took off from southern England. While the first part of the flight to the French coast was under clear skies and bright moonlight, scattered cloud cover and haze appeared once the transports swung over the Cotentin peninsula around midnight. The long columns of aircraft hauling paratroops and towing gliders also ran into a storm of antiaircraft fire. Formations began to break up as Dakota pilots took evasive action, weaving and twisting through tracers and orange shell bursts.

Heavily laden with equipment, weapons and ammunition, paratroopers needed a steady jump platform and a straight, undeviating approach to their DZs (drop zones). They weren't getting it. Instead, the pitching, rolling aircraft knocked men into each other and off their feet. Some were still struggling to get up again when the green lights flashed on.

As a result of being slow to get out the doors, coupled with cloud cover and disorientation that hampered pilots in seeing and recognizing DZs marked by pathfinders, paratroopers ended up scattered all over the Cherbourg Peninsula, some as far as twenty miles away from where they were supposed to land.

Some jumpers dropped directly into flak, antiaircraft, and infantry fire and were dead by the time they hit the ground. Other paratroops, as well as glider troops, plummeted into fields the Germans had flooded against airborne

U.S.S. *West Virginia* and other vessels on "Battleship Row" at Pearl Harbor erupt in flame and smoke under Japanese attack on the morning of 7 December 1941. Navy Cook Dorie Miller and Quartermaster Striker Arles Cole were caught below decks. *(Photo: U.S. Archives)*

Quartermaster Striker Arles Cole saved the life of his friend Dorie Miller who had been knocked unconscious below decks aboard U.S.S. *West Virginia* when the Japanese attacked Pearl Harbor. *(Photo: Cole)*

Port facilities burn during the Japanese attack on Dutch Harbor in the Aleutian Islands on 3 June 1942. *(Photo: U.S. Archives)*

Captain William H. Willoughby, commander of the 7th Scout Company that endured bitter cold on Attu Island. *(Photo: U.S. Army)*

This prisoner was one of only 28 Japanese who chose to survive the Battle of Attu in the Aleutians in 1943. *(Photo: U.S. Archives)*

Boatswain's Mate Roy Boehm, whose destroyer was sunk under him at the Battle of Cape Esperance, survived a horror-filled night in the sea against sharks. *(Photo: Boehm)*

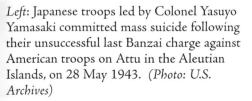

Left: Japanese troops led by Colonel Yasuyo Yamasaki committed mass suicide following their unsuccessful last Banzai charge against American troops on Attu in the Aleutian Islands, on 28 May 1943. *(Photo: U.S. Archives)*

Above: Sergeant Rayson Billey wore his old campaign hat and ribbons for the rest of his life. Famed WWII cartoonist Bill Mauldin called Billey "the bravest man I've ever known." *(Photo: Author)*

Left: WWII U.S. Army cartoonist Bill Mauldin based "Joe" (kneeling) in his famous "Willy and Joe" *Stars & Stripes* cartoons on his friend Rayson Billey. *(Photo: WWII Museum, Oklahoma City)*

Flight Navigator Lieutenant Haig Koobatian's number failed to come up during a catastrophic B-17 bombing raid over Germany. *(Photo: Koobatian)*

Lieutenant Charlie Brown, his B-17 crew either dead or wounded, met a chivalrous German fighter pilot who guided him to safety. *(Photo: U.S. Army Air Force)*

U.S. Army Air Force Chaplain George R. Barber was one of only four chaplains to make the D-Day landing on Omaha Beach on 6 June 1944. *(Photo: Barber)*

"Acting Sergeant" Jack McNiece (*right*), 101st Airborne Division, prepares his men to parachute behind enemy lines on the night before D-Day. (*Photo: McNiece*)

General Dwight D. Eisenhower talks to men of the 101st Airborne Division prior to their insertion behind enemy lines in Normandy on D-Day. (*Photo: U.S. Archives*)

U.S Marine Sergeant Tom Cottick with the first of three Silver Stars he was awarded. He earned this decoration for valor in action in the Marshall Islands with the 4th Marine Division. *(Photo: John Cottick)*

Marines of the 4th Marine Division with a Japanese prisoner on the island of Roi-Namur in the Marshall Islands where Sergeant Cottick earned his first Silver Star. *(Photo: U.S. Archives)*

Sergeant Ruben Rivera was posthumously awarded the Congressional Medal of Honor when he sacrificed his life in a tank battle in France in 1944. Rivera was a member of the 761st Tank Battalion under General Patton, the first and only all-black U.S. Army armor unit to fight in WWII. *(Photo: Joe Wilson)*

Lieutenant Jim Carl and his P-51 fighter, *Quapaw Squaw*, prior to an aerial duel to the death with an ace Luftwaffe pilot. *(Photo: Carl)*

Above left: Corporal Ed Peniche, 101st Airborne Division, fought at Bastogne during the Battle of the Bulge. Wounded along with other members of his 57-mm gun crew, he crawled for help, encouraged by a large wooden cross at a farmhouse. *(Photo: Peniche)*

Above: Ed Peniche returning to the site of his 1944 encounter with death at The Battle of the Bulge, to find the wooden cross near where he was wounded still there. *(Photo: Peniche)*

Glider pilot Staff Sergeant Robert W. Powell crash-landed his CG-4 glider during "The Bridge Too Far" operation in Holland. He awoke from a coma four months later. *(Photo: Powell)*

Victims of the "Wereth Massacre." Eleven black artillerymen of the 333rd Field Artillery Battalion were executed by the SS during the Battle of the Bulge. *(Photo: U.S. Archives)*

Spec 4 James Stewart *(above left)* and Spec 4 William Pritchett *(above right)*, two of the eleven victims of the "Wereth Massacre." The victims' bodies were horribly mutilated by the SS. *(Photo: Charles Gordon)*

Robert K. Hill (*standing, 2nd from left*) and members of his platoon on Iwo Jima. Others include Red McGowen (*standing, 3rd from left*) and Bill King (*standing, far right*). (*Photo: Hill*)

Private Galen Kittleson (*right*) following the "Great Raid" on Cabanatuan, for which he received a Silver Star for valor. He is being congratulated by General Douglas MacArthur. (*Photo: Kittleson*)

Above left: Lt. Colonel Paul Bates, commander of the all-black 761st Tank Battalion, fought with General George Patton's Third Army all the way to Germany. His romance with Army nurse Lieutenant Taffy was one of the great love stories of the war. *(Photo: Taffy Bates)*

Above: Taffy Bates, the indomitable army nurse who treated wounded soldiers from shortly after D-Day all the way to Germany. She and the commander of the 761st Tank Battalion, Paul Bates, married after the war ended. *(Photo: Taffy Bates)*

Left: Taffy and Paul Bates after their wartime romance led to marriage. *(Photo: Taffy Bates)*

Above: Corporal Dale Shaw enlisted in the Army to fight the enemy. Instead, he ended up on Guadalcanal and Guam keeping the Army's machines running. *(Photo: Shaw)*

Above right: Robert Williams (*right*) sailed the South Pacific during the waning days of WWII and was scheduled to be in the invasion force against Japan when the dropping of the atomic bomb forced Japan to surrender. *(Photo: Williams)*

Right: Petty Officer Clinton Nesmith (*left*) helped offload atomic bombs from the U.S.S. *Indianapolis* prior to the bombing of Hiroshima and Nagasaki. *(Photo: Nesmith)*

Lieutenant William Morris, a 21-year-old USAAF B-29 pilot, flew 34 bombing missions over Japan during the final months of the war. *(Photo: Morris)*

Crew members of *Big Time Operator*, the B-29 flown by Lt Morris *(top right)* and Cap Jack Payne *(front right)*. Bombardier Jim Bec is the tall man in the rear. *(Photo: Morris)*

Corporal Leonard "Sack" Owczarzak was at Pearl Harbor when the war began and in the Philippines when it ended, and was assigned to guard Japanese POWs until they could be repatriated. *(Photo: Owczarzak)*

Corporal Leonard "Sack" Owczarzak (*left*) and a Japanese POW at Base S POW camp on Cebu in the Philippines, after the Japanese surrender. *(Photo: Owczarzak)*

Left: B-29s en route to Japan on the last bombing raid of the war. *(Photo: Morris)*

U.S. Army Lieutenant George N. Garrett (*right*), administrative head for the defense at the Nuremberg Trials, assisting military attorneys during the trials. Garrett knew all the major Nazi war criminals and was present on the night ten of them were hanged   (*Photo: Garrett*)

Lieutenant George Garrett's official identification card as administrative head for the defense during the Nuremberg Trials. (*Photo: Garrett*)

operations and drowned. While casualties were heavy, the majority managed to get down safely, even though they had little idea of where they were. In the dark, picked at by the enemy, frequently alone or in groups of three or four, they faced the task of reassembling and working toward their targets.

Although landed in the wrong places, most of the paratroops and glider infantry overcame difficult beginnings to inflict heavy casualties on the Germans while securing nearly all their objectives. By the end of six days in Normandy, they had stabilized both flanks of the Allied beachhead.

* * *

McNasty

ALL TROOPS WERE IN LOCKDOWN BY 5TH JUNE 1944, nobody coming or going, units briefed, and everyone wearing a clean pair of skivvies. You didn't want to get killed with hash marks in your drawers, although Acting Sergeant Jake McNiece, 101st Airborne, figured there would be a lot of fresh hash marks before the night was over.

Father John Maloney, the Catholic chaplain, came around.

"Okay, fellas, let's get down to the nitty gritty," he began. "We're going to be jumping in there about eleven o'clock tonight. Look to the guy next to you. You or him are not going to make it. We're going to lose fifty percent. So in the case of imminent danger of death, I can administer extreme unction. I can do that right now. That way if you get killed, you've already got it done."

While some of the guys thought it a good deal, Jake McNiece stepped back and scowled. To start with, he didn't intend to go out there and get killed. At twenty-five years old and therefore up a couple of years on the average paratrooper in the 101st, he was a rather short, rawhide-tough, half-breed Choctaw Indian who grew up meaner than a starving coyote in the Great Depression Dustbowl of Oklahoma. He was the youngest of ten kids, which meant, as he put it, you had to fight just to get to the dinner table.

"McNasty?" the chaplain asked. "Do you want extreme unction now?"

"You wouldn't happen to have a couple extra bottles of communion wine, would you, Padre?"

The handle "McNasty" had been tagged on McNiece in his capacity as acting sergeant in charge of one of three demolition-saboteur sections in the 506th Parachute Infantry Regiment, 101st Airborne. His permanent rank was actually private, which he had held since he enlisted in the Army in 1942. Private he would probably remain. Every time he won a stripe, he lost it again the next time he got drunk, missed muster, or punched out some NCO or officer in a bar-room brawl. Officers all agreed McNasty was a rogue, but the bastard was the best damned demo man in the army. And he had a set of balls.

Because he was a rogue, every man jack in his thirteen-man demo-saboteur section was also a misfit. If a man screwed up somewhere else, he got transferred over to McNasty's "Filthy Thirteen." McNasty didn't give a shit if you saluted officers, said "sir," or even if you had hash marks in your drawers. All he cared about was could you do your job.

"You don't want them filthy sum'bitches around in garrison," declared the *real* sergeant of one of the other sections. "You gotta keep 'em out of sight of the brass. But when you go to war, you wanna go with the Filthy Thirteen."

The Filthy Thirteen's mission tonight was to parachute onto Drop Zone D with 3rd Battalion, 506th. Once on the ground, McNiece's thirteen plus six others assigned to him, including a Lieutenant Mellen, would blow the bridges that spanned the Douve River near Carentan, saving only the main bridge to hold as a crossing for when the Allies busted off the Normandy beachheads. Carentan was a transportation hub for roads and railroads leading in and out of the Cherbourg Peninsula.

Since it might be days, perhaps even weeks, before the men got another opportunity to shave or bathe, McNasty figured to get the jump on lice and shave his head. He left a Mohawk strip of hair down the middle of his scalp.

"We wear a scalp lock like that down in Oklahoma," he explained. "Whoever kills the other gets to take the scalp as a trophy."

Naturally, he was bullshitting, but everyone in the section nonetheless shaved his head into a scalp lock. They also painted their faces like Indians in a war party. General Eisenhower came around later and walked down the line of aircraft as jumpers rigged their gear and prepared for the night's insertion. When he came to the Filthy Thirteen and their add-on "associates," he caught himself up short and stared at the strange spectacle of troops with bull's eyes painted on their cheeks and hair all shaved off except for strips running down the center of their heads. He broke into a broad Ike grin.

"Give 'em hell, boys," he said.

An Army photographer happened to be present. The photo of McNasty and the Filthy Thirteen in full war regalia appeared in *Stars and Stripes* and on the front pages of newspapers back home. It became one of the most famous and enduring images of D-Day.

A paratrooper preparing for a combat jump might have done better as a pack horse. Into the pockets of his combat jacket and trousers or attached to his web gear went: a pocket knife; spoon; razor; socks; gun cleaning equipment; flash-light; maps; ammunition; a three-day supply of K-rations; emergency chocolate; a compass; two fragmentation grenades; a Hawkins antitank mine; one smoke grenade; two pounds of plastic explosive . . .

He also carried a holstered .45 pistol, water canteen, collapsible shovel, first aid kit, bayonet, gas mask, and jump knife. Over all this went his parachute harness with a main and a reserve. Into a musette bag slung underneath his reserve in front he stuffed spare clothing, more ammo, and anything else he had room for. Finally came his helmet and helmet liner, M1 rifle or Thompson, and his Mae West in case he landed in water.

Other equipment such as extra machineguns and mortars, reserve ammo, extra radios and batteries, and medical supplies went into "para-packs" to be parachute-dropped either from bomb racks underneath the bellies of the C-47s or pushed out the door by jumpmasters when the green jump lights came on. Guys were so overloaded they had to pull each other up off the ground when they sat down. They waddled to their aircraft and helped each other climb aboard.

It was a pretty night with plenty of moon on the way across the English Channel. From the air, it was an impressive scene—sky full of paratroop transports and airplanes towing gliders, ships on the Channel below so thick they were like stepping stones.

Along with scattered rain on the French coast came German flak and anti-aircraft fire. Tracers whipped up out of the darkness like strings of flame. Enemy fire was really tearing up the Dakota occupied by McNasty and his men.

The 3rd Battalion's DZ lay about two miles or so from the three bridges over the Douve River. Pilots were supposed to pull power coming to the DZ and drop the nose so the tail would lift to allow jumpers to clear it. Instead, the plane revved up its good engine, the other having suddenly become disabled, and began losing altitude. McNasty shouted paratroopers to their feet.

"We got to get out of here! Come on, get out!"

The stick pressed together toe to heel like a coiled spring and rushed the door. McNasty positioned himself in the center of the stick so jumpers on the DZ could assemble on him from either end. "Piccadilly Willy" was snug behind McNasty when a chunk of flak exploded through the floor of the airplane and struck Willy's reserve parachute, ripping it from his pack. Wind howling past the door and in through bullet holes and other battle damage deployed the chute. In all the excitement, pushed by paratroopers behind him eager to get out of the plane, Willy grabbed the parachute canopy in his arms and went out the door with it. McNasty never saw him again.

Corporal Chuck Plauda was last man out of the airplane. Three seconds later the Dakota exploded in the air.

Germans on the ground had illuminated the field below by igniting an old barn. Paratroopers tried to steer their T-3 parachutes away from the light. Those unable to get away from it became targets and were dead by the time their boots struck the ground.

McNasty landed in an open area away from the barn and in fact about eight miles from the Douve bridges. Small arms fire chattered and rattled all around him. Rounds buzzed out of clumps like angry fireflies, but none seemed directed at him for the moment. All he knew for certain was that he found himself lost in the middle of a foreign land surrounded by pissed-off Nazis.

He whipped out his jump knife and cut himself out of his parachute harness since unbuckling it took too much time. Keeping low, he took off running toward a distant ink smear of woods, hedgerows, or some form of growth that might offer cover and concealment. So far, he hadn't heard the report of a single American rifle. It gave him a damned lonely feeling. Like the invasion had been called off and somebody forgot to tell him.

The French utilized hedgerows as fences. They grew so thick that even goats couldn't get through them. As McNasty scrambled across his landing field, a group of Germans positioned where three hedgerows formed a T opened up on him, pinning him down in a shallow washout, creating a nasty kind of standoff.

The enemy shot at McNasty; he shot at them. They cursed him; he cursed them back. Then the Germans split up and attempted to come in on him from different sides. Fleeting moonlight revealed a gap in the nearest hedgerow. An earthern dugout blocked it, probably a machinegun nest, but there was no movement around it and nobody was shooting at him from it. He figured it was his only chance to bust out of the mess he was in. He either ate through it or the assholes around him were going to waste his sorry butt.

Out of desperation and to shore up his courage, he yelled something like, "Screw the whole bunch a' ya'all kraut eaters!" Then he shot off a clip from his M1, jumped up, and dodged toward the dugout and the opening in the hedgerow before the Germans realized what he was doing.

On the off chance that there might be somebody in the dugout and that he might be a friendly, McNasty sprawled on the ground and clicked him with his toy cricket. Crickets had been issued to paratroopers as a means of signaling to each other in the dark.

He received no response, neither of cricket nor of gunfire. So far, so good. If there was somebody in there and he was German, he would surely have opened fire by now. That meant the dugout was either empty or some scared-shitless

American GI was hiding in it. Either way, McNasty had to move fast before the asshole buddies out there discovered he had given them the slip.

McNasty clicked again. Still no response. That did it. The only way out of this trap was to go over the dugout, whether it was occupied or not. He rushed it with his bayonet ready, determined to kill the mute sonofabitch if he was in there.

At the last moment, the tenant jerked his head out of his ass. He started screaming, "Flash! Flash! Flash!", the American challenge-and-password, and clicking his cricket like it had gone insane. It was another paratrooper. McNasty jerked up his bayonet just in time and slid into the bunker with the terrified GI.

"What the hell were you thinking?" McNasty scolded.

"Man, they're everywhere. You ought to be careful charging these dugouts like that. They could be full of Krauts."

"I wasn't the one about to get killed, you idiot. One more second and I would have had your ass on the point of my bayonet scooting you across the field. Why didn't you answer my challenge?"

"I been watching what's going on over there with them three hedgerows of Germans. I thought you was a Kraut putting on a show to get me to open up. If you was a Kraut, you know what I woulda had to do?"

"What woulda you had to do?"

"Beat you to death with this machinegun belt. When I jumped and got my opening shock, me and my machinegun parted company. This belt is all I got left to fight with."

McNasty handed him a couple of grenades. "Don't spend 'em all in one place. Follow me. We're on the attack."

The guy, a machinegunner from a heavy weapons platoon, was the first American McNasty had run across so far. The two soldiers slipped out the back of the dugout and cut wide of the hedgerows full of Germans. After they were clear, McNasty pulled out his map and compass and charted an azimuth to the Douve River and its bridges. He had 36 pounds of C-2 plastic explosive in his demo satchel, a thousand feet of electrical wire, blasting caps, a ten-cap detonator, and one man in his sapper force. They were on their way to his objective.

The two troopers gathered other jumpers along their way to the river. They were skirting a big field the Germans had flooded when they heard voices and people splashing through water. The machinegunner almost crapped his pants when McNasty called out to them.

"Are you crazy? They might be Germans," he hissed.

"Germans wouldn't fight a war like that. They have to be stupid paratroopers."

Sure enough, Acting Sergeant McNiece added four more men to his little force. Manual Cockeral was from Tulsa; McNasty had enlisted with him at Fort Sill, Oklahoma, in 1942. The other three were veteran Filthy Thirteens: Jack Agnew, Mike Marquez, and Keith Carpenter. What were the odds of running across each other like that?

A little later, they picked up three cannon cockers from a mortar platoon. They didn't have mortars, but they had six mortar rounds each. McNasty's little demo section was growing.

Now ten men strong, they knocked out a German headquarters, going through it like a bunch of bobcats and collecting weapons enough for everyone. They were still spoiling for a fight when they came across the headquarters of the 501st Regiment. Colonel Howard R. Johnson was desperately short of men. He needed shooters.

"Colonel," McNasty tried to explain, "I got three bridges to blow about six miles from here."

The Colonel ignored him. He pointed. "Take your men and set up a defensive perimeter over in that area."

"You can't use me on the line," McNasty protested. "I won't do it. I have a job assigned to me and a lot of lives depend on it."

"Sergeant, your orders are rescinded," Colonel Johnson barked. "You're a part of this position now."

Muttering under his breath, McNasty led his little band into the darkness—and kept on going.

"McNasty, what the hell are you doing?" Carpenter asked.

"Screw him. We got bridges to take care of."

It was then the acting sergeant revealed he had stolen enough weapons and ammo from Colonel Johnson to finish arming his command. He had planned it all along, concealing the weapons outside the perimeter so they could be picked up on the way out. Not for nothing was he called McNasty.

Someone remarked how they were like Dorothy, the Straw Man, the Lion, and the Scarecrow on their way down the Yellow Brick Road to see the Wizard—and no evil witches or Germans were going to stop them.

They hadn't gone more than a few hundred yards before a shot cracked out of the darkness. Carpenter went down with a bullet hole through the calf of his leg. The shooter took off. Fortunately, it was a clean wound. McNasty poured sulfa powder in it, pasted on a patch, and Carpenter asserted as how he was ready to continue to march.

Several more stragglers from various outfits joined the band. They were moving fast. McNasty wanted to reach the bridges before daybreak.

They were wading one of the flooded fields when a single sniper shot barked from a little shed in the middle of a bog about seventy-five yards away. A GI named Clarence Ware dropped from a bullet that entered between his shoulder blades and blew out his chest.

McNasty slithered on his belly through the shallow water to check out the shed. The sniper had already hauled out. McNasty returned to his men while they carried Ware to dry ground and left his helmet on a tree limb as a marker for when Graves Registration came through.

Ware was the first fatality along the Yellow Brick Road.

French farmers cut deep trenches through their fields for easy drainage after a flood or heavy rainfall. They lurked like traps underneath the German flooding. McNasty and his ragtag demolitioneers were almost within sight of the first of the three bridges, wading ankle-deep water as the eastern sky began to pale into dawn, when McNasty suddenly disappeared in deep water.

One of the mortar men behind him also stepped into the same ditch and went under, the weight of the mortar shells he carried dragging him to the bottom. Water bubbled. McNasty grabbed the guy by his battle vest and dragged him to shallow water.

Then it was back to work again, on the march.

The two wooden bridges that needed to be blown were upstream of the main bridge. One was no more than a footbridge. Both were unguarded, as apparently the Germans never anticipated being attacked so deep inside their lines. It was a simple matter to rig them with explosives and blow them in the dark. By the time the Germans figured out what was going on, the main bridge at Carentan should be in American hands. After that, it was a matter of making sure it stayed that way.

Dawn was approaching at 0400 when the saboteurs reached the primary bridge, a steel-girded seventy-five-yarder spanning from north to south, with the town of Carentan only a little way to the north. At this point, the Douve was fairly narrow. High causeways with dikes ten to fifteen feet high ran past either end of the bridge, providing excellent cover from which to defend—or, for that matter, to attack.

Thankfully, the Germans still hadn't figured out what was going on and the bridge, like the other two, was unguarded. By daybreak, McNasty, his recruits, and the remnants of his Filthy Thirteen had the bridge wired and ready to detonate. It would be blown only as a last resort to stop Germans from sending armor across toward the beachheads.

Shortly after daylight, the Germans sent foot troops from Carentan to see what all the explosions were about. They dismounted and approached the bridge like they were on parade. Concealed behind the dike on the other side of the river, McNasty's bunch waited to expose their presence until the enemy were almost upon the bridge. It was a real turkey shoot. Not many made it back to the cover of their own dike.

All during the daylight hours of 6th June, the Germans and McNasty's men exchanged fire across the river. The American force expanded to around twenty men as more and more paratroopers heard the ruckus and drifted north to help. It was a classic standoff. The Germans hid behind their causeway and dike, the Americans did likewise on their side of the river. Certain death awaited anyone on either side who ventured into the open no-man's land adjacent to the bridge. It would take a major force to break the impasse, as attackers would necessarily be funneled into the bridge's two narrow lanes.

So far, the Germans were too busy concentrating on the Normandy beaches to pay attention to a handful of Americans on the Douve. All day, McNasty kept wondering if the landings were successful—or would the spearhead of the invasion be abandoned in a little Dunkirk of its own, leaving the men to survive and escape the best they could?

A hundred yards or so behind the Germans rose the steeple of a country church that provided perfect surveillance over the American positions. A sniper took over the steeple and began pinging shots, soon nailing one of the mortar guys. McNasty and Jack Agnew, who was a hell of a shot himself, set up their own hide back of the causeway.

"Watch for the bastard and burn him out of there," McNasty encouraged.

It didn't take long. The German was an amateur. The next time he showed himself, Agnew leveled down and cut out the German's middle. His body flopped out the window and hung head down from the steeple until after nightfall. It was Agnew's first kill. He was so excited that he jumped to his feet and started jumping around shouting, "I got the sonofabitch!"

McNasty jerked him back behind the causeway just in time. A burst of machinegun fire chewed up the ground where he had been.

Once during the day, the Germans foolishly broke the stalemate again and attempted to charge across the bridge. American shooters scythed them down. Bodies lay on the bridge in the sun for days afterwards.

McNasty's wool OD trousers and jacket became soaked with sweat. During the afternoon's lull, he removed his outer garments and spread them out on the lee side of the dike to dry in the sun. A mortar round dropped out of the sky, shredding his clothes and blowing sand and debris into McNasty's eyes. He hunkered down and waited for his vision to clear. It was the most helpless and frightening feeling of his life. "Fifteen miles behind enemy lines, surrounded by about a million Krauts, blind, and naked . . ."

He needed a big dip of Copenhagen to calm his nerves, but the two cartons he had brought along were soaked from when he stepped into the farmer's drainage ditch. The snuff had melted. This was getting to be one shitty war.

His vision returned shortly, he scrounged some spare clothing, and felt a little better.

It went on and off like that for the next two days. McNasty's men rationed their ammo, shooting only enough to keep the enemy at bay. They were also running out of food and water. Although they could hear water running underneath the bridge, they dared not try to reach it, not even at night. Apparently the Germans didn't know how many Americans they faced across the river and kept popping flares all night to prevent a sneak attack.

"Mac, what you got to eat?" Agnew called out.

"Nothing. What you got?"

"I got me some cans of cheese. You want a bite of it?"

McNasty's men had been the first Americans to reach the river. They were holding. But times were about to get desperate unless they were reinforced and resupplied soon.

Finally, at the end of the second day, fresh troops began straggling in to the sound of M1 rifle fire. Captain Charles Settle of 3/506th brought up four officers and thirty-eight soldiers. The next morning, five more officers and fifteen men arrived.

Exhausted, hungry and thirsty, McNasty's original little band had been reduced to only eight survivors, the others having either been killed or wounded and removed rearward to a grove of trees that served as a casualty collection point. Against all odds, these Screaming Eagles had accomplished their mission, one of the most daring feats of soldiering during the D-Day campaign.

Follow-up

In addition to fighting on D-Day, Acting Sergeant Jake McNiece parachuted into Eindhoven of *A Bridge Too Far* infamy; into Bastogne as a pathfinder during the Battle of the Bulge; and, finally, behind the Siegfried Line in Germany in direct resupply of the 90th Infantry Division when the Germans surrounded it. He and Sergeant George Blaine were the only two paratroopers of the Second World War to make four combat parachute jumps.

Jake McNiece left the army after the war, still a private after having served three years and five months. His exploits and those of the Filthy Thirteen were later fictionalized and made famous as the inspiration for the movie *The Dirty Dozen*, starring Lee Marvin.

McNiece returned to Oklahoma and eventually retired from the U.S. Postal Service. He and his wife live in Ponca City, Oklahoma.

Chapter 9

Pacific Island-Hopping

ADMIRAL ISOROKU YAMAMOTO, Commander of the Japanese Combined
Fleet, died when U.S. P-38 Lightnings shot down his plane while he was touring
Japanese forces on Bougainville in April 1943. He had prophetically warned
against America's industrial power and had lived long enough to see his fears
begin to be realized.

For much of 1943, the story of the Pacific war was one of the U.S. Navy's
remorseless expansion as the balance of power shifted decisively from Japanese
to American seapower. The U.S. Fifth Fleet commanded by Admiral Raymond
Spruance, who had led the naval victory at Midway, became the most powerful
the world had ever seen—7 battleships, 11 aircraft carriers with 1,000 aircraft,
44 cruisers and destroyers, and 150,000 Marines specially trained for
amphibious operations like those initiated by the Army on Attu and Kiska in
the Aleutian Islands.

Disagreements arose between Admiral Chester Nimitz, Commander of Naval
Forces in the Pacific, and General Douglas MacArthur, Allied South Pacific
Commander, over the best way to conduct the Pacific campaign. Nimitz wanted
to use his expanded fleet and the U.S. Marine Corps to advance northward and
westward through the islands of the Central Pacific to Taiwan and the coast of
China, where U.S. forces would link up with the Chinese for the final thrust
against the Japanese Empire. MacArthur, on the other hand, favored a somewhat different route of attack through the East Indies and the Philippines as the
fastest and most direct route to deliver assault armies to Tokyo's doorstep.

Although their disagreement led to a growing rivalry between the Army and
Navy, the circumstances and vagaries of war increasingly encouraged the two
camps to work together in joint operations. The Marshall Islands campaign was
one in which the Army and the Navy and its Marines linked up in common
cause.

Prior to undertaking the Marshalls, MacArthur championed a sequence of
assaults on New Guinea and New Britain in the latter half of 1943. Nimitz
and his Navy and Marines launched another prong up through the Solomon

Islands north of Guadalcanal. By November 1943, U.S. Marines had captured the main islands of the Solomons and turned their attention to the Gilbert Islands.

Makin in the Gilberts went down relatively easily on 20th–23rd November 1943, but Tarawa, attacked simultaneously, proved a tougher nut that required bitter and costly fighting. The garrison of 4,700 Japanese on Tarawa had tunneled into the heart of the atoll, converting it into a veritable fortress. U.S. Marines suffered 3,000 casualties taking Tarawa, a third of whom were killed, as they burned and dug the enemy out of their holes. In a soon-to-be familiar pattern, all but twenty-eight Japanese on Tarawa fought to the death or committed suicide rather than surrender or accept defeat.

The Marshall Islands campaign entailed important firsts for American forces against the Japanese. For the first time in the conflict, the U.S. moved into actual Japanese territory. For the first time also, American aircraft carriers, which had hitherto mainly been deployed defensively, would go on the offensive. The Battle of Midway, Guadalcanal, and other fierce actions had been defensive operations in support of U.S. ground and sea forces.

A German colony prior to the First World War, the Marshall Islands had been mandated to the Japanese in 1919. Capture of the main Japanese base on Kwajalein atoll and the primary Japanese airfield on adjacent Roi-Namur would afford Allies a launch site for reconnaissance, combat staging, and logistics routing in another major step toward the main islands of Japan.

MacArthur and Nimitz were involved together in the planning and conduct of the campaign. Seizing Kwajalein was assigned to the Army's 7th Division while Roi and Namur, atolls linked by a short causeway and therefore considered the single target of "Roi-Namur," fell to the newly created and untested 4th Marine Division.

Naval Task Force 58, now with twelve fast carriers and eight battleships, advanced on Kwajalein and Roi-Namur well ahead of the invasion forces to "soften" the objectives. Nimitz's swift attacks with his carriers' 650 aircraft destroyed almost every Japanese warplane within striking distance, while his battleships pounded the Roi-Namur airfield and entrenched Japanese troops on both islands right up until Marines and soldiers landed on their respective beachheads on 1st February 1944.

U.S. troops outnumbered the Japanese by more than ten to one in hopes of avoiding another bloodbath like that on Tarawa. Fewer than 400 Japanese soldiers out of a defense force of 7,500 were taken alive. American dead numbered far fewer than the 1,056 killed on Tarawa.

* * *

Marine Sergeant

STANDING IN FRONT OF THE POST OFFICE in Detroit, Michigan, Tom Cottick was about to make one of those pivotal decisions that would change the rest of his life. It was a date he would always remember—24th April 1941. Hitler was kicking butt all over Europe and was two months away from invading the Soviet Union. Yet, no one in Cottick's circle of friends, family, and acquaintances saw the United States entering the war. Let those people "over there" take care of their own problems. Live and let live seemed a good American philosophy.

The question Cottick pondered as he stood at the door of the post office was whether he should continue farming and trucking milk or whether he should change occupations. His net return from farming this year so far was sixty bucks. At twenty-one years old, he didn't smoke, drink, or chew, which meant he was in pretty good shape physically.

He opened the post office door and walked down the hall. Maybe it was time for a little adventure in his life. He came to the U.S. Marine Recruiting Office and went inside to ask where he had to go to enlist in the Navy. "I want to go in and learn a trade," he proudly explained.

The Marine sergeant behind the desk looked him over and stood up, all six-and-a-half feet of him and wide enough to pick up a milk cow and carry her across the road. "Son, you don't want to waste your time with a sissy outfit like the Navy," the sergeant said. "Join a *real man's* outfit and we'll take care of you. You can still see the world and get paid for it."

And so Tom Cottick became one of the few and the proud. He discovered there were two ways in the world to do things—the wrong way and the Marine Corps way. Twenty-one dollars a month pay. Humping thirty miles with thirty pounds of gear on your back. Digging a foxhole in the dirt and sleeping on a bed of gravel.

Months passed. Cottick moved up in rank to sergeant. The Japanese bombed Pearl Harbor. Hitler and Mussolini declared war on the United States. In Britain, Prime Minister Winston Churchill delivered soaring rhetoric over the radio about duty and honor and what lay ahead. "For the best part of twenty years the youth of Britain and America have been taught that war is evil, which is true, and that it would never come again, which has been proved false. For the best part of twenty years, the youth of Germany, Japan, and Italy have been taught that aggressive war is the noblest duty of the citizen . . . We have, therefore, without doubt, a time of tribulation before us . . . Many disappointments and unpleasant surprises await us . . ."

Cottick wasn't sure whether the surprise that awaited him in December 1943 was pleasant or unpleasant. On the one hand, he was curious about war and wanted to do his part in fighting back the Yellow Peril and the Swastika. On the other hand, he had his reservations about the rusty old Liberty ship, looking like it was salvaged from a scrap yard, that, along with others like it, would transport him and others like him across the Pacific Ocean.

The boats pulled out of San Diego crammed with Marines of the 4th Marine Division, an outfit formed, commissioned, and brought on line only three months earlier. Few of the men, and that included sergeants and officers, had ever fired a shot in anger. That was all about to change.

The voyage to Pearl Harbor was rough sailing. Below decks smelled of man sweat, puke, and piss. Troops were overcrowded, unwashed, and underfed. Chow lines started topside on the main deck and were so long that a Marine had time to write a letter home, read a pocket novel from cover to cover, and still win ten dollars in a poker game before he reached the head of the line. By the time troops finished with breakfast, it was almost time to line up again for dinner.

Marines were told only that they were headed for the Marshall Islands by way of Pearl. A place called Roi-Namur. Most of their spare time on the boats was consumed studying maps and mockups of the islands and in briefings on what to expect when they landed. It was all about travel and adventure, the Marines told each other.

Reality didn't sink in for Cottick until the transports reached Pearl Harbor, where the war began for the U.S. on 7th December 1941. One evening, on-board PA systems began booming instructions: "Now hear this. Stand by and no liberty. Make out your wills. Services on deck for men of all faiths. Make peace with your Maker. The Big Day is almost here." It was time to wash out your socks, give a silent prayer to the Almighty, and say goodbye to peace. The Marines were heading for war.

But what the hey. If he got hit, Cottick rationalized in the bluff way of Marines conditioned to believe they were invincible, he didn't have a bank account and he wasn't married. He told his buddies they could split up among them his K-bar knife and other personal gear. All he asked in return was that they write a letter to his folks telling them he wasn't too bad a guy.

Otherwise, it was too late to worry now. Just get in there and give 'em hell.

Over 500 transports delivered the 4th Marine and 7th Infantry Divisions to Kwajalein and Roi-Namur. Three days of naval bombardment and carrier aircraft strikes preceded their arrival. Ships and planes were still pounding

Roi-Namur when the Marines broke over the watery horizon and saw smoke and fire seemingly rising out of the sea and heard the thunder of big 14-inch guns from the battleships. Cottick stood at the rail with other Marines of his 2nd Battalion, 24th Regiment, and watched the show. It was the most terrible and mesmerizing spectacle any of them had ever witnessed.

"Can't nobody live through that," one Marine opined, awe-struck. "We can just walk right on that island and have a seat and a beer. Ain't nobody gonna be left alive."

"That island's not very big," observed another. "How come it ain't sunk yet?"

More than 6,000 tons of heavy explosives were thrown at the island before Marines began to board LCPs, tracked landing vehicles, and other watercraft at dawn on 1st February 1944. To Sergeant Cottick, the operation seemed to be, in Marine parlance, a clusterfuck. Squads and platoons were running all over the decks of their transports trying to find their assigned landing craft, half of which somehow got lost and failed to show up on time. Officers and NCOs shouted at their men and at each other.

"Damnit, First Platoon! Platoon Sergeant, I told you your fucking boats aren't here yet. Your platoon will ride in with Charlie Second Platoon the second wave. Do you read that, Sergeant? Now get these ladies squared away or their asses are mine . . ."

Lack of boats meant the assault waves went in piecemeal toward the smoke and fire of hell. Squad Leader Cottick and his company aboard LCPs dodged through a gaggle of tracked landing vehicles which, for some reason, had come to a standstill offshore. Cottick's boat was among the first to reach the beach. He crouched with his rifle squad behind the boat's steel landing ramp and waited for it to drop. The ride in had been smooth on calm seas. They weren't even getting shot at.

Cottick took a deep breath and looked up at the sky. It was pink from sunrise, pink and peaceful with only a few lazy clouds stationary in the absence of morning winds. The battleships and carriers had pulled back, taking their thunder with them. What followed was a strange and deadly kind of silence. Maybe the Japs were all dead.

Or maybe they were dug in and waiting for the first Marine to show his face.

The jarring bump of the LCP driving up onto the beach snapped him out of his brief reverie. The steel ramp dropped, exposing the frightened and excited men inside to a panorama of smoke swirling among toppled and splintered palms beyond golden beaches of sand.

"Go! Go! Go!"

Fortunately, the enemy chose not to fight on the beach, providing time for the battalions, companies, and platoons to sort themselves out and get organized.

But the enemy wasn't far back in the jungle. Firefights soon broke out, rippling up and down the beachhead in fierce little pockets of sound and fury.

Out front, just inside the tree line ahead of Cottick and his platoon, appeared Japs in their baggy brown uniforms, firing and yelling *banzai* and other warcries. On his way across the Pacific, Cottick often wondered how he would react under fire. Would he freeze up, get rattled, and fall apart? Or would he conduct himself like a Marine?

Although green and untested in battle, he let his training take over and just went along with it. He rallied his squad and charged directly into the fire, shooting his M1 from the hip as he ran, intent on getting his men off the open beach and into the cover of the trees. Several Japanese soldiers dropped where they were in agonized death throes. A wounded Jap reached for his weapon. The Marine running alongside Cottick blasted him through the skull.

"Banzai *that*, asshole!" he snarled.

Back in garrison there had been barracks-room talk about combat, stories told and re-told by the old salts of how war was hell and bodies getting stacked up and all that. Cottick was to discover before the first day was done that words could never express, nor pictures convey, the true horror of combat.

Still, the pre-action anticipation of it was worse than the actual thing. Last night, Cottick had had night sweats and cotton tongue and jitters in his stomach. Once the shooting started, however, a man merely reacted to his training, instinctively and without thought of what *might* happen. "I'm gonna need a bigger gun," Cottick reflected as Marines advanced, pushing the enemy back ahead of them.

Although the growl and harsh stutter of combat reverberated all around him almost constantly, it wasn't like he was personally involved in life or death fighting every moment. Lulls in his sector allowed the company to push forward a few yards at a time without resistance. Tension mounted as Marines covering each other broke their way through jungle growth toward the next opposition. Never knowing what awaited them—a sniper perhaps tied into the top of a palm, an ambush from the side of the trail, a *banzai* attack in force. It was nerve-wracking work.

During a short, fierce firefight, a Browning Automatic Rifle man in Cottick's platoon took a round through the chest. He dropped and didn't move again. Cottick tossed his M1 and snatched up the BAR. It was essentially a one-man light machinegun with a twenty-round magazine. A good weapon for close-in fighting. Cottick had his bigger gun.

An enemy scurried from hiding across Cottick's path. Cottick swung on him and squeezed the trigger. Nothing happened. "Damn it!" The gun had a broken extractor.

Remembering that the weapon came with a spare extractor in its stock, he dived behind a fallen tree and within a few minutes switched out the broken part for its replacement. The next Jap who showed himself was in for a big shock. A full mag of M2 Ball could do some chewing.

Only the north shore of the island remained to be captured as nightfall approached. American troops began to establish their night perimeters and dig in. Officers warned their men to dig deep since Japs were known to be fond of night counterattacks.

A foxhole dug properly was a work of art. Ideally, it accommodated two fighters at one-man-and-a-half wide, one-man-and-a-half long, and six feet deep, if possible. A small "cat hole" in the bottom served as a toilet; you didn't want to have to get out to take a leak or a crap while Japs waited to catch you with your pants down. A six-inch-wide ledge near the top of the foxhole became a storage shelf for weapons, ammo, hand grenades, K-rations, and cigarettes.

The soil on Roi-Namur was not conducive to works of art. Living coral didn't dig worth a damn. Cottick's foxhole was about two feet deep, which he shared with his company commander, a captain.

Marines used the buddy system at night. One Marine tried to sleep, an almost impossible enterprise what with jagged shards of coral sticking up in the bottom of the hole, while his buddy remained alert for sounds or signs of enemy approach. Nights could be hellish. You dozed off for a few minutes, only to jerk awake, scared stiff, half-expecting some wild-eyed Jap with a samurai sword to be sitting on your lap wearing a maniacal pre-execution grin.

There would be little sleep for the American line, at least during that first night. After full dark, the enemy started moving around out in the forest less than a football field's distance away, as though positioning for an attack. Over to the left, an enemy machinegun raised hell every so often. Over a period of about an hour, it killed one American and wounded several more in exchanges of fire.

"Sergeant Cottick, we got to shut that bastard down," the company commander said. "Think you can handle it?"

"I'll walk over and say pretty please? Just kidding, sir. I'll take care of it."

"While you're out there, Sergeant, see if you can find out what the Japs are up to."

Damn! Here he had been shot at, shook up, near-missed, and now this? But he was a Marine, wasn't he? That was why he got the big bucks.

Besides, he was probably as safe out there as he was in this shallow hole. The Japs would anticipate the Americans would hunker down for the night. What they would never expect was some fool jarhead crawling out there among them. Showed how much they knew about Marines.

Cottick shucked his gear and BAR, retaining only his .45 pistol and some grenades in his pocket. The CO slapped his shoulder. "Tom . . .?"

"See you in a bit, Cap. Let the boys know I'm out there so they don't shoot at me."

With that, he elbowed himself over the lip of his foxhole and slithered through the moonless night into no-man's land and toward the Japanese lines. The terrain was pock-marked with mortar and bomb craters and littered with felled trees and palm fronds ripped off during the fighting. Plenty of cover and concealment.

He was scared shitless, as he later admitted to the boys of his platoon. But he didn't need to shit anyhow.

Flares streaked into the black sky at uncertain intervals and exploded in miniature suns as one side or the other lit up the battlefield to try to get some idea of what was going on. Feeling as exposed as a painted whore in church, Cottick hugged the ground and remained frozen until the light went out again.

The machinegun remained ominously silent. He was at the opposing team's twenty-five-yard line with goal almost in sight. It had to be directly ahead, somewhere. He just didn't know where. So he played the possum game and waited.

That was the really scary part, lying there in the dark by himself waiting for something to happen, for the Japs at the machinegun to give themselves away. Very shortly, he began to hear rustling sounds, the clank of weapons, furtive whispered exchanges. All directly in front of him, within hailing distance. The Japs were definitely up to something. That was just what he needed to make sure his goose got cooked—some fanatic officer organizing a *banzai* charge right over the top of him.

He continued to wait. Sporadic exchanges of rifle fire still broke out at various points along a battle line that at this point stretched for some half-mile or so. Gunfire winked. Men yelled and cussed each other across no-man's land.

Finally, the offending Jap machinegun opened up with deafening presence, blossoming flame almost in Cottick's face. He almost jumped out of his skin as bullets chewed the air above his head.

He eased pins from a pair of grenades and immediately tossed the first in an overhand swing. He heard it hit someone. A Jap, startled, yelped. Cottick's second grenade followed. There was no yelp this time. The sergeant squeezed his eyes shut to save his night vision, buried his head in the sand, and tried to make himself as small as a sand crab.

The grenades detonated simultaneously in a bright ball of fire and brimstone. Shrapnel, body parts, and various bits of Jap equipment plopped all over the landscape.

Cottick didn't wait around to assess the damage. The gun nest was obviously destroyed. Like a lizard, he slithered off parallel to the Japanese lines to get out of the immediate vicinity. The second part of his mission, finding out what the Japs were up to, turned out to be a simple matter of crawling along in front of enemy positions and listening.

It didn't take him long to sound-locate concentrations where the enemy were apparently massing for one of their notorious counterattacks. They had a reputation for fighting to the last man, who then committed *hara-kiri*, willing to give everything for the Emperor. Still, the Emperor was god on earth, not a mere flesh and blood man.

The sergeant made his way back to friendly lines, arriving unscathed and bearing vital intelligence on American sectors that should reinforce themselves against expected enemy attacks. His company commander slapped him on the back as he collapsed into his foxhole to catch his breath. He felt depleted, as though he had been holding his breath for the past hour while crawling around out there among the enemy.

Sure enough, whistles shrilled, horns tooted, and Jap zealots screamed at the tops of their lungs and charged out of the jungle and into a withering buzzsaw of American rifle and machinegun fire prepared to mow them down wholesale, thanks to Sergeant Cottick's little excursion across no-man's land. Marines stacked up bodies. Only a few Japanese made it near enough to be bayoneted.

The enemy charged the Americans several more times during the night. No one got much sleep. In between attacks, each of which was less fierce than the one preceding it, a foxhole buddy might doze off while his partner kept watch. The slightest sound jarred him awake, scared stiff and in a hypnotic trance.

Sergeant Cottick was never in his life so glad to see the sun come up—even though it revealed the true carnage of blood and gore that trashed the battlefield, most of which belonged to the enemy.

"Damn!" he said, looking out over the field of corpses.

By early that afternoon, 2nd February, the 4th Marines held Roi-Namur and the Army's 7th Infantry had defeated the Japanese on Kwajalein. The Marines lost 313 men killed and 501 wounded. Out of a Japanese force on Roi-Namur estimated at 3,563, only 90 surrendered.

Nearby on Kwajalein, the Army lost 334 soldiers killed in action. Only 265 Japanese out of a garrison of 4,000 chose to surrender and survive.

Now blooded in combat, the 4th Marines returned to Hawaii to recuperate, refit, and up-train. Then it was time to return to the business of war. The word came down: "Clean your weapons, sharpen your combat knives, write your letters home. It's time you got back to doing what you were trained for."

Follow-up

Admiral Chester Nimitz personally presented Sergeant Tom Cottick with the Silver Star medal, the nation's third-highest award for valor, for his feat in single-handedly knocking out the enemy machinegun and obtaining information that aided the Americans in repelling Japanese counterattacks.

After Roi-Namur, Cottick participated in "island hopping" battles on Saipan, Tinian, and Iwo Jima. He was awarded a total of three Silver Stars for valor, three Purple Hearts for wounds sustained, the Presidential Unit Citation, and was added to the U.S. Marine Corps Honors list.

He left the service at the end of the war and returned to Michigan where he lived until his death in 2003.

Chapter 10

Black Americans at War

ASSUMPTIONS ABOUT THE INFERIORITY OF BLACK SOLDIERS were common in American military thinking prior to the Second World War. African-Americans could be enlisted as cooks, stevedores, truck drivers, orderlies, and in service and support units, but never as combat troops. Only five black commissioned officers served in the U.S. Army in 1940—and three of them were chaplains.

Such thinking persisted in spite of the valiant service of black "Buffalo Soldiers" on the American Frontier in the 1800s. Later General John J. Pershing penned a secret communiqué outlining how black officers (from Northern National Guard units) should be treated in France during the First World War: "We may be courteous and amicable . . . but we cannot deal with them on the same plane as white American officers without deeply wounding the latter. We must not eat with them, must not shake hands with them, seek to talk to them, or to meet with them outside the requirements of military service."

Colonel James A. Moss, commander of the 367th Infantry Regiment, 92nd Division, also held a poor opinion of black soldiers. "As fighting troops, the Negro must be rated as second-class material, this primarily [due] to his inferior intelligence and lack of mental and moral qualities."

"In a future war," said Colonel Perry L. Miles before Pearl Harbor, "the main use of the Negro should be in labor organizations."

Even George Patton initially had little confidence in black soldiers. In a letter to his wife, he wrote, "A colored soldier cannot think fast enough to fight in armor."

On the other hand, General Leslie J. McNair, Chief of U.S. Army Ground Forces, believed the nation could not afford to neglect such a large potential source of manpower. Eleanor Roosevelt became a major advocate for allowing blacks to serve in combat. With her backing, the black press, the National Association for the Advancement of Colored People (NAACP), and the Congress on Racial Equality (CORE) pressured the War Department and President Franklin Roosevelt to permit blacks to serve on an equal footing with white soldiers.

Congress took quick action, what with war looming on the horizon. It passed into law the Selective Training and Service Act of 1940, which stated, "In the selection and training of men under this act, there shall be no discrimination against any person on account of race or color."

Three months later, in October 1940, the White House issued a statement saying that while "the service of Negroes would be utilized on a fair and equitable basis," segregation in the armed forces would continue. Black combat units would be formed, but under white commanders. Such units included the 5th Tank Group, the first all-black armor unit in the history of the American military.

In March 1941, ninety-eight black enlisted men reported to Fort Knox, Kentucky, for training and assignment to one of three battalions of armor— the 758th, the 761st, and the 784th. They trained in light tank operations, mechanics, and related areas of mechanized warfare.

The 758th was the first activated. Soon, as America entered the war and black ranks swelled, a cadre and a core of enlisted personnel were sifted from the 758th to form the second of the three battalions. The 761st was activated at Camp Claiborne, Louisiana, on 1st April 1942, the 784th a few months later. Major Paul Bates, a white officer, assumed command of the 761st Tank Battalion (Light) in May 1943 to prepare it for combat in Europe.

* * *

Panther Battalion

COLD JANUARY RAIN DRIZZLED onto the rolling red-dust hills of central Oklahoma the day Ruben Rivers walked to war. He was hiking to Tecumseh to catch the bus that would take him to enlist because no vehicle could get down his road when it rained, not unless pulled by horses or mules. He seemed reluctant to take each step. He stopped, looking back down the muddy road that led past the ramshackle farmhouse behind the rusty barbed wire fence.

Rivers's little black community of Holtuka insisted this was a white man's war and he didn't belong in it. The only reason blacks were invited in the first place was to cook for the white man and clean up after him while the white man did the fighting. Ruben didn't see it that way. This was *his* country too. Hadn't the Japs attacked Pearl Harbor? Ruben and the two other older boys in the large Rivers family had talked of little else but war since the sneak attack by the Japanese five weeks ago. Ruben was the first of them to make up his mind to go.

He stood in the churned mud of the road looking back at the house. A gawky farm kid seemingly stuck in a stage of growth that was neither boy nor full man, wearing faded overalls, brogans, and a raggedy old winter coat. Rainwater beaded on a smooth honey-brown face that showed traces, perhaps, of both slaves and slave owners. The jaw was strong and well-defined, eyes dark and so straight-staring they turned aside under no man's gaze. A lean young man going to war like millions of others from Los Angeles to Washington D.C.

His little sister Anese stood alone on the front porch waving through the drizzle. A brown little girl wearing a faded feed sack dress mama had sewn for her. Tears and rain in her eyes. Waving and waving. The others were out at the barn tending livestock or still inside because they couldn't stand the heartbreak of actually watching Ruben leave home.

Ruben waved a last time at his baby sister. Then he turned abruptly, batted his eyes, lowered his head into the cold rain, and resolutely trudged in the direction of Tecumseh. He would have to walk the whole distance. He never looked back again. He remembered hearing somewhere that the road away from home led in only one direction. Once you left home, you could never go back again.

George S. Patton Jr. was one of the earliest advocates of armor, beginning when he commanded tanks in France during the First World War. Following D-Day in June 1944, armored conflict between the Allies and Germany developed to a high art of brute force, speed, firepower, and steel-clad massiveness. As battleships were on the seas, tanks on land became the supreme threat, punching into rear areas to destroy command posts and supply depots, rolling over dug-in enemy, spearheading infantry attacks, and moving swiftly to cut off avenues of enemy retreat. Accompanied by lightly armored fighting vehicles such as half-tracks and armored cars, supported by infantry and mobile artillery, tank battalions and divisions formed the nucleus of armies fighting against Nazi Germany in Europe.

The medium M4 General Sherman main battle tank was the major U.S. weapon in the engagement of armored titans. It was armed with a short-barreled, low-velocity 75-mm gun, later modified to the more powerful 76-mm cannon; two 30-caliber machineguns, one ball-mounted in front of the assistant driver, the other in the turret coaxial with the main cannon; and a heavy 50-caliber machinegun mounted on a ring on top of the turret. The 50-caliber could be fired only while the turret hatch was open.

The nimble Sherman compromised firepower and survivability in its emphasis on speed, mobility, and maneuverability. At 35 tons in weight, it was powered by a 450-hp V-8 gasoline engine that allowed it to reach speeds of nearly 30 mph and gave it a range of 100–150 miles. A crew of five men operated the Sherman: tank commander; gunner; loader; driver; and assistant driver/hull gunner.

The 761st Tank Battalion, known as the "Black Panther Battalion," departed Camp Hood, Texas, with fifty-four Sherman tanks and fifteen smaller M5 General Stuart tanks on 9th August 1944 for overseas deployment. The outfit's patch and emblem was a black panther superimposed against a silver shield above the motto "Come Out Fighting."

Only the week before, on 1st August 1944, General George Patton's Third Army became operational in France, fifty-six days following the Allied landings at Normandy. Never one to tarry, Patton unleashed an American blitzkrieg that raced 200 miles through the gap at Avranches to reach the outskirts of the port of Brest in just six days.

By the end of August 1944, the Third Army had liberated more than 500,000 square miles of territory and swept 400 miles all the way to Verdun and the Meuse River, and come within sixty miles of Germany. Patton hoped to reach the Rhine River by the first week in September and from there head on to Berlin ahead of Russians probing in from the east. Then he ran out of fuel and his army stalled for nearly two months against fierce German resistance.

When he learned that the 561st Black Panthers were to be assigned to his army, he snorted in characteristic Patton style and, apparently disregarding his earlier comments about the capability of black soldiers, said, "I don't give a damn what color they are. Can they fight?"

On 28th October 1944, the 761st caught up with Third Army at St-Nicolas-de-Port, east of Nancy. A few miles ahead, the front had lain quiet most of the morning and the rain had sucked back into a swollen, bruised overcast. Colonel Paul Bates, the white battalion commander, called formation.

A bunch of Jeeps loaded with MPs and 50-caliber machineguns rolled in. A three-star general jumped out of one of the Jeeps, received Colonel Bates's salute, then vaulted onto the hood of an armored car. He stood there with his feet spread apart, fists on hips, as his eyes sharply surveyed the ranks. Sergeant Ruben Rivers knew from the two ivory-handled pistols holstered on the general's belt that he was looking at the legendary General Patton.

When he began to speak, the Panthers were shocked to discover that he had a very high-pitched voice that sounded like an angry woman with a bad cold. Many people suspected he used profanity in order to be taken seriously.

"Men," Patton began, "you are the first Negro tankers to ever fight in the American army. I have nothing but the best in my army. I don't care what color you are, so long as you go up there and kill those Kraut sonsofbitches. Everyone has their eyes on you, and is expecting great things of you. Most of all, your race is looking forward to your success. Don't let them down, and, damn you, don't let me down. They say it is patriotic to die for your country. Well, let's see how many patriots we can make of those German sonsofbitches."

He concluded with, "There is one thing you men will be able to say when you go home. You may all thank God that thirty years from now when you are sitting with your grandson on your knee and he asks, 'Grandfather, what did you do in the Second World War?' you won't have to say, 'I shoveled shit in Mississippi.'"

The Black Panthers of the 761st pushed forward across France, operating with Third Army's 26th Infantry and the 4th Armored Division. It was rough going against rain, mud, cold, snow, driving sleet, and an enemy who bitterly contested every inch of ground. The Panthers learned to live with war and its constant stench, taste, sights, and threats.

When Sergeant Johnnie Stevens went to the rear to recuperate after being wounded on Hill 309, Sergeant Ruben Rivers took his place as a tank commander in Captain David Williams's Able Company. It became a byword that Rivers would lead the way whenever it was time for the 761st to "Come Out Fighting."

Air reconnaissance assets reported the Germans were staging for a big fight in the defense of Guebling, France, in November 1944. Roads behind the enemy's main line of resistance at the town were clogged with vehicles and infantry sent up to relieve and reinforce panzer troops.

Rivers's tank hit an antitank mine on the way to Guebling. The explosion hurled the tank sideways, blew off the right track and suspension, and damaged the running gear. It also shredded flesh off Rivers's leg. Most of his knee was gone. His shank bone gleamed startlingly white.

Company A's trailing elements found Rivers and his crew crouching behind the disabled tank for cover. Medics cleaned and dressed Rivers's wound and attempted to administer morphine for pain. Rivers pushed them away.

"I ain't needin' that stuff," he protested. "I gotta be alert. We got a job to do."

"The only place you're going with that leg, Sergeant, is back to the aid station," the medics insisted.

"That's what you think."

When Captain Williams learned that his sergeant refused to be evacuated, he took a morphine syringe and approached where Rivers was smoking a cigarette while sitting in the snow and muck with his back against his ruined tank. The captain knelt without a word and started to insert the needle. Sergeant Rivers grabbed Williams's wrist.

"Please, sir. No."

"Ruben, you've got a million-dollar wound. You're getting out of this war and going home."

"Captain, you're going to need me."

"I'm giving you a direct order. Medics, bring up a stretcher."

"Sir, this is one order I'm gonna have to disobey."

"Listen to me, Ruben. There's no turning back once we cross that bridge up there. The Jerries are over on our right flank. The 4th Armored is getting murdered."

"Who said anything 'bout turnin' back, sir?"

A plume of smoke puffed from behind a stone barn about 100 yards away as the Germans lobbed in smoke to mark an artillery target. High explosives were sure to follow. Rivers hobbled over to a tank commanded by Corporal Henry Conway, whom he outranked, and took it over. He turned back toward Captain Williams.

"Sir, what we waitin' for? The Krauts is about to throw a party."

Just as cool as could be, in spite of his pain, he mounted the tank and stood with his head and shoulders thrust out the open turret as the iron beast rumbled off. Captain Williams shook his head in admiration.

The town of Guebling, a German stronghold, lay on the other side of a narrow river whose bridge had been blown by the retreating enemy. A small village on the near side, a mere scattering of houses, had to be cleared before engineers could lay a portable bridge across the stream.

The lead echelon of tanks led by Rivers blazed its way into the village. Resistance was stiff but comparatively brief. Lieutenant Bob Hammond, Rivers's platoon leader, not knowing what Rivers had done, radioed a command to his willful sergeant.

"Don't go into that town, Sergeant. It's too hot in there."

"Sorry, sir," Rivers's response came, quick as a flash. "I'm already through the town."

Germans threw everything they had at the American attack in a desperate effort to hold Guebling. A battlefield was a violent, insane, horror-filled cauldron of evil sights, sounds, and odors. Sergeant Rivers on point led Able Company and accompanying infantry right down the middle of the road toward town. Bogy wheels, tank tracks, helmets, backpacks, rifles, arms, legs, and blood flew in all directions. Screams came from everywhere. Rivers kept his engines wound tight and his guns hammering, leaving wispy trails of gun smoke hanging in the cold air of his passage.

Tanks were not supposed to fight other tanks if it could be avoided. They were to bypass armor and attack enemy objectives in the rear. The way the battle unfolded, however, Able Company had no choice but to engage anything that got in the way.

A pair of German Panther tanks scuttled out of hiding at the edge of town and commenced firing at near-point-blank range. Rivers's land battleship shot back and charged directly at the enemy wagons.

"Damn you, don't slow down!" Rivers challenged his driver.

Both sides continued to fire as fast as they could reload. The distance between the stationary German tanks and the single charging American Sherman narrowed rapidly. One of the German machines exploded from a direct hit. The other, damaged, stopped firing. Shadowy figures bailed out of it and hightailed it toward their rear.

Able Company's mission for the day was to secure a crossroads on the edge of town and hold it until dawn when it would be used as a staging area to resume the attack on the rest of Guebling. Rivers took on a second pair of German tanks at the crossroads, but they withdrew before either side inflicted significant damage. However, his tank struck a mine and became the second knocked out from under him during the current drive.

Just before dark, Rivers, as point for Company A, commandeered a Sherman driven by Tech4 Jonathan Hall and crewed by PFC Frank Jowers, PFC Ivory Hilliard, and PVT Everett Robinson. Having secured the crossroads, Able Company set up defenses in anticipation of a possible counterattack.

Here on the outskirts of Guebling, residences stood shoulder to shoulder, most of them constructed of stone and plaster with red tile roofs. Nearly every house had a basement or root cellar. Tanks formed a ring around the intersection, with guns thrust outward like the horns of threatened African Cape Buffalo.

Johnny Holmes saw Ruben Rivers standing outside his tank concealed behind some damaged houses. Obviously in pain, the sergeant hobbled to the corner of the nearest house to look out and study the battlefield. Satisfied, he labored slowly back to his machine, dragging his bad leg. Someone appeared in the tank turret to give him a hand back inside.

Holmes shook his head. "That Rivers. That crazy bastard."

There was a lull during a night so cold that moisture in the air froze and sparkled and snow crunched underfoot. Captain Williams, as was his custom, paid a visit to each tank in his company. He found Rivers nibbling on a K-ration while sitting in a wicker chair with his bad leg propped up on the side of the tank to relieve his pain. His temperature was spiking around 100.

"He's got gangrene," medics informed Captain Williams. "He needs to go back to a field hospital. He'll be lucky if he only loses his leg."

"Ruben, I'm giving you another order," Captain Williams said.

"Tomorrow's gonna be tough, sir," Ruben said in that quiet way of his. "Another day ain't makin' any difference."

"Ruben . . . Damnit!"

U.S. infantry, battered and bloody from the day's fighting, had established a defensive perimeter along with the tanks at the crossroads. Hostile artillery fire began walking all through the infantry and tanks, erupting buildings, setting some afire, cratering the streets. The breather was over. The Germans were coming, and, boy, were they pissed off.

"Sir, I be all right," Ruben said. "Give me one more day and I be goin' back. I promise."

"Who the hell ever believed black men wouldn't fight?" wondered Williams.

Fighting in Guebling continued throughout the night as both sides held and defended positions. The battle shifted like a wave from place to place at either flank of the crossroads, kicking up first in one sector, then dying down only to reignite elsewhere. Parachute flares lit up the dreary urban terrain, exposing awesome and terrible doomsday panoramas.

Daylight slowly arrived, cold and frosty with thin crusts of sleet over snow in those few places that hadn't been trampled or shelled. Fog eddied and oozed in a vacant field south of the crossroads. Things had been comparatively quiet for the past hour.

As Rivers looked, he became aware of something moving in the fog, something large and indistinct but whose rumbling sound signature he recognized immediately. His spine seemed to turn to ice.

"Tigers!" cried Lieutenant Bob Hammond, Rivers's platoon leader.

As Hammond and his gunner, Tech5 Roderick Ewing, readied their 76-mm cannon for combat, a Tiger appeared from out of hedgerows on the other side of the field and belched flame that seemed to scorch light out of the morning.

Hammond's wagon detonated like a match as the round impacted the gunsight and twisted the turret nearly off its mount. Hammond and Ewing died instantly, their bodies torn and scorched. The rest of their crew escaped the tank with minor injuries. Staff Sergeant Teddy Weston raced his tank forward to counterfire, but he likewise suffered a disabling blow. He and his crew dismounted and fled to cover at the crossroads.

German antitank positions concealed on the far side of a slope beyond the hedgerows lit up the gray morning sky. Barrages of explosions stomped all over and around the intersection. German assault guns rumbled out of the fog to join the attack initiated by the Tiger, an awesome sight that seemed to be generated by something evil in the mist.

"Pull back, pull back!" Captain Williams radioed, seeing what was left of Able Company about to be dismantled.

"I see them. We'll fight them," Rivers responded.

His tank darted from cover, joined by a Sherman commanded by Sergeant

Walter James. Outnumbered and outgunned, the two iron steeds charged, diverting the German onslaught in order to allow Americans caught in the open to withdraw and regroup.

Captain Williams shouted into his radio, attempting to bring back the two tanks before it was too late. "Move back, Rivers!"

Rivers and James continued their charge across the field toward the enemy armor, all guns blazing. For a few minutes, the American Shermans held their own. They seemed to exist in a charmed atmosphere as they tore furiously through fiery blasts of light and smoke. Brilliant tracers bounced off their thick hides.

Then a shell caught Ruben Rivers's tank and cracked it like an eggshell.

"Pull up, driver! Pull back, driver! Oh, God!"

Those were Rivers's last words. A second AP shell finished the job. It struck the turret and almost ripped Rivers's body into two. Blood gushed into the crew compartment as survivors struggled to quit the vehicle. Ivory Hilliard, who also occupied the turret with Rivers as a gunner, was so disoriented from the concussion and his own injuries that when he hit the ground he took off running in the wrong direction, toward German lines. That was the last anyone saw of him alive.

Coming to his senses after seeing Rivers's tank destroyed, Staff Sergeant James scurried his tank back to the crossroads, from where defenders were already laying defensive fire and calling in artillery support. Rivers's tank continued to smoke and smolder out there on the field of battle for the rest of the day as American forces rallied, repelled the attack, and secured Guebling.

The Black Panther who refused to quit was dead, having sacrificed his life in order to delay German armor until GIs could get prepared to defend.

Follow-up

In 1997, fifty-three years after Sergeant Ruben Rivers gave his life on the battlefield at Guebling, President Bill Clinton posthumously awarded him the Medal of Honor, the nation's highest medal. In 1998, the 761st Tank Battalion (deactivated) received a Presidential Unit Citation, the highest award that a command can receive. In 2009, a section of Oklahoma State Highway 9 was named in Rivers's honor.

Chapter 11

Fighter Combat

THE FIRST LARGE-SCALE AMERICAN BOMBING RAID deep into the Reich with fighter protection all the way took off on 11th January 1944 with meteorological reports of clear skies over north-central Germany. Previously, because of their limited range, P-38 Lightnings and P-47 Thunderbolts had to turn back and leave bombers unprotected over their targets. The P-51 Mustang with its longer range was just beginning to have an impact that would change the character of the Allied air war.

Targets on that date for the U.S. strike force of 663 B-17 Flying Fortresses and B-24 Liberators were Luftwaffe airplane and parts factories at Oschersleben, Halberstadt, and Brunswick. The fighter escort consisted of eleven groups of P-47s, two groups of P-38s, and a single group of forty-nine P-51 Mustangs. Even after the short-range American fighters had to turn back, the Mustangs proved more than a match for the Luftwaffe interceptors, destroying fifteen enemy planes while suffering no losses of their own.

Major James Howard, leader of the Mustangs, took on a force of thirty German fighters single-handedly while other American fighters were busy elsewhere. He shot down four German Bf 109s and Me 110s and chased off others. He was one of the few fighter pilots to win a Medal of Honor in aerial combat over Europe. He credited part of his success to the amazing little P-51 Mustang.

The development of the Mustang, considered the best all-around fighter plane of WWII, was due not to the Americans but instead to the British. A U.S. airplane manufacturer built it to British specifications in 1941, prior to the U.S. entering the war. The early model lacked power at high altitudes. Americans also considered its liquid-cooled engine more susceptible to damage by enemy gunfire than the air-cooled engines that powered Lightnings and Thunderbolts.

In 1942, the British fitted the Mustang with a bigger engine—a Rolls Royce Merlin—that made the Americans take another look. Flight tests showed the newer-model P-51B could attain a top speed of 440 mph, an altitude of 30,000 feet, and outrun, outclimb, and outdive any fighter the Luftwaffe could field. Its economical engine burned only half the gasoline of other U.S. fighters. "Drop tanks" containing 108 gallons of fuel under each wing meant the Mustang could fly all the way to Poland and back to England, a distance of 1,700 miles round trip. Long-range bombers could finally have fighter protection all the way to and over their targets.

Allied tactical air forces pounded the Luftwaffe relentlessly in the air and on the ground during the months prior to the Normandy invasion in order to attain vital air superiority. Massive wide-ranging air assaults also knocked out roads and rail lines, bridges, enemy convoys, troop movements, artillery emplacements, armor, and other targets of opportunity. By the time the invasion armies broke out of Normandy, the Allies were masters of the sky over France and much of Germany. German infantry bitterly claimed to have developed a foolproof method to identify aircraft overhead: if a plane was silver, it was American; if dark in color, British; and if it could not be seen at all, it was German.

Mustangs flew 213,873 sorties during the war and 2,520 were lost to all causes, including enemy action. In turn, Mustangs shot down 4,950 enemy aircraft, a feat second only to the carrier-borne Grumman F-6F Hellcat used in the Pacific war. The 354th Fighter Group in Europe destroyed more enemy aircraft in aerial combat, 701, than any other U.S.A.A.F. fighter group in the war. Major George Preddy with a final tally of twenty-three victories was the top Mustang ace when he was killed on Christmas Day 1944 during the Battle of The Bulge.

Reichsmarschall Hermann Göring, commander of the German Luftwaffe, was quoted as lamenting how, "When I saw Mustangs over Berlin, I knew the jig was up."

* * *

Quapaw Squaw

LIEUTENANT JIM CARL, a lanky P-51 Mustang pilot from Quapaw, Oklahoma, felt the power of G-forces as he dived his *Quapaw Squaw* into the attack on a heavily defended German airfield. Antiaircraft guns laced tracers and explosive across the sky like psychedelic spider webs as the fifteen planes from Carl's 354th Fighter Group buzzed and dived in and out of the mêlée, like supersonic gnats over a dead carcass.

Carl sprayed a 50-caliber swath of destruction into parked Bf 109s caught by surprise as the squadron came in low and fast on-target. The Germans didn't have top-line radar. He pulled out of his run and circled at 1,000 feet with the airfield below his left wing and the French countryside stretching into low green hills and forest all the way to Paris. Not a bad day's work, he thought, what with the squadron planting bombs and chewing up everything in sight with their quad-50s.

Several shattered Messerschmitts spewed flame and smoke into the air. A fire truck at the end of the asphalt runway near some concrete revetments had overturned and burst into flames. Tracers zipped up from hardened antiaircraft sites.

Fighters usually made only one run on an airfield, at the most two, since they were normally well-fortified and well-armed. Squadron Leader Major "Pinky" O'Connor was on the radio calling off the attack when Carl noticed an undamaged Bf 109 partly hidden underneath a tree off to one end of the landing strip.

"Hallum Two," he radioed his squadron leader. "Hallum Two, I'm making another run. An overhead against the bogie hiding under the tree."

"Roger, Squaw Man."

Carl dipped a wing into a belly-wrenching dive, almost straight down at the parked airplane. He felt the smooth stutter of 50-caliber machineguns throughout his body as he gnawed up turf, the tree, and the Bf 109. He zoomed through the black-and-red ball of gasoline fire he had ignited and pulled up in wild, weaving flight through streams of tracers attempting to bring him down.

While all this was going on, Pinky O'Connor was raising hell at the opposite end of the airfield, creating a diversion. When the squadron returned to base near Cherbourg, Carl discovered Pinky had almost as many holes in his Mustang as Carl had drilled through the Bf 109 underneath the tree.

"What the hell were you thinking?" Carl scolded him. "You didn't have to make another run."

"I did it to give you a chance," Major O'Connor replied with a shrug.

That was the kind of guy Pinky was—ballsy, cavalier, and he took care of his pilots. It was he who gave the squadron its moniker: "The Red Ass Squadron." It came about after a particular long escort of B-17s on a bombing raid. As Pinky landed back at base and got out of his one-seater, he groaned, "Aieee! Is my ass ever red."

It wasn't long after the airfield raid that Pinky got shot down. He parachuted out right into the hands of an SS gun crew.

Jim Carl lost a lot of good friends during the last year of the war.

The 354th Fighter Group had been activated on 15th November 1942 and deployed to England a year later to fly escort for B-17s and B-24s on long-range bombing missions into Naziland. During its short tenure operating out of Lashenden, Kent, the 354th lost twenty-three aircraft while killing sixty-eight enemy fighters.

Two weeks after D-Day, the 354th moved into France to support the Allied advance, basically following General George Patton across France, into Belgium and the Battle of the Bulge, and then across the Siegfried Line into Germany. While the Group's primary mission was to go up against Hitler's Luftwaffe, it soon ran out of serious opposition in the air and took to busting and strafing targets of opportunity. The P-51 proved excellent in ground support, but it suffered more losses in this role than in air-to-air combat, partially because its liquid-cooled engine system could be punctured by small arms fire.

Carl was fresh out of flight training when he arrived in France in July 1944. Like most pilots thrown into the mix, he had accumulated a minimum number of hours in the P-51. A pilot had to learn on-the-job fast once he arrived. Otherwise, he didn't make it.

"If you get through five missions," Pinky O'Connor bluntly told replacements, "you will probably get smart enough to survive."

Carl, who eventually flew eighty-six combat missions, began to count off until he reached the magic number five.

His first mission was flying wing to "Pop" Young on a bomber escort. At twenty-five, "Pop" was older than most of the other flyers. It was Carl's first experience with flak and AA fire. It was so thick puffing and popping and streaking all over the sky that it seemed a miracle even a single airplane could get through it. He was reckoning to himself that nobody was going to get back alive—and this his first mission!—when Pop Young developed engine trouble and had to turn back. As his wingman, Carl escorted him back to base.

Four more missions to go.

Carl's second saw an attack on a moving freight train steaming across some flats. He and the *Quapaw Squaw* took their place in a string of Red Ass Mustangs making their runs. German troops in green-and-gray on flatcars unlimbered their cannon and machineguns on the attacking fighters.

Flying in line-ahead, one Mustang directly in front of him and trailed by another, all traveling at more than 400 mph, Carl rolled in ahead of the moving locomotive and strafed the train all the way back to its caboose. Tracers from Kraut machineguns flashed no more than six feet in front of his nose. A train wheel flew into the air and zipped past his cockpit. He flew so low he saw the expressions on the faces of the flatbed AA crews before they and their car were chewed into kindling and splinters, blood and bone chips. On his climb-out,

Carl looked back over his shoulder and saw the train derailed, cars overturned and smoldering, surviving troops racing for cover.

Miraculously, he was still alive after completing his five magic missions. Maybe he was going to make it after all.

He acquitted himself well in several air-to-air encounters. During one big dogfight, the 354th Group took on a superior force of German Bf 109s and Me 110s. Thirty-eight Mustangs joined the scrap, along with fifty-one German fighters. Planes of both teams all mixed together at 20,000 feet, ducking and darting and sweeping, muzzles flashing and flaming, shouting and yelling through the radios. It was total bedlam with no time to think, not at such speeds, when what was a gnat against a distant cloud one moment quickly became a flying dragon spitting fire.

When it was over and the Germans were hightailing it home with their figurative tails between their figurative legs, Lieutenant Carl took a deep breath and looked around. It was really beautiful this high up, with great pillows of cumulo-nimbus contrasting against the deep blue of the sky, the rounded green curvature of the earth below. There were only a few holes in the *Quapaw Squaw* and, best of all, he was alive and *feeling* alive.

A few days later, about forty planes from the 354th were at 10,000 feet approaching a ground target when someone called the alarm over the radio: "Bogies!" German Messerschmitts swarmed out of the clouds above like frenzied hornets.

"Break left! Now!" ordered the Group leader, Major Carl Depner.

The Group turned as one, dumping bombs in the turn to lighten their loads for combat. Mustangs climbed in waves and busted through the bogies with guns blazing. Carl laid on his trigger. His guns failed to function. He found himself surrounded by vampires and not even a wooden stake. All he could do was fly like hell in the middle of a chaos of screaming airplanes all shooting at each other. Trying to stay out of the way while all around him airplanes exploded in bright balls of fire or streaked toward earth trailing smoke and flame.

Major Depner's wingman, Boze, was shot down and killed. Moments later, Depner got hit. He pulled out of the fight and headed for home. Fire in the cockpit forced him to bail out. That was the last anyone heard of him.

These were the only two American planes lost in the scrap, while the Germans had at least fifty blasted out of the air.

And Carl fired not a single shot. He couldn't even throw rocks.

A replacement pilot named Homburg joined the outfit. He was supposed to have been a real hotshot back in the States. "It's a different situation over here than it is back home flying where they aren't shooting at you," Carl warned him, recalling his own learning missions.

New pilots weren't issued their own airplanes for a period of time. Homburg requested to fly Carl's *Quapaw Squaw* on a routine sortie that predicted little contact. Carl relented and flew a spare on Homburg's wing.

"If you see the squadron start to weave," Carl cautioned, "you start to weave too because that means they got radar on you. You take care of my *Squaw*."

The Red Asses took off and headed east over France, just outside the Siegfried Line. Shortly, Carl heard humming in his earphones and recognized it as enemy radar. Mustangs immediately took to jinking across the sky to make themselves more difficult targets for German 88s on the ground.

Homburg froze, forgetting everything he had ever known. Carl saw flak explode in front of the *Quapaw Squaw*, followed by a second bracketing him in the rear.

"Dive! Dive!" Carl shouted into his mic.

The third round split the difference in the bracket. The *Quapaw Squaw* burst into flame and streaked toward earth like a meteor. That was Homburg's first, and last, mission.

Lieutenant Carl named his new Mustang *Quapaw Squaw II*.

Some pilots got shot down more than once and lived to tell about it. Captain James Edwards, a big, tall boy and winner of two Distinguished Flying Crosses, got busted out of the sky twice and wrecked two more planes while trying to bring them home riddled by gunfire. "You keep losing airplanes," Carl told him, "they'll make you start paying for them."

Most fighter pilots, of whichever side in the conflict, developed a grudging respect, even admiration, for pilots of the opposite uniform. Shooting each other down was nothing personal. It wasn't killing a *man* as much as it was killing a *machine*.

Unlike bomber crews who flew a designated number of missions and went home, a fighter pilot flew until the war ended, he got shot down and captured, or he died. Jim Carl had sixty missions or so in his logbook when he ran up against a Bf 109 jock who proved his equal, maybe even better than equal.

The Red Asses were sweeping out ahead of Patton's Third Army when a dozen or so Bf 109s bounced the Mustangs from out of the sun. Although the savage-looking 109s weren't quite equivalent to the little mosquito-like Mustangs, they could be formidable when driven by a top-line pilot who knew his way around the sky.

As Carl tacked on to one of the lead 109s, the German began putting his Messerschmitt through maneuvers Carl wouldn't have thought possible until now. The fight began with Carl on the guy's ass, streaking through the air at more than 400 miles per hour. Every time the German zigged, Carl zigged with him and tried to catch him in his sights. He choked down on his stick and pressed the trigger of his quad-50s, sending fire slashing after his foe.

The Bf 109 seemed to dive before the bullets reached him.

The guy suddenly switched positions with Carl in a maneuver so skillfully executed that it left Carl breathless with astonishment and shock. Now the German was on the American's ass. Tracers flashed past Carl's cockpit as he feinted, bobbed, and weaseled across the sky, trying to shake the 109 before it caught him. Only one thing saved him from certain destruction: while the guy might fly like a superhero, he couldn't shoot for shit. Had it been otherwise, the American wouldn't have had a chance.

The two fighter planes fought it out for what, to Carl, seemed an eternity. First one took the advantage, then the other, lashing viciously at each other. Each unable to administer a fatal blow.

It became personal. After a bit they circled each other warily about three miles apart, each striving to fight out of the sun while forcing the other to fight into it.

They charged each other like gladiators, weapons blazing. Bullets spanged into Carl's fuselage. The two planes passed wing tip to wing tip at a combined speed of more than 800 mph. Carl caught a glimpse of his rival's face—a young face in a brown aviator's cap, ear pieces loose, the expression on his face intense and concentrated. A young *American-looking* face, nothing like the gross caricatures on the *Know Your Enemy* propaganda posters. This guy was as human as Carl. Carl couldn't let that stop him. The only way this could end was with the death of one or the other of them.

He thought his flaps were ripping off as he pulled into a sharp turn that placed him back on the young hotshot's ass. The German dived almost straight down toward earth in a "playing chicken" move. Carl kept on his tail, his aircraft vibrating at speeds beyond its red line. The first one to chicken out was going to find himself at a crucial disadvantage. Pulling out of a dive at such low altitudes where there was no maneuver room bled off immediate speed that would allow the "non-chicken" to sweep him into his sights.

Carl's only hope was to stay on the guy.

Bobbing and weaving, making himself a difficult target, the German seemed prepared to lead them both directly to hell rather than relinquish the field. The ground rushed at Carl. He glimpsed individual trees and fences, a farmhouse, some geese flying.

At the last instant, just when it appeared both planes would crash, the Messerschmitt pulled up and leveled off just above a tree line. Tree branches quaked and bowed from the Bf 109's hurricane-force slipstream. The German had "chickened." Evasive maneuvers this low to the ground were difficult to perform. The German's escape lay in climbing to a more favorable level.

Carl anticipated it. As the Messerschmitt pulled up, losing velocity, Carl caught him in his sights and squirted him with all his guns. The Bf 109 tumbled through the low air, tail over nose, and burst into bright flame as it struck the ground. Burning parts of it showered off in all directions. No way could a pilot live through a crash like that.

A certain sadness overcame Lieutenant Carl as he pulled back on the throttle of *Quapaw Squaw II* and circled the field. He thought he would have liked to have met the German and congratulated him on a duel well fought.

Follow-up

Jim Carl left the U.S. Army Air Force after the war with two Distinguished Flying Crosses and promotion to lieutenant colonel. He flew civilian commercial aircraft for a few years before becoming an Oklahoma Highway Patrol officer. Retired from the OHP, he now lives near Tulsa, Oklahoma.

Chapter 12

Market Garden

"HAD THE PIOUS, TEETOTALING MONTGOMERY wobbled into SHAEF [Supreme Headquarters Allied Expeditionary Force] with a hangover," declared General Omar Bradley upon hearing of General Bernard Montgomery's suggestion for Operation Market Garden, "I could not have been more astonished than I was by the daring adventure he proposed."

The "daring adventure" evolved to a large extent from the rivalry between British General Montgomery, Twenty-First Army Group Commander, and American General George Patton over who would be the first to "piss in the Rhine River," as Patton put it.

The British wanted to concentrate available resources in support of a fast, narrow thrust into Germany. Americans preferred a slower, broader approach, mopping up resistance as they went. After Patton ran out of fuel for his tanks in France, due to long supply lines stretching 400 miles back to the Normandy beaches, General Dwight Eisenhower, Supreme Allied Commander, took another look at Montgomery's proposal.

Montgomery's plan called for the Allies to strike north instead of east, advancing from Belgium into Holland, thus getting behind the Siegfried Line's northern end before turning east again toward the Reich's industrial Ruhr and northern plains. Paratroopers and glider-borne infantry would capture key bridges that spanned the Rivers Maas, Waal, and lower Rhine at Arnhem, Nijmegen, and Eindhoven, thus gaining control of vital communications and transportation points. Paratroops and glider infantry would hold the bridges long enough for tanks of the British XXX Corps to break through from northern Belgium to seal the bargain.

What ultimately threw the proverbial monkey wrench into Montgomery's plan was a breakdown in Allied intelligence that failed to locate and identify the German 9th and 10th SS Panzer Divisions which had moved to the Arnhem region for refitting.

On the morning of 17th September 1944, 1,600 air transports, over 2,000 British and American gliders, and 900 fighter planes flew out from England.

This would also be the second of three large-scale deployments of gliders, the first having been during the Normandy invasion and the last the Rhine crossings in March 1945.

These inexpensive, engineless, disposable little aircraft constructed of wood or of metal frames covered in a kind of fabric and carrying troops or equipment were towed to their intended targets by military transport planes. Once released, they glided swiftly down into open terrain where, hopefully with minimal losses, they offloaded cargo and infantry.

The Soviet Union built the world's first military glider in 1932, followed by the Germans in 1940. By mid-1940, both Japan and Britain had active glider programs, followed by the United States in 1941. The shock of the attack on Pearl Harbor prompted America to ramp up its program. By 1942, the U.S.A.A.F. had more than 6,000. By the end of the war, the United States would have trained nearly 7,000 glider pilots and built 14,612 gliders.

Most American gliders were the Waco CG-4 model constructed of metal and wood frames covered in fabric. Manned by a crew of two, the CG-4 carried a load of 3,700 pounds, which meant thirteen combat-equipped infantry or an equal load weight of equipment. The larger Waco CG-10 had a cargo capacity nearly triple that of its little brother.

Shortly after 1300 hours on 17th September, the U.S. 101st Airborne Division began jumping north of Eindhoven and the 82nd around Nijmegen. Further north, the British 1st Airborne Division had a change of plans because of perceived German defenses at the Arnhem bridge. Instead of jumping within a short distance of the bridge, the 1st inserted with most of the glider force in fields eight miles away, where it reverted to a conventional ground role in its approach to seize Arnhem.

The two American divisions promptly accomplished their assigned tasks, while the British paratroopers ran into deep trouble. At first, the British paras marched triumphantly through the countryside where the Dutch greeted them as heroes. However, Panzers of the 9th and 10th SS Divisions swarmed all over them once they reached the bridge, as was later made famous in the book and movie *A Bridge Too Far*. Their problems were compounded when German resistance along the single-lane road that led to Arnhem bogged down the British XXX Corps that was supposed to link up with the paratroopers.

On 27th September, after a bloody ten-day struggle over the bridge, the battered remnants of the 1st Airborne stole back across the lower Rhine under cover of darkness, leaving their wounded behind to be cared for by the Germans. The Arnhem bridge, the key to the entire operation, remained in German hands until April 1945.

The Allies lost 1,200 dead in the botched operation and 3,000 taken prisoner. Generals Bradley and Patton were proven right in their skepticism of Montgomery's scheme. Attention returned to Patton's broad-based sweep through the Nazi-occupied hinterlands toward the Rhine.

* * *

A Bridge Too Far

A RADIO HAM OPERATOR IN CIVILIAN LIFE, Robert W. "Bob" Powell enlisted in the U.S. Army Air Force in November 1940 and trained in military radio communications. Following Pearl Harbor, he was working at a radio station in the tower at English Field near Amarillo, Texas, when a colonel walked in with a message he wanted sent. Sergeant Powell perked up. The message noted how an Air Force glider pilot school was about to be launched.

"Sir, may I ask a question?"

"Yes?"

"What in the world is the Army going to do with a bunch of sail planes?"

The colonel stared at him as if to ask, "Where the hell have you been?" He said, "Sergeant, we're starting the school right here at English Field. In about two months you'll see a tent city out there with about 400 brand new glider pilot students. Why are you asking?"

"Sir, I have sail plane experience."

"How much training do you have?"

Powell possessed both a standard airplane pilot's license and a sail plane license dating to 1939 when he was a student at the Spartan School of Aeronautics in Tulsa, Oklahoma.

"May I see them?" the colonel requested.

Powell showed him.

"Sergeant Powell, give me your name, rank, and serial number."

Two weeks later, Powell received new orders: "You are hereby relieved from your current assignment and appointed senior instructor at the English Field Glider Pilot School."

The Waco CG-4, without amenities or luxuries, was a simple flying machine with a thin fabric skin over a framework. It contained two pilot seats behind a Plexiglas windshield. An altimeter and an air speed indicator dominated the uncomplicated instrument panel, while the only controls were foot pedals for the ailerons and a stick that worked the elevators and vertical stabilizer. Pilots were on their own, without a radio, once the tow craft cut them loose near their target.

For the next two years while war raged in Europe, North Africa, and the Pacific, Staff Sergeant Powell trained pilots Stateside, assembled gliders in North Africa for the Sicily invasion, which he missed, and finally transferred to England where he flew ranking Army officers around the country in little Piper Cubs. It was easy duty; he spent most of his time "scrounging around for something to eat and a beer."

One day in August 1944, his commander took him aside. "Sergeant, we're running out of glider pilots. We're taking some of our bomber pilots and training them to fly gliders."

D-Day had claimed a toll in both gliders and the men who flew them.

Powell was back in gliders, this time not only as an instructor but also as a combat pilot. He began training and being trained for a mission classified Top Secret. Several thousand transports, fighters, bombers, and gliders were being amassed all over Britain. Troops were finally briefed on Operation Market Garden on the morning of 17th September 1944.

Powell began wondering about his long-term career path when ground crews loaded a 75-mm pack howitzer, crates of ammunition, and containers of gasoline into the cargo hold of his CG-4. He would be the lone occupant of what was essentially a flying bomb waiting to be ignited by enemy flak or ground fire.

"There'll be somebody to offload when you get where you're going," he was informed.

"What do I do then?"

"Get out the best way you can. We'll give you another plane and you can do it all over again."

The great armada of warplanes and towed gliders headed out over the English Channel toward Holland. Cloud cover closed in so thick Powell could barely make out the red light on the tail of the C-47 pulling him. He would be let loose when the light turned green. There was no turning back after that, no way to go except down.

Soon, his bladder let him know he had neglected to make a latrine call before he took off. A glider was not equipped with a relief tube. He had little to do for the next hour except sit there and shiver from the cold, battle with his bodily urges, and peer into the surrounding cloud fog while he waited for the light to turn green. If he could even see the light. Which, of course, made no difference. The C-47 was going to cut him loose whether he could see the light or not.

The thing was, seeing the light helped you prepare to release your end of the tow line before it whipped back and ripped off your wing or something.

The fleets of warplanes dropped down to 1,000 feet when they drew near their destination. They were now below the clouds and exposed to every German in the country with a rifle, pistol, or slingshot. Everybody on the ground seemed to be taking potshots. It occurred to Powell that since he was positioned toward the tail of his formation, the enemy would be well prepared to lay it on thick by the time he flew over.

Flak huffed and puffed. Tracers lashed across the sky. Planes all around burst into hellfire. Gliders that caught fire were let go from their mother planes, green lights or not, to shower the earth with a meteor storm. This was Powell's first time under fire. One round in the right place and his glider would go up like a load of dynamite.

"These sonsofbitches are trying to kill me!"

His landing zone, according to pre-mission briefings, was a large field a few miles from the bridge over the Rhine near the Dutch town of Arnhem. Aerial photos of the LZ had shown a short-grass, oblong field surrounded by a fringe of small trees and only a few smaller trees on the field itself. The green light popped on as the field Powell assumed to be the right one loomed in his Plexiglas. The release went smoothly, considering conditions. He loosed his end of the tow line and it floated away. He now had sixty seconds to get down safely.

Hundreds of gliders jammed the air like gaggles of geese all trying to land on the same tiny pond, only not as coordinated and disciplined as geese. Powell's blood turned to ice as he realized that the "few smaller trees" on the field were ninety feet tall and clustered everywhere. When had the briefing photos been taken? In 1844?

Gliders darted everywhere as they tried to get down while avoiding trees and each other. Powell picked an opening and headed for it. With the limitations of his aircraft, it wasn't like he could kick in a little power to clear a tree line or a rock pile. Once you were committed to a particular course, you were *committed*.

Trees filled his windshield. He jinked to one side to clear another glider that skidded below him and smashed into a tree. Dust and debris obscured the field as planes slid in, some of them tumbling when they struck washouts, rocks, or trees.

"Damn! It's a real screwup!"

Suddenly, he noticed how an entire forest seemed to loom directly in his landing path. He had already used up his airspeed and lift. His only recourse was to yank back on the stick to slow the plane as much as possible and pancake it in rather than nose it in.

Limbs and leaves and tree bark exploded as the glider connected with earth. Powell heard the crash as though he were a distant observer. Pain wracked his body—and, after that, nothing.

He came out of a coma sixteen weeks later at a hospital in France. His leg was in a cast. Bandages encased his head, including his eyes. It was the most terrifying moment of his life. "Help me! Where am I? Am I blind?"

He was not blind, but he was beat up bad and had lost four months of his life while in the coma. When bandages were removed from his eyes, he looked over to the pillow next to him and saw a Bronze Star and an Air Medal pinned to it.

"What's that?" he wondered.

A nurse explained. "Some lieutenant came in, put them there, saluted you, and left."

Powell never learned who brought the medals or who picked his battered and unconscious body off the landing zone. He had no recollection of what happened after the crash or how he ended up in the hospital. No records existed to explain it. All he remembered was going down in Holland and then waking up four months later in France. It would remain an unsolved mystery into his old age.

Follow-up

Robert W. Powell remained in the U.S. Air Force after the war. He participated in the 1948–9 Berlin Airlift and served in both the Korean and Vietnam Wars. He retired in 1966 with the rank of full colonel. He lives in Oklahoma where he serves as the curator of the Broken Arrow Military History Museum, which he founded in 1989.

Chapter 13

The Battle of the Bulge

DURING THE WINTER OF 1944, U.S. Army Private Joe Schectman penned a letter home to his parents from the Ardennes Forest of Belgium. "We are billeted as comfortably as we were in England," he wrote. "Of course, there's no telling how long I'll be in this paradise. But as long as I am, I'll be safe."

Within two weeks, he and some 83,000 other Americans spread thin across a 100-mile front in the Ardennes would be battling for their lives as the Führer initiated Operation Autumn Mist, a bold plan that almost succeeded.

The Ardennes Forest was the classic invasion route used by the Germans in 1940. It was difficult terrain—dense woodlands and mountain-hills slashed by valleys and ravines. At this point in the war, it was the last place through which the Allies expected the Nazis to strike. The U.S. forces were even using the area for rest and relaxation centers for their weary combatants. More than a dozen recreation centers equipped with Red Cross clubs, gyms, and movie theaters were scattered throughout Luxembourg and Belgium. As Private Schectman explained in his letter, soldiers here felt perfectly safe.

Hitler launched Autumn Mist out of frustration from months of bad news. His Allied enemies were closing in from almost every direction. In the East, the Russians had smashed twenty-five German divisions; in Italy, Allied forces seized Rome and were attacking German lines 155 miles further north; Patton and Montgomery in Belgium and France were rolling toward the German borders. So far, through five years of war, Germany had lost over 3 million men killed, wounded, or missing. Even Hitler had to admit the war was lost unless he turned it around in a dramatic fashion.

During a special meeting on 16th September 1944, the Führer, looking worn and hollow, surprised his military advisors by suddenly proclaiming, "I have just made a momentous decision. I shall go over to the attack." He stabbed his finger at the tactical map on the wall. "Here," he continued. "Out of the Ardennes, with the objective—Antwerp."

He explained that he would counterattack in a powerful blitzkrieg of the sort that had proved successful in 1939 and 1940. The blitzkrieg would break

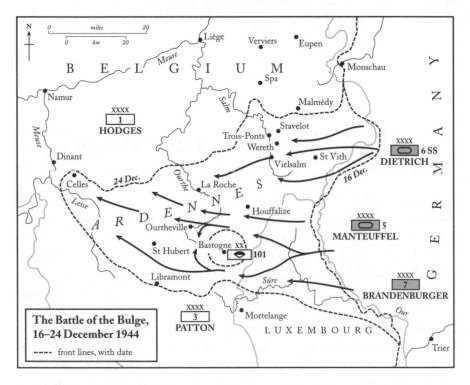

The Battle of the Bulge,
16–24 December 1944

---- front lines, with date

through the thin shell of American defenders in the Ardennes of Belgium and Luxembourg and storm across the Meuse River to seize the Belgian port of Antwerp, which General Montgomery had captured two weeks previously. The thrust would split the American and British armies and drive the British into the sea for "another Dunkirk." Once he defeated the Allies in the West, he could concentrate his forces against the Russian offensive. If all went well, his enemies would be forced to sue for peace.

While Adolf Hitler was plotting victory, General Eisenhower thought the war was almost over. He made a wager with General Montgomery that it would be over by Christmas. On Sunday morning, 16th December, Eisenhower received a message from Montgomery reminding him of the bet. Eisenhower responded that he would pay up on Christmas Day, not before.

At precisely 0530 on that same December morning, an American sentry in the Ardennes Forest reported "pinpoints of light" suddenly flickering all along the German lines as German artillery opened up in the first salvo of the Battle of the Bulge. Out of the freezing mist appeared 200,000 Germans supported by 1,600 artillery pieces. The Germans expected a quick victory in that they outnumbered the American forces by nearly three to one and had taken them by total surprise.

By evening, the Germans had pushed twenty miles into Belgium and encircled Bastogne, a key crossroads and rail and communications center that, if taken, would have provided Hitler an open run to Antwerp and success. On 21st December, German troops challenged the Bastogne garrison commanded by General A. C. McAuliffe to surrender or suffer total annihilation. "Nuts!" McAuliffe responded.

It was Bastogne that derailed the Führer's juggernaut.

General Eisenhower rallied Allied troops north and south of the German incursion and sent them rushing toward the new front. That included the 101st and 82nd Airborne Divisions, the 10th Armored Division of Patton's Third Army, and parts of several other units. It was the 101st, arriving in Bastogne during the night of 21st December, that stopped the German tide and created the pivot point around which stiff Allied resistance formed.

By Christmas Eve, hampered by snow, cold, muddy roads, and critical fuel shortages, the Germans had turned to the defensive. Hitler's "secret strategy," the last major German offensive of the Second World War in the West, had failed.

Hitler admitted defeat on 8th January 1945 and authorized abandonment of the Bulge Pocket, although sporadic fighting continued for another week. Autumn Mist cost Germany 10,749 dead, 34,225 wounded, and the loss of 600 armored vehicles. It also robbed Germany of its last resources and opened the way for the Allied advance to Berlin.

* * *

The Cross

THE 101ST AND 82ND AIRBORNE DIVISIONS had been pulled off the line for refitting following seventy-two days of combat. They were enjoying two weeks of R&R in northern France when they suddenly received orders to deploy immediately to Belgium to help stop a German offensive in the Ardennes. Word had it that this might be tougher than the Market Garden fight. To make matters worse, this was turning out to be the coldest winter on record.

Grumbling and bellyaching, 101st Airborne paratroopers loaded onto open trucks to race across the frozen landscape to kick the Germans back. Private First Class Ed Peniche, nineteen, and Corporal Darrell Garner, twenty, hitched their rolling 57-mm antitank gun to a deuce-and-a-half truck and clambered aboard. GIs were packing in so tightly there was standing room only. If one man's butt itched, the man next to him had to scratch it.

Peniche, a diminutive Mexican immigrant only an inch or so above five feet tall, was born in Yucatan, the eldest child of eight from a devout Catholic family. He came to the United States in December 1942 to stay with an aunt in Paducah, Kentucky, and acquire an education not available in Mexico. After completing high school, he enlisted in the U.S. Army on 27th September 1943 and volunteered for the elite airborne.

Now, on 16th December 1944, the 101st's convoy of trucks roared all night, passing into the Belgian town of Bastogne shortly before dawn with a long rumble and roar in a swirl of snow. All was quiet. Snow caked the streets and most lights in town were extinguished.

At daybreak, the paratroopers were on the outskirts of Longchamps where their task was to block the main road intersection between Bertogne and Bastogne. Sergeant Joe O'Toole, squad leader for Peniche's antitank-gun section, placed his 57-mm guns in the grounds of a farm overlooking the road intersection, facing the expected direction of the oncoming enemy. The unnerving thunder of big guns from toward the front was evidence that the Germans were near. Orders for the 101st were simply: "Defend and hold the roadblock—at all costs."

"Sounds like the Krauts are really pissed off," Garner said.

The farm on which O'Toole set up his AT section consisted of a small rock-and-wood cottage and a barn. The owners had moved out because of the German offensive. O'Toole warned his men to stay out of the house, although they could use the farm barn for warm-up. Peniche and Garner gathered straw from the barn to line their foxhole and help ward off the terrible cold that seemed as much a threat as approaching panzers and their big guns.

Then they waited.

Corporal Garner took a stroll to expend nervous energy and stimulate the circulation in his freezing arms and legs. He returned with good news for his buddy. "Ed, there's a cross and crucifix in front of the house."

Sure enough, a crucifix of black metal attached to a four-foot-tall wooden cross stood in the garden. While artillery growled ominously in the background, Peniche, being a devout Catholic, knelt to pray.

The weather grew colder. Snow continued to fall. Ice crystals floating in the air glistened. Paratroopers put on every scrap of clothing they possessed but fires were prohibited since smoke gave away their positions.

Snow kept falling so thick on the second night that visibility was cut to mere feet. Big wet flakes the size of golf balls that filled up foxholes and rose to knee-deep. Even walking to an adjacent foxhole proved exhausting. A soldier threw up his arms in exasperation. "I am so tired of this miserable shit!"

Having grown up in sunny Yucatan, Peniche was afraid he would freeze to death.

While Sergeant O'Toole's emplacement had little to do except snipe at an enemy recon patrol now and then, paratroopers elsewhere fought a series of thrust-and-parry engagements against probing German infantry and armor. Six miles northeast of Bastogne at Noville, Americans stopped the 2nd Panzer Division cold, but then had to pull back to higher ground in the village of Foy, a mile nearer Bastogne. Brief battles also raged in sectors near where Peniche and the other AT and antiaircraft gunners held vigil.

Suddenly, several German half-tracks and a line of infantry in winter camouflage emerged around a bend in the road several hundred yards away from the 57-mm AT section. American infantry forward of the gun emplacements raked the intruders with heavy machinegun fire. Sergeant O'Toole issued the order to fire the 57s. The skirmish, though brief and concussive, didn't last long. The German reconnaissance withdrew, leaving behind one of its half-tracks blazing so fiercely it melted snow for yards around.

Finally, even worse than the weather, if that was possible, came the daunting news that the 101st Airborne had been cut off and surrounded, trapped inside a lumpy circle some five miles in diameter. Assuming the Americans were running out of supplies and ammo, advancing Germans demanded the division's surrender. General Anthony McAuliffe's reply both amused and rallied the tough men of the Screaming Eagles.

The entire Longchamps–Monaville region exploded in bloody and ferocious fighting as Germans of the 9th Panzers struggled to break through the American main line of resistance and rush on toward their objective at Antwerp. American machineguns, mortars, antitank cannon, and artillery sawed back at the attack. Peniche's 57-mm gun boomed at white-camouflaged Panther and Tiger tanks, delivering armor-piercing rounds on target until the barrel glowed from heat.

One of the first rounds from his gun picked the turret off a tank and put it out of action. Subsequent rounds destroyed another tank on the road and damaged a third, which withdrew dragging a torn track.

Machinegun bullets thumped into the shield that protected Peniche and Garner behind their 57. Concussive mortar shells stomped all around them. A piece of shrapnel caught Peniche in the left leg as he dashed back from picking up fresh shells at the ammo dump near the barn. He ignored the pain as he crouched behind the gunshield to fix fuses to shells for Garner to fire.

German mortar fire homed in on Sergeant O'Toole's guns. An airburst over the sergeant's fighting hole wounded him so severely he couldn't get up again. Simultaneous explosions knocked Peniche's gun out of commission. One of its wheels flew past Peniche and slammed into Garner. The detonation tossed Peniche through the air and deposited him in a snowdrift.

Groggy, his ears buzzing, Peniche couldn't get up for what seemed an eternity. He seemed to exist in a vacuum, a sort of momentary trance in which he no longer felt afraid.

He was in a bad way. His left shoulder was dislocated, his jaw out of place and swelling, and shrapnel in the muscles of his legs burned like fire. Mud and blood were splattered all over the snow.

As reason and reality gradually returned, the little Mexican heard Sergeant O'Toole groaning. He pulled himself through the snow to find O'Toole lying in the bottom of his hole with shattered bones protruding from his right thigh and leg. The syringe the sergeant had used to inject himself with morphine dangled from his hand. He looked pale and shocked.

"Ed . . . Ed, stay down . . . Don't get hit," he babbled.

That was when Peniche spotted Garner stunned and sitting right out in the open while deadly bullets and mortar shells played all around him. Peniche crawled over and dragged his buddy to the cover of O'Toole's foxhole.

He had to make some kind of decision. He could either think of his own skin and stay down in the hole with O'Toole and Garner, perhaps letting them die, or he could make his way through the pounding barrage of German shells and seek help for them. The choice was easy.

Although consumed by pain and terror, he set out on his belly through the thick snow and ice while he prayed in both English and Spanish. Sheer bedlam reigned as he made his way toward the battalion command post located beyond the farmhouse on the lee side of a hill. He paused at the calvary to ask for the Lord's help. Bullets thudded into the front of the house and kicked up plumes of snow all around him, but he and the cross remained untouched.

He felt panic subsiding while he prayed, in its place a sense of peace and well-being. His pain became more bearable. He knew, *knew*, everything was going to be all right.

"My buddies are hurt out there," he reported to medics at the command post. "God is protecting them until you can reach them."

Follow-up

Sergeant Joe O'Toole and Corporal Darrell Garner survived the Battle of the Bulge, as did Private Ed Peniche. Peniche was awarded the Bronze Star with "V" for valor for overcoming danger and his wounds to seek medical aid for his friends.

After the war, Peniche served a brief stint in the Mexican Army, co-founding his native country's parachute school, before he returned to the United States in 1952 and reenlisted in the U.S. Army. On 25th February 1953, he became a naturalized citizen of the United States. In October of that year he married Deanie Baggett of Paducah, Kentucky. They parented three sons.

Peniche retired from Army active duty as a Sergeant First Class in 1970 after having served three combat tours in Vietnam. He earned an MA degree from Murray State University in Kentucky in 1971 and was a college professor at Central Virginia Community College for twenty-two years, where he was awarded the title Professor Emeritus. He eventually retired from teaching at the age of seventy-four. He and his wife live in Kentucky.

"I am most proud that I lived the American Dream," he says. "This is the greatest country on Earth."

* * *

Massacre at Wereth

THE LAUNCH OF HITLER'S OPERATION AUTUMN MIST on 16th December 1944 created confusion and panic in GIs rousing for what they at first thought would be another uneventful day in the wooded, snow-covered hills of the Ardennes. The enemy artillery bombardment ended as twenty German divisions, supported by tanks, emerged from freezing fog in their attack against stunned Allies. The outcome of the Battle of the Bulge would remain in doubt for most of the rest of December.

When the shelling began, the all-black 333rd Field Artillery Battalion had two forward observation posts deployed in the German town of Bleialf. Both OPs overlooked a portion of the Siegfried Line. Their job was to keep an eye on the enemy out front and, when called upon, plot targets and direct fire for big 155-mm howitzer batteries located in the rear in the vicinity of St-Vith, Belgium.

For weeks, the 333rd had not been called upon for much other than manning radios and telephones and maintaining their vehicles, guns, and equipment. And now, on a dark morning so bitter cold that curses froze in the air, the Germans had taken it upon themselves to act up. It wasn't long before the Americans realized the attack was not just an inconvenience call from the Führer; it was a full-scale offensive.

The 333rd began laying artillery fire onto the attacking Germans. The battalion had twelve guns with eleven men usually assigned to operate each piece. The 155s lit up the horizon as black cannoneers got to work to the rhythm of their battle song, "Low Down Babe."

"Fee Fi Fo Fum, I smell the blood of the Boche," chanted Corporal David Smith of New York. "Rommel, count your men," chimed in another gunner, then added after a roaring salvo, "Rommel, how many men you got now?" Many of the shells bore chalked messages such as "From Harlem to Hitler with Love."

Most of the soldiers of the 333rd had worked together in the sweep across France, having landed in Normandy one month after D-Day. In September 1944, the battalion moved into the Ardennes in support of the 106th Infantry Division of the U.S. Army's VII Corps.

Singing and shouting as they worked, the black artillerymen were like a well-drilled professional football backfield in synchronization with the deafening sound of their guns. A projectile slammed into the gun's breech. The crew whirled in unison to accept the bagged propellant as it flew forward from man to man. The breech slammed shut. Number One man yanked the firing lanyard. A flash and a roar and the whistle of the ninety-five-pound projectile as it left the gun's muzzle. "Hey, Hitler! Take that one up the ass!"

The 333rd held the unofficial record of having fired three rounds in an incredible forty seconds. One of the outfit's batteries had scored a direct hit on a Tiger tank at a range of 16,000 yards. *Nine* miles.

In spite of relentless pressure from the German advance, the OPs at Bleialf continued to direct fire into a "target-rich environment" throughout the first day of the attack. German infantry were entering the little town by 1100 hours, advancing block by block, but the OPs held out until 0600 the following morning, December 17th, when, under cover of fog, snow, and pre-dawn darkness, the two officers and seven soldiers of the outposts attempted to withdraw. Neither the officers nor their men were ever heard from again.

In the meantime near St-Vith, the 106th Infantry was taking such a pounding from the Germans that when the 333rd proposed to move back to alternate positions, the 106th's commander requested that some guns be left behind to continue delivering fire support. Service and C Batteries, along with the 333rd Battalion's commander and operations officer, remained at St-Vith while the rest of the battalion withdrew to support the 101st Airborne Division at Bastogne.

At 0800, December 17th, Service and C Batteries received orders to pull back. Battalion Commander Lieutenant Colonel Harmon S. Kelsey and Operations Officer Captain Kline L. Roberts loaded their people onto three deuce-and-a-half trucks and blasted off for Schoenberg. Enemy mortar and artillery rounds danced all over the landscape, hammering out death and disarray.

Desperation turned to panic when enemy halftracks loaded with machine-gun-spitting infantry cut off the small American convoy before it reached friendly lines. Officers ordered men of the two batteries to dismount, destroy all guns and equipment, and attempt to escape on foot. About sixteen men eventually found their way to friendly lines. The others were either killed or captured.

During the turmoil, eleven black GIs became separated from the main body. Disoriented and frightened, armed only with two rifles and a bar of soap, they struck out, walking northwest through deep snow in hopes of escaping. Germans were in no mood to extend mercy or compassion toward prisoners.

Americans captured at a crossroads near Malmedy had been marched into a field to await an escort to the rear. Half an hour later, an SS task force arrived and executed seventy-one of the prisoners. Survivors feigned death or lay unconscious until nightfall when they crawled away from the gore to limp into Malmedy.

Unaware of such activities in the area, the eleven young black men of the 333rd approached the ten-house Belgian hamlet of Wereth. They hesitated, crouching on the outskirts of the village as nightfall began to descend upon the battlefield. Eleven frightened, hungry, exhausted, and disoriented American GIs who had little idea of where they were: Staff Sergeant Thomas James Forte; Corporal Mager Bradley; Private George Davis Jr.; Private George Moten; Private Due Turner; Private Jim Leatherwood; Private Curtis Adams; Spec4 William Pritchett; Spec4 James Stewart; Private Robert Green; and Private Nathanial Moos.

The region of Belgium around Wereth had been part of Germany prior to the First World War, after which it was ceded to Belgium. Most of the people still spoke German and viewed themselves as German citizens. Unlike the rest of Belgium, they had welcomed being conquered by Hitler in 1940 and did not necessarily see Americans now as "liberators."

With night approaching and no shelter against sub-zero temperatures, the eleven 333rd artillerymen finally ventured from hiding and approached the nearest house. It belonged to the Bürgermeister, Mathius Langer, who took in the Americans and gave them food and shelter. Present in the house were Langer's wife, his daughter, and a neighbor woman.

Unlike many in his community, Langer was ardently pro-Allied; he had sent his draft-age son into hiding so the Germans could not conscript him and was providing sanctuary for two Belgian deserters from the German Army. On the other hand, the visiting neighbor was just as ardently pro-Nazi. She left the Langer house immediately after the black GIs arrived.

An hour later, an SS patrol driving a halftrack rumbled into the little settlement and stopped in front of the Langer house. The SS seemed to know exactly what they were after, causing Langer to suspect his neighbor had turned in the lost GIs.

"We only wanted to help the men get warm," the frightened Langer explained to the SS.

"When we are finished with them," the SS commander said, "they won't feel cold any more."

U.S. Army Major James L. Baldwin, who was later assigned to investigate the incident, took witness statements from village residents.

"I am the Bürgermeister of Wereth and live there," Mathius Langer said in his statement. "On 17th December 1944, eleven black American soldiers arrived at my home at 1600. They came on foot with their hands in the air, carrying a blue flag. Apparently, they believed that the Germans were in the village. They had two rifles but didn't look as if they would use them. When they discovered that there were no Germans present, they stayed a half hour to an hour and ate the food I gave them.

"Then, four or five Germans came in a car, looking for the blacks, who came out and put their hands in the air. The Germans searched the blacks, took off their helmets and made them sit down on the ground, which was extremely cold and damp.

"They stayed like that until it was night. At nightfall, the men were lined up in the street and were made to run in front of the vehicle driven by the Germans."

The eleven artillerymen were herded up a small cow path in the snow to the corner of a nearby pasture.

"Neither I, nor any member of my family, saw the black soldiers again living," Langer's statement continued. "The next day, they were found dead at some 800 meters from my house, along the road."

Two civilians, who had left before the arrival of the Germans and who tried to return towards Valender, heard gunfire after nightfall. When they came back the following morning, they found the eleven bodies.

"I don't know who the Germans were, nor to which unit they belonged," Langer concluded. "They wore SS insignia on the collar and drove a little amphibious vehicle. They came from Halenfeld. I think that they were soldiers from the Hohenstaufen [SS Division], but I don't remember their insignia. I am sure they were SS. I didn't see them again after they left my house . . ."

Snow soon covered the bodies, which remained entombed in ice until mid-February 1945 when villagers directed a U.S. Army Graves Registration unit to the site. Autopsy reports revealed that the men had been brutalized before they were executed.

Adams, Green, and Stewart had their skulls fractured by blows to the backs of their heads. Pritchett's jaw was fractured in two places. Four fingers had been *pulled* off Forte's hand. Others had their eyes bayoneted out and fingers severed in order to remove rings. Track marks showed how some of them had been run over by the German vehicle before all were eventually shot.

The SS had had orders to roam the battlefield and strike terror into the hearts of the Americans. Apparently, that was what they were doing at Malmedy and in "The Massacre of the Wereth Eleven." No one was ever held accountable for the war crime.

Follow-up

The 333rd Battalion suffered more losses in action at Bastogne and leading up to Bastogne than any other artillery unit. Six officers and 222 men were either casualties, taken prisoner of war, or executed. The handful of 333rd survivors and their five remaining guns joined the all-black 969th Field Artillery Battalion to become a decisive factor in the defense of Bastogne.

On 3rd January 1945, General Maxwell D. Taylor, Division Commander of the 101st Airborne, recommended the 969th Field Artillery, which included the 333rd, for a Distinguished Unit Citation. It was the first DUC awarded to a black combat unit.

Seven of the eleven black servicemen murdered at Wereth were buried in the American Cemetery at Henri-Chapelle, Belgium. The other four were returned to their families for burial after the war. In 2001, Belgian citizens, led by the children of Mathius Langer, erected a monument at the site of the massacre to honor the memory of the Wereth Eleven. It is the only memorial in Europe dedicated to black GIs.

Chapter 14

Iwo Jima Ordeal

IN EUROPE, THE ALLIES WERE EDGING their way toward Berlin following Hitler's major defeat in the Battle of the Bulge. In the Pacific, Admiral Chester W. Nimitz and General Douglas MacArthur were "island hopping" ever nearer the Japanese mainland.

After Americans captured the Marshall Islands in early 1944, Japanese leaders countered by establishing an inner line of defense that extended from the Carolinas and Marianas to Japan via the Volcano Islands and westward to the Palau Islands and the Philippines. America penetrated this defensive line by seizing the Mariana Islands in the summer of 1944, which put Japan within reach of B-29 bombers.

As part of Operation Scavenger, B-29s began flying almost daily bombing raids from the Marianas against the enemy mainland. Along the B-29 flight path lay the tiny one-mile wide by five-mile long island of Iwo Jima controlled by the Japanese. An early warning station on the island allowed the Japanese to alert Tokyo of incoming bombers. Iwo Jima also provided a haven for Japanese naval units, an air base from which Japanese fighter planes scrambled to intercept American long-range bombers, and a launching platform for Japanese air attacks against U.S. forces now in control of the Marianas.

The American capture of Iwo Jima would eliminate these problems and provide a staging arena for Operation Downfall, the eventual invasion of the Japanese main islands. The island's three airfields would also provide a refuge for damaged B-29s returning from Japan, and would provide a base for P-51 Mustang fighters to use in escorting and protecting bombers.

Obviously, Japanese commanders felt the island had to be held to support their own operations. General Tadamichi Kuribayashi, placed in charge of defending Iwo with 22,000 soldiers and marines, converted the island into the most fortified warren of caves, tunnels, pillboxes, and camouflaged positions ever devised in the history of warfare. Some eleven miles of tunnels connected the various hidden artillery and infantry positions, allowing troops to respond en masse by scurrying along secure tunnels to reinforce points

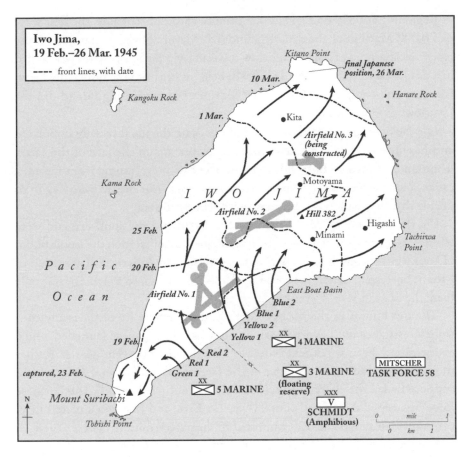

**Iwo Jima,
19 Feb.–26 Mar. 1945**

---- front lines, with date

Kitano Point

*final Japanese
position, 26 Mar.*

10 Mar.

Hanare Rock

Kangoku Rock

1 Mar.   •*Kita*

*Airfield No. 3
(being
constructed)*

Kama Rock   •*Motoyama*

I W O   J I M A

Airfield No. 2   ▲*Hill 382*

25 Feb.   •*Higashi*

•*Minami*   *Tachiiwa
Point*

P a c i f i c   *20 Feb.*

O c e a n   *Airfield No. 1*   *East Boat Basin*

Blue 2

Blue 1

Yellow 2

Yellow 1   XX
19 Feb.   ⊠ **4 MARINE**

•*Red 2*

Red 1   XX
captured, 23 Feb.   *Green 1*   ⊠ **3 MARINE**   **MITSCHER**
                               XX   *(floating*   **TASK FORCE 58**
N   *Mount Suribachi* ▲   ⊠ **5 MARINE**   *reserve)*   XXX
                                              V
                                         SCHMIDT
Tobishi Point   **(Amphibious)**

0   mile   1
0   km   1

under pressure. Or they could abandon a position, only to pop back up behind the enemy.

There were hundreds of hidden artillery and mortar positions, and land mines were sown all over the island. Static heavy weapons such as machineguns, artillery, mortars, and dug-in tanks provided mutually supporting, interlocking fire that could touch every inch of the island. Two semi-independent sectors— one in the north along the Motoyama Plateau and Hill 382, the other around and *inside* Mount Suribachi to the south, were prepared to repel any invasion.

It was a devious system and, as U.S. Marines soon discovered, a deadly one.

"Softening up" the objective began in June 1944 and continued for nine months, right up until D-Day, which was slated for 19th February 1945. While it seemed as if nothing alive could survive such a relentless pounding, hundreds of tons of bombs and thousands of rounds of heavy naval gunfire had left the Japanese defenders almost unscathed in their deep tunnels. They were prepared to inflict losses on U.S. Marines unprecedented up to this point in the Pacific War.

Beginning at 0859 on D-Day, one minute ahead of schedule, the first wave of 70,000 Marines of the 3rd, 4th, and 5th Marine Divisions landed on the black volcanic sand of the beach below towering Mount Suribachi. They landed in a deadly calm, as General Kuribayashi held his fire until the beach filled with Marines and equipment. Only after Marines began pushing inland did the Japanese respond with blistering fire.

For the next forty-two days, Iwo Jima became the most heavily populated and heavily contested 7.5 square miles of real estate on the face of the earth. Thousands of men on both sides fought it out with everything from mortars, tanks, and machineguns, to knives, clubs, and fists. The enemy were dug in so deeply that they had to be burnt out with flamethrowers.

On the morning of 23rd February, Suribachi and the southern end were effectively cut off from the rest of the island. Joe Rosenthal took the iconic photo of four Marines and one Navy corpsman raising an American flag on top of Mount Suribachi, the most-reproduced and famous photo to emerge not only from the Second World War but from any war.

The area known as "the Meatgrinder" on the northern tip of the island continued resistance until, worn down by attrition, the Japanese launched a final counterattack against Airfield Number 2 on the night of 25th March. Rather than commit traditional *seppuku* in the face of defeat, General Kuribayashi supposedly led the charge himself and died shouting *"Banzai!"* The Japanese force was wiped out. Army pilots, Navy SeaBees, and Marines suffered fifty-three killed in action and 120 wounded in the ninety-minute fight.

Iwo Jima was declared secure at 0900 on 26th March 1945.

Of the 22,060 Imperial soldiers who began the battle, 21,844 died either from fighting or ritual suicide. Only 216 were captured, most of them having first been rendered unconscious or helpless from wounds. Iwo Jima was the only U.S. Marine Corps battle in which overall American casualties (26,000 killed or wounded) exceeded those of the Japanese. However, Japanese combat *deaths* were three times the 6,800 Marines killed.

American commanders initially assumed that not a single Japanese remained alive inside the island's caves and tunnels. That turned out to be a false assumption. Many Japanese soldiers hid underground for months, coming out only at night to scrounge for provisions. The last two finally surrendered in 1951.

As America continued to prepare for the invasion of the Japanese mainland, top Pentagon planners designated Iwo Jima as an emergency landing point for B-29 bombers en route to or from Japan. What no one outside the top echelon of government and the Manhattan Project knew was that this "emergency landing point" was intended as a backup site for B-29s carrying atomic bombs.

* * *

On the Island

CORPORAL ROBERT K. HILL, 2nd Battalion, 23rd Infantry Regiment, 4th Marine Division, had had enough of trying to sleep below decks on his way across the Pacific from Pearl Harbor to . . . Ordinary grunts seldom knew the "Big Picture." They just went wherever they were told to go and shot whoever they were told to shoot. Except that Bob Hill knew where the 4th Marines were bound even before the division loaded aboard troop transports, 400–500 leathernecks to the boat, and took to sea out of Pearl. Gunnery Sergeant Bill King from New Jersey told him.

"Okay, Hill," the gunny said in his "wise guy" Joisey-speak, "nobody knows where we going, unnerstand? 'Cept the officers. But I know where we headed. I am gonna give youse one letter uncensored to tell youse mama where we going. You can't tell nobody else, unnerstand? Not youse best buddy or youse ho' downtown. It's Iwo Jima."

Hill didn't know Iwo Jima from hog spit, but at least his mama back in Wagoner, Oklahoma, could keep up with him if Iwo Jima came up on the radio. She had a map of the world and he reckoned she had followed him on it from Kwajalein and Roi-Namur up and down and back across the Pacific. Sometimes she knew where the 4th Marine Division was going before he did, all from listening to President Roosevelt and whoever on the radio.

"Sand beaches, lots of sunshine, and pretty girls," he wrote to try to keep his mama from fretting.

Before the 4th loaded up and set out from Pearl, Gunny King told him, "Hill, youse on the Reserve list this time."

"Gunny, uh . . .?"

"Yeh, Hill? What's on youse mind this time?"

"Gunny, Baker's wife just had twins. He's on the Forward list. Whyn't I take his place and you put him on Reserve since I'm not married and got no kids that I know of?"

Hill, a corporal and squad leader at nineteen, was the second-youngest Marine in his company. Already a combat veteran, he was mean, lean, green, and gung-ho. He didn't figure the Japs had a bullet big enough to write his name on.

"Damn, Hill," Gunny King grumbled. "I'll do it. But damned if I don't think youse wouldn't be satisfied if we buried youse in a new suit."

Corporal Hill certainly wasn't satisfied with the arrangements for getting to Iwo Jima. There was some mean weather with squalls and seas so high ships dropped out of sight in the troughs. He was one of a handful who didn't get just puke-green seasick, which explained why he couldn't sleep below where guys were stacked five bunks tall. You had to pity the poor bastards in the lower bunks. The toilets got stopped up in the heads and everything stank of puke, shit, man sweat, and farts.

Out of self-preservation, Hill took his life preserver and slipped topside to sleep in one of the tarp-covered lifeboats in the fresh sea air. One of the Navy officers caught him there and kicked him out of the boat. Hill bobbed and grinned and slipped away to sleep in a lifeboat on the other side of the ship. The officer was smarter than Hill gave him credit for. "I catch you again, Marine, and I'm writing you up for Captain's Mast. You'll go to the brig."

So Hill went below decks—but not to the fetid bunk area. He strung up a hammock in the ammunition hold and was lying kicked back in bed smoking a cigarette when the same lieutenant caught him again. Sure enough, he went to Captain's Mast, non-judicial punishment. He didn't end up in the brig, but he did slave in the laundry, pressing uniforms for the rest of the voyage.

It was almost a relief when he heard the thunder of big guns in the distance and saw the horizon flash against the night like lightning. Somebody was kicking the shit out of somebody else. Hill figured the Japs were getting about what they deserved.

According to briefings, Iwo Jima was to be a twenty-four-hour operation at most. The Navy had been working over the island for weeks, and were still at it. Battlewagons were spitting chunks of fire as transports pulled to anchor a mile or so offshore. Troops lined the rails of hundreds of transports and watched the rest of the day and night as Navy guns and airplanes hammered the tiny piece of terra firma and smoke and fire roiled from it.

A light, cold drizzle fell on D-Day, 19th February 1945. Just enough to keep troops wet and miserable. Mount Suribachi, the 550-foot black cone on the island's southern tip, dominated the landing beach. It seemed to be waiting in ambush. Surely, though, nothing on this little hunk of rock and volcanic dirt could withstand the beating it had taken.

Then why, Hill wondered, was it going to take three full Marine divisions—the 3rd, 4th, and 5th—to run the Japs off it.

"Now hear this, now hear this!" blared transport PA systems. "Chaplains will offer a moment of prayer before you board your landing craft . . ." That was how you knew when things were serious. Not an eye remained open or a head unbowed.

Shivering, laden like a mule with combat gear, Corporal Hill joined the scramble over the sides of the transports, down the loading nets, and into assigned landing craft. Hill's company would go ashore like a troupe of monkeys on the fourth wave, which gave the first three waves time to really piss off the Japs. If there were any Japs left inside that cloud of smoke, fire, and dust.

Attacking bombers and Navy guns lifted their assault at the last moment. Marines charged ashore—and were greeted by a strange, eerie silence. They suffered nothing worse than a sprained ankle. Immediately, they began digging fighting holes in the loose volcanic soil, but the holes filled back in almost as soon as they were dug. Not a single hostile round issued from the Japanese lines.

Officers walked up and down the beach. Others glassed Mount Suribachi and the interior with binoculars. You could almost see from one end of the island to the other. Puzzled commanders studied maps. Ordinary leathernecks stood up, arched their backs, and looked at each other.

"Maybe they all got killed," seemed to be the growing consensus.

No such luck. The Japanese were merely waiting to catch everyone on the beach before they started the slaughter. All hell had broken loose by the time Corporal Hill arrived with the fourth wave. It was just like he figured. The first landings stuck a stick in the hornets' nest and now the hornets were riled.

Safe from aerial bombing and naval gunfire in their tunnels and caves, the Japs were ready. Enemy machineguns crisscrossed the beaches with deadly interlocking fire, mowing down advancing Marines like sheaves of rice. Rockets and artillery pulverized the beaches. Unable to dig foxholes in the loose ash, Marines were sitting ducks, their only option to go forward as fast as they could. While they fought from above ground, the Japanese defended from below ground. The cloying stench of blood and death, of fear and horror, of cordite and smoke hung toxic in the Pacific air.

For the next six weeks Marines measured their advances in yards. Sometimes no more than a yard or two a day, and that bought dearly in lost lives. The defenders were there to fight to the very last man. The 3rd Marines held in reserve had to be called into the fight on D-Day plus four.

As soon as 2/23rd (2nd Battalion, 23rd Infantry) landed, it broke inland toward its objective—the main airfield located north and east of Suribachi. Gunny Bill King, the "old man" of the outfit at forty-six, and platoon leader Lieutenant Leonard Thomas, shouted the platoon into battle formation. Squad leaders like Corporal Hill did likewise with their squads under platoon control. Men had been cut down all over the terrain as soon as steel ramps opened on landing craft and the fourth wave rushed ashore. Some slumped to the ground to lie silent and motionless. Others went down hard with bloodcurdling screams and a lot of kicking and flailing of arms.

Numerous Japanese defensive positions stood between Lieutenant Thomas's platoon and its objective. All had to be beaten down and gone through. Japanese sprang out of tunnel openings in fierce ambushes. Enemy heavy artillery crews up on Suribachi opened reinforced steel doors, fired, then closed the doors again against counterfire. Bunkers once cleared had to be cleared all over again after Japs scooted back into them via the many tunnels that honeycombed the island.

The Japanese threw everything they had at the Marines, including the "flying shithouse," a monstrous box full of explosives, nuts and bolts, and scrap steel launched by a device that resembled a medieval catapult. It blew giant craters wherever it landed and sprayed shrapnel in all directions.

Sergeant Fred Harris, the company's master gunner, was sprinting to another position about ten feet away when a spray of heavy machinegun fire caught him, smashing his head like a pumpkin and blowing off his left arm at the shoulder. He always wore a big Marine Corps ring. His buddy, Sergeant Miller, found his arm and removed the ring to send to his wife.

Corporal David Ray from San Francisco trapped a bunch of Japs in a cave.

"Hill, you keep firing on the front end," he said. "I'll run by and throw a charge in on them."

The opening of the cave was dug into the side of a black bluff about twenty yards away. Ray sprang to his feet with a canvas satchel full of plastic explosive, the fuse lit, and made a run for the cave like a quarterback heading for goal. Hill emptied a clip from his M1 into the cave to keep the Japs pacified. Corporal Ray tripped and almost fell as he raced past the cave's entrance and flung the satchel.

The bag bounced off the side of the entrance and back toward Ray and Hill. Both Marines hugged the ground. The satchel exploded with a concussive whump that filled the air with debris and shrapnel. Miraculously, except for having the breath knocked out of them from the detonation, both Marines escaped relatively unscathed. Gunpowder burns, cuts, scrapes, and minor bone fractures didn't count in this kind of fighting.

While the dazed Marines were working on another plan, along came a Sherman "Zippo" tank with a flamethrower that could shoot dragon's breath for a hundred yards of more. It lit up the cave with flame. Burning Japanese ran out like screaming roman candles. Hill and Ray and some of their platoon mates chopped them down, mercifully putting them out of their agony.

Every Marine in 2nd Battalion carried a little address book listing the names, addresses, and next-of-kin of every man in the outfit. That was for when some-one got killed, so his buddies and officers could write letters to his wife, mother, or whoever. There were going to be many letters written after this fight.

By evening of D-Day, Suribachi had been cut off from the rest of the island. Marines dug in for the night wherever they happened to stop. Japs came out of their burrows to attack, but U.S. Navy ships offshore kept firing starburst shells to deny them the cover of darkness. Everyone expected a Japanese *banzai* charge, their standard final defense on Tinian and other islands, but the first night remained relatively quiet.

Wide-awake, watching shadows, Hill and his squad that included red-haired "Red" McGowen, Emile Valentech, and Marvin "Jew Boy" Franklin, crouched in shifting-sand foxholes and waited out the hours until daylight when the fight started all over again.

It took four days for 2nd Battalion to battle its way to the airfield and secure it. Four days of firefights, flamethrowers, and Zippo tanks to burn Japs out of their holes. Four days of grenades, bayonets, and hand-to-hand struggles. Curiously enough, none of the expected *banzai* charges developed. At least not until later when the Japs were pushed back into the "Amphitheater" at the northern end of the island and they became cornered and desperate.

As Lieutenant Thomas's platoon cautiously approached the airfield against sporadic opposition, a Jap bullet slapped Franklin. The impact threw his rifle into the air and flipped him over. Medics stretchered him off to a hospital ship waiting at sea. "Good luck, guys," Franklin said as he was hauled away from the squad. "I guess I'm one of the lucky ones."

As soon as 2nd Battalion secured the airfield, Navy SeaBees arrived to start repairing it for the Air Force to use in their campaign against Japan. Hill's squad was tasked with airfield security.

Different challenge-and-response passwords were issued every twenty-four hours as the campaign stretched toward the end of February and Japanese defenders retreated into final enclaves at the island's north end. While on watch one night at the north end of the airfield, Bob Hill and Red McGowen spotted two figures approaching in the dark. They assumed the intruders to be Japs trying to sneak through the lines, but you had to be certain before you lit up anyone.

Hill snapped the selector switch of his .45 Thompson submachine gun to full auto while Red and he crouched breathlessly and waited for the shadows to get closer.

As soon as the strangers were within a couple of hundred feet or so, Hill issued the challenge. "Halt! Chevrolet."

The reply to "Chevrolet" was supposed to be "Dream." Japs had difficulty pronouncing the English "R."

There was no response. "Them are Japs," Red hissed. "Shoot 'em."

"Let them get a little closer to be sure."

They waited some more. "Halt! Chevrolet."

Still nothing.

Hill took up trigger slack. One of the visitors suddenly called out, "Hill, that you?"

They were Valentech and another guy from the platoon out patrolling the perimeter. They had forgotten the password. Red went off on them.

"What's the matter with you crazy sum'bitches? We almost killed you."

"Nah," Val scoffed. "I've seen how you guys shoot."

Not all wounds and injuries were clearly visible. One kid in the squad named Blevins couldn't take the stress of continuous fighting any more. He crabbed out, went catatonic. It was called shell-shock. In his mind, he went off somewhere away from the island. Hill stashed him in a cleared Japanese bunker at the end of the runway where he could be safely fed and watered and left alone until he either recovered or could be evacuated.

One night on watch, McGowen and Hill ran out of cigarettes. "I know who's got some," Hill recalled. "Blevins over in the Jap hole."

Hill slipped over to the bunker. Without identifying himself, thinking Blevins was still off traveling around in his head, he crawled through the low tunnel that led into the larger chamber. Suddenly in the darkness, he felt a muzzle press hard against his forehead.

Damn! Blevins was back. "Put that damned gun down, Blevins, and give me some cigarettes," Hill demanded.

One night, an enemy probe caught Hill and platoon leader Thomas out in the open. They made a run for the cover of a big steel wagon wheel when the fireworks started. Nearby, a U.S. tank unleashed on an enemy position north of the airfield. The enemy unloaded back at the tank, catching the two Marines in a crossfire. They dashed for a shell crater to get out of the line of fire. A shell exploded nearby as they dived for shelter. Both heard the high-pitched shriek of a big piece of shrapnel whizzing between them.

Panting from the run and the near-miss, the Marines grasped each other's shoulder as though to reassure themselves that they were still alive. The only word they could think to utter was, "Damn!"

They stayed in the hole until daylight and things quieted down again. Hill kicked around in the sand at the bottom of the crater and picked up a snapshot of an unidentified young woman some Marine must have lost. Written on the back of the photo was an inscription poignant in its simplicity: "Every moment has its unbelievable moment."

Hill stuffed the photo in his pocket and kept it.

Follow-up

Most of the Japanese on the island died fighting, including the Japanese commander who led a final charge on the night of 25th March. Iwo Jima was officially declared cleared the next day.

Corporal Hill sometimes wondered why so many people had to die for possession of a place like this. He got his answer after SeaBees repaired the airfields and B-29 Superfortresses started using it. One afternoon, a B-29 returning from having bombed Japan landed and skidded down the runway without landing gear, one engine gone, and its fuselage all shot up. The crew were dead except for the pilot, navigator and one of the gunners. These three wouldn't have made it back either except for the runway on Iwo Jima.

Bob Hill survived the war and returned to run private businesses and raise a family in Oklahoma, where he still resides.

Chapter 15

Prisoners of the Japanese

AFTER RETAKING THE ADMIRALTY ISLANDS in February and March 1944, General Douglas MacArthur planned to make a 500-mile leap directly to Hollandia on the coast of New Guinea. He hoped that would bring him closer in time and distance to realizing his greatest aim of returning to the Philippines, as he had promised in 1942 when the Japanese destroyed his army and took prisoner some 70,000 American and Filipino soldiers.

To add to his ground forces in the Southwestern Pacific, MacArthur activated the Sixth U.S. Army under the command of General Walter Krueger on 22nd January 1943. Since Krueger was a Texan, the Sixth Army operated under the code-name Alamo Force.

Three months later, on 22nd April 1944, Krueger's army participated in the most ambitious amphibious operation undertaken so far in the Southwest Pacific when 217 ships carrying 50,000 combat troops and 30,000 support personnel invaded Hollandia, the largest anchorage on the north coast of New Guinea. The 11,000-man Japanese garrison hightailed it into the central jungle highlands rather than stand and fight.

Krueger, like MacArthur, was suspicious of intelligence sources outside his control. MacArthur so distrusted the Office of Strategic Services that he refused to allow OSS agents south of the equator. In November 1943, Krueger created out of this atmosphere of distrust and secrecy his own unit within the Sixth Army to be used for intelligence gathering and other special operations.

The Alamo Scouts participated in New Guinea action by conducting behind-enemy-lines recon and intelligence work. In October 1944, the Scouts rescued a former Dutch governor, his family and their Javanese workers—sixty-six men, women, and children—who were being held by the Japanese in slave labor in the village of Maori in Cape Oransbari in northwest New Guinea.

Nearly three years after he fled the Philippines, on 20th October 1944, MacArthur waded ashore on Leyte near the town of Tacloban with a body guard of Alamo Scouts and broadcast to the Filipino people: "I have returned." It took 100,000 GIs more than two months of hard fighting to secure Leyte from the Japanese. Americans lost 3,508 men killed in the action, compared to 55,344 Japanese dead. One U.S. soldier observed how "the Japanese fought to die, and the Americans fought to live."

The bulk of American land and naval forces now concentrated on MacArthur's next move—landing on the main Philippine island of Luzon where Manila was located. His first incursion took place at Lingayen Gulf, 100 miles north of Manila, on 9th January 1945. Other American landings quickly followed—at Subic Bay west of Bataan, at Corregidor, and southwest of Manila by parachutists.

Instead of resisting at the Luzon beachheads, the Japanese under General Tomoyuki Yamashita pulled back toward the middle of the island. Soldiers of General Krueger's Alamo Force were among American elements that swept through the final defenses of Manila to liberate the capital on 4th March 1945.

MacArthur was afraid that large numbers of American prisoners of war, survivors of the Bataan Death March being held near the city, would be massacred as the Japanese withdrew into the mountains.

* * *

The Raid

GALEN CHARLES KITTLESON, ELDEST OF EIGHT surviving barefooted offspring, struggled through the Great Depression in an old white two-story farmhouse through the cracks of which a cat might squeeze without losing hair. He grew up a skinny little kid who weighed less than a 100-pound sack of feed oats until after he started high school in nearby St Ansgar, Iowa. He was tough, though, and strong for his size.

"I'm going to be an Iowa farmer, just like my pops," he would proudly proclaim.

Pearl Harbor occurred during basketball season at St Ansgar Independent High. It was a distant thing, akin to a revolution in India or a famine in Africa. The war fever that swept the nation barely touched the Kittlesons and their neighbors in the corn and hay fields of Iowa. At least not until the area's young men began disappearing into the Army.

On Saturday nights in downtown St Ansgar, fewer and fewer young men gathered to appraise the girls strolling in the streets. "Have you seen Angus?" someone might ask.

"He joined the Army, what I hear."

That was how war came to St Ansgar. Galen graduated from high school in the spring of 1942. Soon thereafter, he marched into his local draft board. He ended up a paratrooper assigned to General Walter Krueger's Sixth Army's 503rd Parachute Regiment in the South Pacific, where he volunteered for Alamo Scout training.

On 26th January 1945, two weeks and four days after General Douglas MacArthur invaded Luzon, a thin GI major in worn uniform riding an even thinner and more travel-weary bay horse halted his mount at the edge of Sixth Army headquarters near Calasio south of the Lingayen Gulf. Corporal Willie Wismer and Private Galen Kittleson watched him walk his horse through the middle of the tent city blistering amidst rocks, tall grass, and dust. General Krueger's headquarters tents were located on the far side of the encampment.

"Wonder who that is?" Kittleson mused.

"Don't you know nothing, private?" Wismer chided. "Don't you recognize the most famous American guerrilla chief in the South Pacific?"

During early 1942 when the "Battling Bastards of Bataan" were being systematically pounded and starved into submission, Lieutenant Robert W. Lapham and thirty-five other GIs volunteered to infiltrate Japanese lines, make their way north through fifty miles of enemy country, and blow up enemy aircraft at Clark Field. Bataan surrendered when they were only ten miles from their target. The small combat force split up to escape and evade and headed for the hills.

Lapham made his way to Nueva Ecija Province and began recruiting guerrillas from the Filipino natives. Promoted to major by the U.S. War Department, he eventually commanded a guerrilla force numbering more than 2,000. His guerrillas and other guerrilla bands like his, many of which were also led by Americans, continued to fight against the occupying Japanese army while awaiting MacArthur's return.

Now, he had urged his spent horse through thirty miles of Jap-infested terrain to bring crucial information about the Bataan Death March survivors at Cabanatuan. He was escorted to the tent of Colonel Horton White, Krueger's intelligence officer.

"Sir," he began without preliminaries, "there is real danger, *imminent* danger, that the prisoners at Cabanatuan will be massacred out of vengeance when our units start approaching the camp." Lapham went to a map and pointed out locations as he spoke. "There are approximately 9,000 Japs in this area either withdrawing toward the mountains or establishing defensive positions. The road in front of the prison camp is heavily traveled by tanks and vehicles. There are 5,000 more Japs in and around the town of Cabanatuan and a strong enemy force bivouacked here along the Cabu River less than a mile northeast of the camp.

"Japs use the camp as a stopover, a way station. At any given time, there may be between 100 and 300 Japs inside the prison compound. Sir, it may look impossible, but it's not. These Americans *must* be rescued. We owe it to them to at least make the effort."

As usual, Willie Wismer picked up the news first from somewhere. He burst into Kittleson's squad tent. "I know where the Alamo Scouts are going next," he blurted out. "You boys remember the Bataan Death March? Kit, you weren't even out of high school then."

As usual, Wismer's intel was right on. Lieutenant Bill Nellist, Kittleson's team leader, gave the required briefing. "We're going behind Jap lines to rescue 500 GIs being held at the Cabanatuan POW camp. Headquarters figures the Japs may murder all the prisoners unless we can get them out. Be ready to move out at 1630 hours this afternoon to our forward positions in Guimba."

Guimba, the Sixth Army's most forward position, was twenty-five miles northwest of the POW camp.

The thirteen Alamo Scouts—a baker's dozen—held on to the slatted sides of the two-and-a-half-ton truck and coughed and hacked at dust swirling underneath the tarp with them as the truck weaved and rattled violently through military traffic toward Guimba. Each Scout was acutely aware that they were embarking upon one of the war's most perilous and spectacular operations. Never before in American history had U.S. soldiers been called upon to rescue such a large number of POW from so deep inside enemy territory. Everyone had to be in position to kick off the raid by 1930 hours the day after tomorrow, 29th January 1945.

"We're bringing out every GI, even if we have to carry them on our backs," Lieutenant Nellist vowed. "Colonel Henry Mucci, commander of 6th Ranger Battalion, is overall commander of the operation."

Major Lapham and one of his guerrilla chiefs who spoke English greeted the Scout officers at Guimba. While officers conferred inside a hut, the teams ate a meal of black beans and rice around a big iron pot on a fire outside. Nellist came out of the hut. "Boys, get some sleep if you can. It's gonna be a long night."

A half moon drove black shadows across the stubble of dry rice fields at 2100 hours when thirteen Scouts of the Nellist and Rounsaville teams and about fifty of Major Lapham's guerrillas set out on foot from Guimba. Colonel Mucci and his Rangers were exactly twenty-four hours behind the Scouts. The Scouts and guerillas would lead the way to establish advance surveillance on the prison camp. It would be a twenty-four-mile forced march.

As the Scouts' most reliable point man, Kittleson took the lead along with two Filipino guerrillas who knew the way to the village of Balincarin. Most of the distance lay over harvested rice fields, now dry, or through prairies of tall kunai and cogon grass. They had to cross several streams and ravines and two main highways. To be discovered meant compromise of the mission and a probable quick and brutal death for the small band. They had to travel fast in order to reach Balincarin by daybreak.

About nine miles into the march, they approached the National Highway that ran from Manila through Cabanatuan town and on to San José. As Kittleson approached the thoroughfare, he caught the unmistakable clanking of tanks. He went to all fours and crawled up a ravine for a look. A pale moon obligingly broke out from behind drifting clouds long enough to reveal three tank silhouettes, now stopped on the road, guarding a small bridge about thirty feet long. A convoy of Jap trucks rumbled by, their cats' eye lights winking.

The raiders had only one choice; they had to cross the road, and the only path seemed to be to crawl underneath it through the bridge culvert pipes. "Do we have another option?" Lieutenant Thomas "Studs" Rounsaville asked rhetorically.

Kittleson thought the Japs up on the road must be deaf not to hear the pounding of his heart. Nonetheless, in less than fifteen minutes, everyone was under the bridge and across. Apparently, the sentries were too busy smoking and joking to pay attention to mice stealing the house from around them.

They arrived like nomads at Balincarin at daybreak. The village was typical: huts; poor natives; naked kids playing in the dust; pigs, donkeys, and carabao. More partisans were waiting there, along with a guerrilla leader named Pajota. "My men observed a Japanese unit of division strength this morning going north on Highway 5 in front of the prison," Pajota reported. "Another 1,000 are bivouacked near the Cabu Bridge."

After a brief rest and more bowls of rice and beans, the Scout team saddled up and a guerrilla guide took them for their initial appraisal of the POW camp. They climbed a jungle rise out of Balincarin, then descended into lowlands along the Pampanga River. Kunai grass grew more than head tall, providing excellent cover. The river was about 200 yards wide in places, but it was lazy and shallow. They waded across at a narrow point. Beyond rose a low knoll covered with tall grasses. Cautioned by their guide, the raiders crawled to the top of the knoll, parted the grass, and peered out.

The camp sat in the open about 700 yards away. All Kittleson could see from this distance were the tops of high fence poles and roofs of thatched palm fronds or tin. There was a guard tower to the left corner of the front gate. Some dusty Jap trucks passed by on the road in front of the camp.

What unsettled the Scouts was not the stockade itself, but the open terrain that surrounded it. It was farmland—flat, cultivated fields of turnips, sweet potatoes, or something similar. There were patches of kunai here and there, but otherwise even a lizard would have had a tough time making it unseen from the river to the camp's front gates.

Filipinos labored in the fields in the bright, morning sunlight. There was a single hut isolated in the field a short distance outside the prison gate, on this side of Highway 5. It appeared unoccupied. Cabanatuan Town lay out of sight along Highway 5 to the southwest, four miles away. Cabu Creek Bridge where a large contingent of Japanese troops had dug in was less than a half-mile from the prison to the northeast.

It was going to be a tough operation.

In the meantime, Colonel Henry Mucci led his 6th Rangers out of Guimba at 1400 hours on 28th January, not quite twenty-four hours behind the lead Scout element. His force consisted of Charley Company reinforced with a platoon from Fox Company, 121 soldiers in all. It was a large number of men to move through enemy country, but their luck held.

The Rangers linked up in the predawn of 29th January with Filipino guerrilla chief Captain Eduardo Joson and about eighty of his fighters in the *barrio* of Lobong, some miles west of Balincarin. From there, now numbering more than 200, they continued to their staging area at Platero about a half-mile to the Scouts' rear and a mile-and-a-half from the POW stockade.

Nellist and Rounsaville Teams continued surveillance on target. Scouts had spent the night in tall grass along the Pampanga River, sharing watches. Bill Nellist and Lieutenant Studs Rounsaville left their men to watch the prison compound while they hiked to Platero to meet with Colonel Mucci and Captain Pajota to round out the operational plan.

Colonel Mucci was concerned about the intelligence they had gathered so far. "We've got to get someone close to the front gate," he said. "We're going to bolt through that entrance, so the gate is the key to the entire operation. Which way does it open—in or out? How is it secured? Where are the exact locations of the watch towers? How are they manned? How many Jap sentries? How is the fence constructed . . .?"

That afternoon while the sun burned straight overhead, Lieutenant Nellist and Pontiac Vaquilar, who was short and dark and could easily pass for a native, shucked their green uniforms in exchange for the loose off-white garb of the local peasants. They stuck .45 pistols underneath their garments and pulled on wide-brimmed straw *buri* hats to conceal their faces. Pajota promised that none of the farmers working in the fields would betray the Americans.

Thus disguised, the two "farmers" ambled across an open plot of young sweet potato plants and made their way toward the hut that sat not 200 yards from the compound's front gate. Farmers used it as storage for their implements and other supplies. It was isolated and exposed to the compound and the road that ran in front. Kittleson and other Scouts watched breathlessly from hiding as the lieutenant and Vaquilar reached the hut, fooled around outside for a minute to allay suspicions, then stepped inside. Cracks in the bamboo walls provided an unobstructed view of the prison gate. Nellist took out a notebook and began plotting and drawing and making notes.

The front gate was about nine feet high and made of sawed lumber. Strands of barbed wire ran from its supporting posts in double eight-foot-tall fences around the entire stockade, which was about twenty to thirty acres in size. Nellist marked on a sketch the locations of sentry towers and noted that neither of the two he saw in front was manned—at least not in daytime. The buildings appeared to be of one- and two-story bamboo with thatched palm roofs, while others were of concrete with corrugated tin roofs.

That night, with Nellist's information in hand, Colonel Mucci called together his element leaders to finalize the attack operations order. Major Lapham's partisans were to provide security and a blocking force around the camp while the U.S. Rangers and Alamo Scouts conducted the actual raid. Guerrillas from Pajota's force would establish a roadblock at the Cabu Creek Bridge to stop Japs from crossing the creek to the prison compound. Joson's guerrillas, along with a Ranger bazooka team, would establish a similar blocking post on the road 800 yards southwest of the camp to catch Jap elements that might attempt to break through from Cabanatuan Town.

"We need a half-hour to shoot our way into the camp and herd out the prisoners," Mucci said.

The rest of the raid worked this way. From an assembly point at the Pampanga River, the Rangers and Scouts would cross the 700–800 yards of open fields under cover of darkness to reach the prison's main gate before 1930 hours. Rangers Lieutenant William J. O'Connell and Lieutenant Melville H. Schmidt received the main task of breaching the front gate with their two respective platoons and the Alamo Scouts. Lieutenant John F. Murphy would lead a platoon crawling all the way around the left of the prison camp to the rear gate.

"Lieutenant Murphy initiates attack by opening fire on the guards at the back gate," Colonel Mucci directed. "That should provide a momentary distraction to allow platoons to take out the Jap guards at the main gate and bust into the compound."

"Lieutenant O'Connell's platoon sweeps the Jap side of the compound to the right of the road inside. Lieutenant Schmidt and his platoon take the left side, the POW side. Murphy breaks through the rear gate and covers Schmidt with a crossfire while one of Schmidt's squads rounds up the prisoners and gets them out the front gate pronto. Alamo Scouts and a squad of Rangers have in the meantime secured the front gate and will start the prisoners in batches of fifty toward the river where we have one hundred-fifty Filipino irregulars waiting with all the carabao carts we can round up by tomorrow night.

"Remember, these boys have been in that shit hole beaten and starved for nearly three years. If they can't walk to the river, carry them. We don't leave one of them behind. Not a single one. I will fire two red flares from my Very pistol as a signal that all the prisoners are out and at the river."

That was also the signal for Pajota to withdraw to the northwest and Joson to the southwest. Hopefully, that would lure Jap forces after them and widen the gap through which raiders would make their return march to Guimba with the rescued POW.

"We attack tomorrow night. I think that the date of 30th January 1945 will be long remembered. Go with God—and bring our boys home. They have not been forgotten."

Private Kittleson cradled his Thompson submachine gun in the crook of his arms and used his elbows and knees to draw himself across the uneven field like a lizard with its front feet removed. He heard other indistinct scraping sounds around him in the dry rice beds and sweet potato fields as 121 Rangers and thirteen Alamo Scouts crawled toward the POW camp.

Lieutenant Murphy's platoon detachment separated from the main body to worm its way around to the back gate.

Suddenly, the night silence shattered. The clear gonging of a bell reverberated out of the prison camp. The raiders froze in place. Had they been detected? Nothing happened. No floodlights, no enemy troops pouring out the gate. Only later did they learn that the gonging came from a ship's bell improvised by a U.S. Navy POW who sounded the watch at periodic intervals.

After what seemed an eternity condensed into an hour, raiders slipped into the drainage ditch that paralleled the road in front of the stockade. Cigarettes glowed where guards twenty yards away were smoking at the gate.

Kittleson peered across the road through the barbed wire directly into the compound. He discerned Japs in their underwear lounging in the open doorways of lighted barracks. Oriental music with its peculiar counterpointing flavor lilted out of the wire and drifted with the breeze across the raiders' heads. Apparently, the Japs felt secure here twenty-five miles behind the front.

He waited for the attack signal.

Meanwhile, Lieutenant John Murphy and his Ranger detachment slithered along a filthy sewage ditch to within fifteen yards of the back gate. It was 1920 hours by Murphy's watch, ten minutes away from H-hour. Rangers rested their rifles on the outer strands of barbed wire and began selecting targets among the unsuspecting Japs inside.

Lieutenant Murphy took bead on a Jap sitting with two others on a back stoop by the gate. He checked his watch. It was time. He squeezed the trigger. His carbine barked and spat flame. His target jumped like an electric bolt had shot through his body. He fell off the stoop. The rest of the platoon opened up with a murderous crescendo of rifle fire to secure the guard towers.

At the front gate, Kittleson scrambled out of the ditch a few paces behind Ranger Sergeant Ted Richardson. Everyone charged. It was Richardson's job to smash the oversized padlock on the gates to allow troops to throw them wide and surge inside.

He struck the lock with the butt of his rifle. It refused to yield. He backed off a step, whipped out his .45 pistol and took aim. Before he could fire, a Jap on the other side of the gate shot at him through the fence. The bullet struck the sergeant's pistol. The weapon spun from his numbed hand.

Kittleson added the guttural sound of his Tommy gun to the racket of a half-dozen automatic weapons busting loose at the same time. Lead scythed through the wooden gate, exploding splinters as more fire killed the Jap who had shot Sergeant Richardson.

Richardson shook his stinging hand. He picked up his pistol. It still worked. He fired bullets into the lock, busting it. Kittleson and several others heaved at the gate. It caught on something. A Jap corpse. He must have been behind the gate when the Scouts and Rangers opened fire.

"Pull it toward us!" Kittleson shouted.

Rangers stormed through the opening, bounding over the dark clumps of three Jap guards lying dead near the entranceway. They disappeared down the road beyond, scattering into the maelstrom of their own creation. Kittleson knelt in the road with Willie Wismer as the raucous din of sharp battle erupted inside the compound.

Only the fact that raiders knew their assignments and missions to precision prevented total confusion. Squads and teams broke off to conduct their tasks. They worked swiftly and mostly in silence.

As Murphy's detachment crashed through the rear gate, a Jap mortar squad began lobbing rounds. Murphy spotted the tube flames. His Rangers opened fire on the mortar, silencing it, but not before three high explosive shells detonated in the roadway and in the ditch among the Scouts and Rangers at the front gate waiting to guide POW to safety.

Kittleson hit the dirt face down. Explosions hopped around the front gate in succession, with roars and blinding flashes of light. The ground shook violently. Shrapnel shrieked overhead and pelted the road with hot metal.

Lieutenant Studs Rounsaville was hit. "I'm with him," Nellist called out. "Everybody hold where you are."

Nellist crawled to his friend's side. Rounsaville groaned. "You're wounded, Studs? Where you hit?"

Rounsaville paused. "In the ass."

The mortars had scored other casualties. Scout Alfred Alfonse took a full load of shrapnel in the gut. He lay on the ground writhing in agony, in bad shape. One of the Ranger medics injected him with morphine. Ranger litter bearers started to the river with Rounsaville, Alfonse, and a Ranger whose inner thighs had been ripped open by shrapnel.

The battle continued inside the compound; no further shells fell outside the gate.

A short distance down the road at the Cabu Bridge, battle was also joined. The earth tremored as Captain Pajota detonated mines that chewed big chunks out of the bridge. The partial destruction prevented attacks by tanks, but girders remained to provide footpaths for determined infantrymen. Pajota's machineguns opened in a deadly crackle as Jap officers urged suicide platoons across the girders toward the guerrillas. *"Banzai! Banzai!"* That seemed the only battle doctrine the Japs knew.

The guerrillas held.

The Japanese at the compound were caught in total surprise. Panicked enemy darted around like defenseless chickens trapped by foxes on a hen house raid. Here and there, individuals resisted, but, demoralized and caught off-guard, few of the 250 Jap troops managed to rally anything like an effective defense. Lieutenant O'Connell's men on the Japanese side of the inner road were stacking up bodies against the anvil provided by Murphy's Rangers pouring through the back gate.

Sergeant Richardson, his hand still numb from having his pistol shot out of it, led two fighters running through the front door of a Jap officers' quarters. Two officers caught in their underwear in a common area stared in shock at the blackened faces rushing at them. Richardson and his men took advantage of their hesitation to stitch them with bullets.

Shouting and roaring with adrenaline and excitement, Richardson and his Rangers kicked in doors and sprayed the tiny rooms with lead. Japs screamed. Windows shattered. Tracers punched through thin walls and blazed through the night like souped-up fireflies gone berserk.

The first POW any of the rescuers saw was a darkened figure who leaped to its feet and thrust arms in the air on the Japanese side of the compound. PFC Provencher swung his Tommy gun and was ready on a trigger squeeze. "Don't shoot! I'm an American!"

Japs often spoke English in combat to confuse Americans. "Look at me, I'm an American," the ragged figure insisted. He really was a Bataan Death March survivor. He was in the Jap area tending a generator providing electricity to the officers' quarters.

"Get to the front gate as fast as you can," Richardson instructed.

The scarecrow shambled off toward the gate. "God bless you. Thank God you've come."

In another part of the Japanese side of the camp, two trucks packed with Jap infantry roared toward the main gate. A Ranger bazooka man exploded the first truck, then the second as it skewed sideways to avoid colliding with the first. Streaks of burning gasoline tentacled from the explosion, setting nearby buildings on fire. Amid screams of terror and anguish, mini-bonfires tumbled from the blazing trucks—human torches. A scene of horror. Some of the torches mindlessly stampeded in all directions, shrieking and fanning their flames. Others staggered around screaming until they collapsed to burn on the ground.

Thinking the Japs were starting to execute them, prisoners were either too petrified from fear or too physically weakened to resist. A few attempted either to hide or recover hidden weapons for a last-ditch fight, but the majority, clad in their underwear, pressed themselves against split bamboo floors and waited in mute stupor for the end of their long torture.

POW Lieutenant Merle Musselman, a company surgeon, was sitting on the steps of the camp dispensary when violent gunfire erupted. He feared Japs were slaughtering inmates. Thinking he might save some of them, disregarding his own safety, he ran on weakened legs toward the camp surgical ward that housed 100 patients. To his consternation, he discovered all the beds empty. He staggered outside, bewildered, where a huge man in green with a blackened face startled him.

"Get the hell to the front gate," the invader ordered. "You're being rescued."

POW Airman George Steiner fled the barracks to hide just as an attacker demolished a guard tower with a long pipe that shot flame. Steiner had never seen a bazooka. His bladder let loose. He tumbled into a drainage ditch off the latrine and began crawling in the filth toward the fence. A strong hand jerked him out of the ditch. To his surprise, the apparition spoke English with a deep Southern drawl.

"Ya'all get to the front gate, hear? It's a prison break. We come to get ya'all out."

POW Sergeant Bill Seckinger hit the floor as bullets shrieked and punched holes into the walls of the POW billets. "It looks like they're killing us all," someone yelped.

"Tear the legs off your bunks," Seckinger snapped. "Get anything you can. Some of them are going to die when they come in." The man was so debilitated he could hardly walk, but he wasn't going down without a fight.

Then came a drawling, "Ya'all are free. Head for the front gate."

A POW named Jackson didn't let the inconvenience of having only one leg slow him down. He jumped into a drainage ditch and actually reached the front gate on one leg and the stub of the other.

A number of prisoners were too weak and debilitated to get out of their beds. They struggled feebly as GIs rushed in to rescue them. One Ranger gently lifted a man in his arms and started toward the door. The skeleton thrashed about and attempted to stand on his feet.

"I gotta go back in," he protested.

"We have to keep moving," the Ranger said.

"No. I have to get some documents." The man seemed demented from his long confinement.

"Documents are not important now," the Ranger insisted.

"You don't understand. I need those documents to court-martial the man who ate my cat. He *ate* my cat."

Backlighted by burning buildings, tattered skeletons and scarecrows began emerging from the inferno toward the open front gate. Staggering and hobbling and crawling, like zombies emerging from catacombs and graves into unexpected light. Blinking, weeping, laughing, thanking God and their liberators in a repetitive heartfelt litany. All hollows and angles and stench and running sores and lost limbs . . . like the gates of hell had been cast open. Dead men returned to life.

The sight broke Private Galen Kittleson's heart.

Follow-up

Kittleson and the other Scouts and Rangers escorted or carried POW across the river. They were far behind enemy lines with a long way to go to reach home, burdened now with 516 enfeebled men who would have to be hauled out in carabao carts through enemy land.

All of them made it out safely.

During the raid, two Scouts and two Rangers were wounded. One Ranger and the Ranger battalion surgeon, Captain Jimmy Fisher, were killed.

Private Galen Kittleson remained in the Army to serve with the U.S. Army Special Forces through the wars in Korea and Vietnam. He was one of the raiders who flew into North Vietnam on the Son Tay Raid to free POW in 1970. He retired from the Army in 1978 as Command Sergeant Major of the 7th Special Forces Group. He returned to Iowa where he lived out his remaining years as a farmer and cattle rancher. He died in 2006.

Chapter 16

Love in War

DURING OPERATION TORCH, the invasion of North Africa from 8th November 1942, sixty nurses attached to the 48th Surgical Hospital, U.S. Army Nurse Corps, clambered over the sides of their transports and into small landing craft that motored them ashore. The ladies wore battle pants and jackets, helmets, canteen belts, and carried full combat packs when they waded onto the beach with the rest of the assault troops near the coastal town of Arzew.

In the middle of the night, after a day huddling in sand dunes against enemy fire, they moved forward into an abandoned civilian hospital to set up shop. There was no electricity or running water. Doctors operated under flashlights. Lack of beds left many wounded soldiers lying on the concrete in pools of blood. One nurse became so outraged at snipers firing through the hospital windows that she had to be restrained from rushing outside to give "them bastards a piece of my mind."

Spartan conditions were standard operating procedure for many of the nearly 60,000 Army nurses, all female, who served during WWII. Nurses were placed on the front lines, at least near enough that sixteen died from direct enemy fire—six at Anzio, six when a Japanese suicide plane attacked the hospital ship *Comfort*, and four flight nurses. Thirteen others died in weather-related airplane crashes. Overall, 201 nurses died or were killed during the course of the war, while sixty-seven were captured when the Philippines fell and were held by the Japanese until their rescue in February 1945.

Formally established by Congress in 1901, the U.S. Army Nurse Corps kept its nurses well to the rear of the front lines during the First World War. Of the more than 10,000 who served in Europe through 1917–19, none died from enemy action. However, over 200 fell to diseases such as influenza.

There were fewer than 1,000 nurses in the Army Nurse Corps and 700 in the Navy Nurse Corps when the U.S. entered WWII after Pearl Harbor. That number increased sixty-fold by the end of the war. Over 200 black nurses also served in segregated units, tending black soldiers.

After D-Day in June 1944, the number of Army nurses in the European

Theater reached a peak of 17,345. The first of them landed on the beachhead four days after D-Day. Hospitals such as the 12th and 14th Field Hospitals followed combat troops across France where they worked out of tents and often slept on the ground under hostile fire.

* * *

Taffy and the Colonel

FOR A WHITE ARMY OFFICER, commanding a black outfit was considered the most devastating thing that could happen to his career. Other white officers viewed Major Paul Bates with a mixture of curiosity and pity when he assumed command of the all-black 761st Tank Battalion at Camp Claiborne, Louisiana, in May 1943, the battalion known as the Black Panthers. At the Officers' Club, which he rarely patronized, he was sometimes greeted with snickers and snide remarks. "Decide to come join the white folk, Major? How're the darkies down on the plantation?"

One evening during a concert at the post theater, Major Bates lit up a cigar at intermission and stood alone at one end of the lobby to avoid offending anyone with his smoke. He became amused by the antics of a very young brunette nurse imitating ballet steps in front of a dance poster. She bounced up on her toes and awkwardly pirouetted with arms arched above her head. Stumbling, she giggled and bounced off the wall. Major Bates caught her before she fell. "Be careful, little girl, or you'll break your neck."

"I won't," the brunette replied, still laughing. "Taffy will show me how to do it."

"Who might I ask is Taffy?" She indicated her friend, a tiny slip of a nurse lieutenant with blond hair and a disconcerting way of looking straight into a man's eyes.

By the time intermission was over, Taffy, Melaney, and Paul Bates were in animated conversation. At curtain call, Major Bates invited the women to the O Club for a nightcap. Melaney couldn't go since she was not wearing proper Class As. Taffy also started to decline, but Melaney pulled her aside. "Don't be silly. Did you *look* at him? He's gorgeous."

The major was thirty-four, Taffy ten years younger. She was surprised to discover he was the dashing white commander of a black tank battalion, a command for which he seemed to have a passion. He leaned across the table toward her, gripping his drink with both hands. "I'm finding out black men have a heritage of undeserved attributes that are all on the downside," he said. "I never look at them that way. I make up my own mind. You get a feeling for your men, no matter their color, when you know you are on the same playing field." Taffy and this tall man also seemed to be on the same playing field.

The wartime romance between Taffy and Paul Bates, who was soon promoted to lieutenant colonel, continued. Sometimes over great distances. Taffy remained at Camp Claiborne when Paul's 761st moved to Camp Hood, Texas, for further training. Several times she caught a bus to Camp Hood or Paul traveled to Claiborne so they could be together.

By some luck of the draw, Taffy's 14th Field Hospital transferred to Camp Shanks in New York to prepare for overseas deployment one week after the 761st arrived at nearby Camp Kilmer, New Jersey, also for deployment. Paul managed to get a full day off to spend with her in New York. Hovering over them, as over other lovers during the war years, was the specter of violent death in battle. There was a chance they would never be together again. "I won't be able to see you any more before we go overseas," Paul said. "We're being alerted for movement."

H.M.S. *Esperance Bay* carrying Paul's 761st docked at Southampton, England, in October 1944. A week later, the hospital ship transporting the 14th Field Hospital arrived at the same port. A dock worker rushed aboard calling out Taffy's name. "Oh, my God!" Taffy's friend Melaney exclaimed with delight. "He's found her already."

Colonel Bates had sent a message: "I was here yesterday to wait for you, but you didn't make it."

The 761st had shipped across the English Channel that very morning to link up with General George Patton's Third Army.

One week later, the 14th Field Hospital followed. Five months had passed since D-Day. The beaches of Normandy, now 350 miles behind the fighting, were a receiving and processing center for supplies and men pouring over from England. A tent city of olive-drab green had sprung up on high ground once occupied by the German defenses.

Even garbed in OD uniform and without makeup, the young blond nurse making her way through the debris and wreckage that still littered Omaha Beach produced quite a stir during her brisk walk from the landing stage. Taffy pushed aside the flaps of a tent that housed Personnel. A young lieutenant behind a field desk glanced up, surprised by his visitor's extraordinary beauty and unexpected arrival. She smiled sweetly; a feminine smile always produced results in locations composed mostly of women-starved males.

"Lieutenant," she said, "has a Negro tank battalion passed through within the past week?"

"You must be Taffy, ma'am."

Taffy laughed. A woman's laughter was a delightful thing in the middle of a war.

"Goodness! Has Paul told everyone about me?" she exclaimed.

"Pardon me for saying so, ma'am, but I would tell the *whole* world if I had someone like you." He blushed and quickly added, "The 761st is staging further inland. They're fixing to move out to the front. Their colonel has been down here every day asking about the 14th Field Hospital."

The 36th Engineer Battalion, to which the 14th Field was conjoined, moved up to stage in a field near Ste-Mère-Église. Service units such as engineers, hospitals, quartermasters, ordnance men, and all the other outfits required to support the insatiable appetites of armies on the move usually tagged along to the rear of combat troops.

Barely had the 14th bivouacked than Colonel Bates drove up in a Jeep. Taffy threw herself into his arms with little cries of happiness. By this time, their romance had spanned two continents and nearly two years. Both knew theirs was more than another wartime fling. They strolled hand in hand, pausing to kiss in the light French rain, happy faces wet and the war far away for that short time. The 761st would be moving up within the next few days. "Promise me you'll write every day," Taffy requested. "Just write 'I'm alive' so I'll know you're okay."

The 761st moved forward to St-Nicolas-de-Port, near the German border, followed by the 14th Field twenty miles behind. Paul sent a staff command car for her when he knew his battalion might be resting. From here on, his tanks would be in constant combat. He and Taffy might not be able to see each other again for a while.

It was shortly after dark when the command Jeep, buttoned down against a cold, driving rain, growled through the ankle-deep mud in which the field hospital was mired. A slight figure dressed in fatigues, poncho, and steel helmet ran out and jumped into the Jeep. The driver, a black corporal named Forbes, headed back to the front, following tank tracks chewed through dark, dangerous countryside patrolled by both Germans and Americans.

The unnerving journey ended when a figure suddenly stepped out of the darkness and blocked the road. "Who dat?" it challenged, rifle at the ready.

The driver unzipped his side window and stuck his head out in the rain. "Dat me. Forbes."

"I knows you, Forbes. Who dat with you?"

Taffy struggled to open her canvas door, no easy task. She finally escaped the vehicle and stood in the pouring rain, a skinny little thing in a too-big helmet and a poncho that went slickety-slick in the breeze. The sentry couldn't see much because of the dark and the rain. Forbes got out and walked up to him.

"Dat's the Colonel's lady," he said.

The sentry didn't understand. "If the Colonel want a lady," he stubbornly insisted, "let him go and get one hisself."

"Man, it's Lieutenant *Taffy*."

Colonel Bates ran down from the bivouac area.

"I just be doing my job, Colonel," the sentry explained. "Them Germans is sneaky."

"You did exactly right, Corporal."

By right of his rank and position, the commander of the 761st rated a pup tent all to himself. He shared it that rainy night before the battalion launched itself into the war.

Field hospitals could accommodate up to 150 patients at a time and generally were assigned about eighteen nurses, plus doctors, surgeons, orderlies, and other medical and administrative personnel. Constant relocation as the 14th trailed Patton's Third Army across Europe meant nurses were always scrubbing, cleaning, and disinfecting in order to provide sanitized facilities that could handle large numbers of critically wounded and sick patients. Nursing experiences ranged from intense boredom during lulls in fighting to periods of exhausting activity whenever units were engaged.

High numbers of casualties occurred in pockets of enemy resistance. Litter bearers and ambulances filtered the wounded back through front-line aid stations to the field hospitals. Wounded young soldiers passed through in heart-breaking streams of blood, gore, and tears, their bodies horribly maimed, limbs severed, paralyzed, destroyed physically, emotionally, and mentally.

Taffy grew accustomed, if not exactly inured, to suffering. A nurse who wore her heart on her sleeve could not function.

Mail moved slowly. Even though the 14th trailed only a few miles in the rear of the fighting, sometimes days passed before she received Paul's letters all collected in a bundle. She relied on wounded black tankers to keep her abreast of the 761st and the men she was getting to know so well through Paul.

She learned of Paul's being wounded from a medical aide who got through to her on a field phone. He had been evacuated straight to England. All she knew was that he had been shot during action near Morville, his ankle shattered by a machinegun bullet. The news threw her into a frenzy. In her mind, he could have lost a leg, he could be in severe permanent pain, paralyzed, even *dying*.

Willing to take any risk to reach his bedside, she was stuffing an AWOL bag when the hospital commander intercepted her. "Taffy, we're at war. You'll be court-martialed."

"I have to go to him."

"Taffy, from what I know of Paul Bates, he wouldn't think highly of any soldier who deserted his post, no matter the reason. You're needed here. There are wounded and sick boys coming through. The Negro tankers ask about you every time. Seems they've even named one of their tanks after you."

She was strong-willed, but the sense of what he said took the wind out of her. The commander placed a kindly hand on her shoulder. "Taffy, he'll come back. When he does, he'll find you wherever you are."

At least, as long as he remained in England, she didn't have to worry about some terrible day when a new load of casualties came in and there lay her Paul.

The 14th Field Hospital followed Patton's Third Army and thus the 761st Tank Battalion all the way into Belgium and the Battle of the Bulge. Paul and Taffy hadn't seen each other since that rainy night when Paul sent the staff Jeep for her.

One morning in mid-February 1945, Taffy was busy catching up on paper-work at a field desk when the flap of the hospital tent opened. It was a rare day when the sun shone with such brilliance that the reflection on snow was enough to blind. The silhouette of a tall soldier filled the opening. The sun against snow blasted an aura all around him. "Taffy."

"Paul! Oh, my God!"

They had only a few hours together. Paul was on his way to Holland to resume command of the 761st. He had turned down a promotion to full colonel and command of a white infantry regiment in order to return to his black tankers. "The job's not over, Taffy," he said. "What kind of man and officer would I be not to return to the men I've trained and fought with?"

The end of the war was in sight, only months away, perhaps even weeks. The legions Hitler sent to conquer the world were now reduced to fighting for their own homeland. Allies entering the Rhineland rebuilt bomb-damaged roads and rail lines and moved up immense quantities of ammunition, gasoline, and foodstuffs from coastal ports to feed and resupply nearly 4 million troops. Colonel Bates's 761st fought its way through the Siegfried Line and crossed the Rhine at Oppenheim.

One woman rose to the minds of the 761st tankers whenever they contemplated feminine loyalty. The Colonel's lady became their perfect idealized woman for whom men crossed oceans, built countries, and fought wars. She was what all dreamed of—a beautiful woman, faithful, and waiting. Far from begrudging Colonel Bates his romance, the tankers lived it with him vicariously. They had watched the relationship blossom at Camp Claiborne and continue to grow over the years into storybook proportions. Taffy and the Colonel were the prince and princess who, one day, would live happily ever after.

They kept in contact with each other whenever possible through field telephone, which was an iffy kind of commo under the best of circumstances. The signal had to be patched through different systems every few miles. Messages were relayed, since person-to-person was almost impossible. Taffy would wait as one operator patched into another, then another, and another. Each voice grew weaker until finally she heard nothing except intermittent static.

Eventually, the voices began to return, the relay growing stronger the nearer it came.

"Okay, we got him on the phone," the local operator would finally say.

"He's on the phone . . . ?"

"He's waiting . . ."

"Tell him I love him."

The message went back to the front in relay. "Tell him she loves him."

After a few minutes, Paul's message returned to her. "Tell her he loves her."

Once there was a pause and a chuckle. "Lieutenant Taffy, we *all* love you."

Taffy was working in France at a general hospital when the war ended. Paul sent her a letter and a map of where the 761st had settled in Steyr, Austria. "We're headquartered in the post office," his message read. "I'll try to get to you, but who knows when. You try to get to me."

The Army Air Corps had built an airstrip of sorts in a field near the hospital, which accommodated mostly small single-engine Piper Cubs flown by recon and artillery observers. One of the young pilots had arrived overseas too late to get in on the war and his share of perceived glory. Taffy explained to him that her "husband" was commander of a tank battalion headquartered in Austria. "If you can get me there," she bargained, "I'll make it worthwhile."

"What I'd really like," the pilot said, "are some war souvenirs. I'll never get any now."

"It's a deal. I'm sure my husband can get more war souvenirs than you can put on a ship."

Pilot and passenger flew the Cub from France across the Alps to Austria, a rough flight that had Taffy sick much of the time out the window. The pilot finally found Steyr, a small Alpine town surrounded by farmland, but no airfield. He circled until he located a pasture sufficiently level and large enough for a landing.

Every child in town, it seemed, rushed down to watch the airplane land. Taffy got out of the Cub, feeling much better now but still a mile from her destination. She selected a twelve-year-old boy with a bicycle upon whom to practice her German.

"Do you know where the black soldiers are?" she asked him. "Are they in the post office?"

"Yes."

"Can you take me there?"

The Austrian boy grinned broadly and patted his handlebars. Taffy was as pretty as she was small.

Colonel Bates was coming out of the post office with his battalion staff when he looked up and saw a blonde on the handlebars of a bicycle coming down the street. He froze with an unlighted cigar between his lips and a lit match between his fingers. His staff roared with laughter when Taffy hopped off the bicycle, kissed her young chauffeur on the cheek, and sauntered up to the Colonel. "Taffy, is that really you?" he finally gasped.

"It's me. Paul, you'd better light that cigar before you burn your fingers. Now, are you going to marry me or what?"

Follow-up

Colonel Paul Bates and Taffy were married and moved to Florida after he retired from the Army, and lived there until his death. Taffy still lives in Florida.

* * *

The End in Europe

ADOLF HITLER's "THOUSAND-YEAR REICH" appeared on the verge of collapse by March 1945. Fighting gradually petered out piecemeal as Germans surrendered all across the fronts. General George Patton complained that it wasn't German resistance holding him up so much as it was the sheer numbers attempting to surrender.

On the night of 22nd March, General Patton secured a bridgehead across the Rhine by sending across the 11th Infantry Regiment in boats. True to his vow, he urinated in the river in symbolic victory not only over Hitler but over his rival General Montgomery as well. He phoned General Omar Bradley.

"Brad, for God's sake, tell the world we're across. I want the world to know Third Army made it before Montgomery started across. I can outfight that little fart anytime."

Having accepted that Germany was losing the war, Hitler issued a "scorched earth" order that everything in the path of advancing Allies would be destroyed. Captured Allied airmen would be executed. "Flying courts martial" would likewise execute German soldiers accused of cowardice or desertion. Allies came upon lampposts festooned with German corpses left by the SS in its final efforts to terrorize the German people into continued resistance.

On 11th April 1945, the U.S. Ninth Army reached the Elbe River at Magdeburg, sixty miles from Berlin. It was there, to Patton's frustration, that General Eisenhower held up the Western advance, having decided that Russia be allowed to take the German capital. Millions of German women and children were about to experience the terror to which Hitler's hordes had subjected much of Europe. Soviet troops smashed their way through the Eastern Front and advanced on Berlin in an orgy of rape and murder.

"Kill! Kill!" exhorted the Russian poet Ilya Ehrenberg. "None of the Germans are innocent, neither the living nor those yet born. Follow the advice of Comrade Stalin and wipe out the Fascist Beast in his lair for ever."

At 0300 hours on 16th April, 2½ million Russian troops with 6,250 tanks and self-propelled guns and 7,500 aircraft opened fire on German positions defending the capital. The Battle for Berlin was on.

In what he knew to be his last stand, Hitler concentrated his remaining forces on the Oder River opposite the Russians. Nazi propaganda chief Josef Goebbels issued a stirring proclamation to the city's population: "I call on you to fight for your city. Fight with everything you have got, for the sake of your wives and your children, your mothers and your parents. Your arms are defending everything we have ever held dear . . ."

As the Tripartite Pact collapsed, communist guerrillas in Italy caught and hung Benito Mussolini on 28th April 1945. Now too the Soviets had Berlin encircled and were squeezing in on the Reich Chancellery, in the cellars of which cowered Adolf Hitler, his mistress Eva Braun, the Goebbels family, and various other high-ranking Nazis.

Adolf Hitler married Eva Braun in the early hours of 29th April. The not-so-happy newlyweds committed suicide the next day. Josef Goebbels and his wife followed suit, killing themselves after first poisoning their six children. The Thousand-Year Reich ended in a bunker underneath the ruins of the nation's capital after a bloody twelve-year run. Germany surrendered on 7th May 1945.

News spread quickly in Britain. Large crowds gathered in London's Trafalgar Square to celebrate VE-Day, 8th May.

"I walked down the Mall and stood outside Buckingham Palace, which was floodlit," recalled playwright Noël Coward. "The crowd was stupendous. The king and queen came out on the balcony, looking enchanting. We all roared ourselves hoarse. I suppose this is the greatest day in our history."

Similar celebrations occurred in New York's Times Square—although they may have been premature.

Chapter 17

Preparing for Armageddon

JAPAN FOUGHT ON WITHOUT ITS TRIPARTITE PACT PARTNERS following the Allied victory over the Nazis in Europe, even though the Emperor's government faced a continuing crisis triggered by the fall of Saipan in July 1944. Prime Minister Hideki Tojo, learning of military plots to assassinate him, resigned. General Kuniaki Koiso took over as prime minister on 19th July 1944 and promised the Japanese people that they now had "the opportunity to smash the enemy and win the war. The time for decisive battle has arrived."

In spite of Koiso's reassurances, Japanese defenses in the Pacific continued to fall like proverbial dominoes: Guam in August 1944; Manila in February 1945; followed by Okinawa and Burma . . .

American B-29 bombers began striking the Japanese mainland during the summer of 1944. By early 1945, B-29s were firebombing the main island almost at will. General Curtis LeMay ordered a raid that burned out more than fifteen square miles of Tokyo on the night of 9th March, killing 83,000 people and injuring 100,000 others.

Now Koiso's government fell in turn and Admiral Kantaro Suzuki took over. But Suzuki still rejected Allied demands for unconditional surrender. Military leaders, considering surrender deeply dishonorable, wanted to fight to the last man. Furthermore, they determined that the *bushido* code should apply to civilians as well as to the military. Japan would be defended at all costs under the slogan "The Glorious Deaths of One Hundred Million."

Anticipating an American invasion, Prime Minister Suzuki continued Tojo's final plans for the defense of the homeland. First off, the nation's 8,000 remaining warplanes and hundreds of explosive-packed boats and human torpedoes were prepared to sacrifice themselves in suicide missions for the Emperor. On land, Japan created People's Volunteer Units, People's Volunteer Combat Corps, Patriotic Fighting Corps, and other similar organizations composed of old men, women, and children. Many of these units were armed only with bamboo lances.

In addition, civilians were to have bombs strapped to their bodies that would

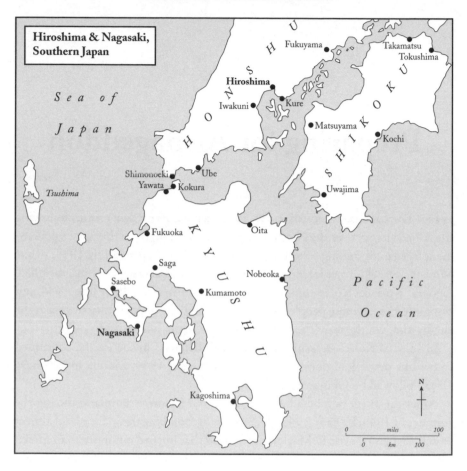

detonate when they threw themselves at tanks. Even young women and children were recruited to sacrifice themselves for the homeland. As former Prime Minister Fumimaro Konoye pointed out, the Army's aim was for civilians and military alike to dig "themselves caves and . . . fight from every little hole or rock in the mountains." Americans were expecting another three years of war and at least a million Allied deaths in invading Japan.

However, scientists and physicists in Britain and the United States were preparing a top secret project that would, if it worked, bring the war to a speedy conclusion. As early as the summer of 1940, facing invasion, Britain's Prime Minister Winston Churchill ordered the formation of a committee to study the feasibility of an atomic bomb. In America in 1939, refugee scientists from Europe, including Albert Einstein, had warned that Germany might be near to developing such a device and urged President Franklin Roosevelt to begin research.

It wasn't until after Pearl Harbor that Roosevelt acted. In early 1942, he formed the ultra-secret bomb-making Manhattan Project with General Leslie

R. Groves in overall command and Robert Oppenheimer heading up the scientific contingent. The workforce eventually grew to 60,000 people and included over half the physicists working in the English-speaking world.

President Roosevelt failed to live long enough to see the culmination of the project. Nor did he see the end of the war. He died on 12th April 1945, less than a month before VE-Day. Vice President Harry Truman succeeded to the Presidency.

There was no guarantee the bomb would even work—which meant it had to be tested. There were even fears that the blast would set off a chain reaction to turn the globe into a fireball and bring about the Apocalypse and the destruction of mankind.

Considering these fears, apprehension bordering on terror ruled the night of 15th July 1945 when hundreds of physicists, lab assistants, technicians, soldiers, politicians, and others brought hampers and beer to the hillsides overlooking a test site on the Alamogordo Air Force Base in New Mexico. If the world was going up in a blaze, they were apparently determined to ride into oblivion on beer fumes and a prayer.

Shortly before daybreak on 16th July, a gigantic fireball, brighter than the sun, erupted into a telltale mushroom cloud. Robert Oppenheimer was moved to recite a sentence from Hindu scripture: "I am become death, the destroyer of worlds."

* * *

Keep 'Em Running

DALE SHAW AND HIS GIRLFRIEND MILDRED grew up on neighboring ranches in the scrub oak hills of south-central Oklahoma, often riding together stirrup to stirrup in those days before the free ranges closed. As for hundreds of thousands of Americans, the war came along and separated them, as it did other young people around the globe. Shaw was on the streets of nearby Hartshorne on that Sunday in December 1941 when he heard about Pearl Harbor. It was as if a pall of anger, fear, and dread settled over the little town. War had come even to the protected heartland of America.

Tears flooded Mildred's eyes. "Dale . . .?"

"I don't know," he said.

Young men began to disappear from all around Hartshorne, from its ranches, one-cow farms, little wide-places-in-the-road towns and communities, Shaw's buddies . . . Willard Griffin, Bud Frye . . . Willard would lose both legs; Frye his life in Europe . . .

Seven months after Pearl Harbor, Shaw still hadn't been drafted and was still torn about whether to go to war or stay back with Mildred for as long as he could. He was out in the barn milking one evening when his neighbor Dub Fite rode up on his bay gelding. Dub dismounted and tied his horse. He wore baggy jeans, a faded chambray work shirt, clodhopper shoes, and an old fedora hat he had picked up somewhere.

"I'm joining the Army, Dale," he announced forthrightly. "If you go with me, we'll stay together."

"Don't let them know you can shoot," Shaw's dad counseled the young men. "You don't want the infantry."

Like most country boys, Dale Shaw had learned to shoot almost as soon as he could walk. During the Great Depression, his mother often sent him down into the bottoms with his .22 rifle so the family could have a nice fat squirrel for breakfast.

In Boot Camp, he did exactly what his dad told him not to do—shot a near-perfect score with the heavy-kicking Springfield '03 during shooting qualification. So did Dub. Both figured that would put them square-dab in the middle of the war shooting it out face-to-face with Japs and Germans. Instead, since they had grown up with machinery and could take a piece of baling wire and make a Ford Model-T run again, the boyhood friends were assigned together to the 958th HAM (Heavy Automotive Maintenance) Company on Guadalcanal. They arrived on the island only months after the Japanese were relieved of that piece of real estate following major land, naval, and air battles. Their job was to repair trucks, Jeeps, electrical generators, and about anything else that had a motor.

They were well behind friendly lines, their only contact with the enemy being the occasional stray Japanese who still haunted the island and sometimes ambushed an unsuspecting American soldier. One night the Japs even blew up an ammo depot near the airfield, a spectacular explosion that flapped the tent Shaw and Fite were living in at the time. It felt like a sudden burst out of a good, hot thunderstorm back in Oklahoma. Otherwise, the few Japs left on Guadal-canal kept a low profile. Live and let live. If they raised too much ruckus the Americans would get fed up and hunt them down.

Shaw generally had enough to eat, he got regular sleep, and nobody shot at him. He sometimes felt guilty about living such a life of luxury, relatively speaking, while other GIs and Marines were fighting and dying all over Europe and the Pacific. He read all about it in *Stars and Stripes* and *Guinea Gold*.

> Bombers in the Southwest Pacific struck heavy blows in the Aitape area of
> New Guinea on Sunday when they dropped 284 tons of bombs on coastal

villages, bivouacs, supply areas, and adjacent islands. Rabaul also received a hammering . . . (*18th April 1944*)

French and Belgian people were warned yesterday by the Supreme Commander of the Allied Invasion Forces [General Eisenhower] that they could expect heavy attacks on their railways and communications centers soon. "I advise you to keep away from probable targets because the attacks will be heavy," he said in a broadcast on the European service of the BBC . . . (*18th April 1944*)

Cooks, drivers, batmen, clerks, and virtually every man the Germans have at their disposal are being flung into the fierce delaying action being fought by Axis troops in and around the doomed port of Sebastopol [Russia] . . . (*20th April 1944*)

The U.S. Navy Secretary (Col. Knox) indicated in Washington yesterday that Allied air raids on the Kurile Islands, northeast of Japan, could be interpreted as a "softening up" process preliminary to U.S. landings. "The invasion of part of the Kuriles may be expected—but nobody knows when," he said . . . (*21st April 1944*)

Hitler's 55th birthday yesterday was marked by a prayer from Reichmarshal [*sic*] Goering and a speech by the Nazi Propaganda Chief Goebbels. "May faith give strength to this man whom we will follow to the end," was Goering's prayer . . . (*21st April 1944*)

The 3rd Marine Division and the Army's 77th Infantry liberated Guam in August 1944. A month after most of the fighting ceased on this largest island of the Marianas chain, the 958th HAM transferred to Guam where Shaw and Fite helped construct another large maintenance facility. As on Guadalcanal, a few enemy soldiers held out in the island's hills and caves, but they were rarely more than a nuisance as they scrounged for food. The last Japanese soldier to surrender, Shoichi Yokoi, came out of his cave on Guam in January 1972, twenty-seven years after the war ended.

Shaw continued to feel as though he might not be contributing all he could to the war effort, him being only a support guy and not on the front line. Still, deep down, he realized soldiers on the front lines could not fight unless they received beans and bullets provided by supply trains that stretched from the farms, fields, and factories of America across the Atlantic and Pacific to battle zones literally around the world.

"The guys who keep things running, who provide the supplies, are as vital to the war as the man firing the rifle," support commanders assured their soldier-workers. "We are a national effort, from Rosie the Riveter and the farmer growing cotton for uniforms to mechanics who keep airplanes flying and tanks on the attack. We all must work together if we are to win this war."

B-29s from Guam began striking targets all over the western Pacific as well as on mainland Japan. Before daybreak every morning, Shaw heard the roar of the big bombers taking off heavily loaded. He sometimes went out to the runway and counted them as they departed. He counted them again when they returned. There were almost always fewer coming back than going out.

Follow-up

Dale Shaw returned to Oklahoma after the war and married Mildred, his high school sweetheart, who is now deceased. Shaw lives on his ranch in Buffalo Valley with his daughter, Sharon Moore.

* * *

"Little Boy"

FROM A QUONSET HUT MINE SHOP on Tinian Island, Navy Petty Officer Second Class Clinton Nesmith, an explosives technician, helped assemble mines and load them onto minelayer boats, submarines, refitted ships, and bombers for planting in the shipping lanes around Japan. They were devious devices that could be pressure-set to detonate beneath larger ships, or they could be deployed to take out number-designated ships in a fleet convoy.

Tinian Island, captured from the Japanese in the summer of 1944, was the busiest airbase of the Pacific War. Squadrons of the 58th Bombardment Wing flew combat and reconnaissance sorties from the island into the heart of the Japanese Empire. The B-29 runway ended off a cliff overlooking the ocean. Loaded Superfortresses on takeoff dropped out of sight off the precipice and skimmed the waves before they gained enough lift to claw altitude on their way to Japan. Rescue boats patrolled the end of the runway to pick up bomber crews who failed to make it. Nesmith watched five planes go over the cliff and into the drink on a single morning.

Since ships were always arriving at Tinian, no one paid much attention when the heavy cruiser U.S.S. *Indianapolis* (CA-35) delivered five civilian technicians and a number of large, heavy crates to the island on 26th July 1945. Since Petty

Officer Nesmith was an explosives tech, he helped offload cargo marked as "Top Secret." Specially constructed pits had been excavated into a taxiway for its storage. Only the five civilian techs were allowed to go near it.

One of the civilians bunked next to Nesmith in the Quonset huts designated as quarters for Navy and Air Force ordnance and explosives people. Curious, Nesmith questioned him about the *Indianapolis'* hush-hush delivery. The tech merely smiled and replied, "I don't know." All Nesmith ever learned was that, whatever the cargo was, it would "win the war."

After dropping off its shipment, *Indianapolis* departed Tinian bound for Guam for further orders. At Guam, CINCPAC (Commander-in-Chief, Pacific Fleet) ordered the cruiser to link up with the battleship U.S.S. *Idaho* in Leyte Gulf, the Philippines, to prepare for the invasion of Japan. Unescorted, *Indianapolis* departed for Leyte—and vanished.

Shortly after midnight on 30 July, halfway between Guam and the Philippines, a Japanese submarine sank the cruiser. About 900 of the ship's company of 1,196 made it overboard and into the water in the twelve minutes it took the ship to sink. Due to Navy SNAFUs and carelessness, survivors of the *Indianapolis* were in the ocean for almost five days before they were rescued. Subjected to constant shark attacks, starvation, gut-shrinking thirst, exposure, and wounds, only 317 survived from those who initially made it into the water. It was the U.S. Navy's greatest sea disaster and single loss of life in its history.

Survivors only learned the nature of their run to Tinian after they returned to civilization and heard the news.

On the afternoon of 5th August 1945, Petty Officer Nesmith was among the military techs who loaded a huge bomb twelve feet long and weighing nearly 9,000 pounds into the bomb bay of a B-29 named *Enola Gay* piloted by Colonel Paul Tibbets and co-pilot Major Robert Lewis. To prevent detonating the bomb prematurely, flight crews would wait until the plane was in the air to complete the assembly of the monster bomb and arm it.

Enola Gay and its escort of six other B-29s and a contingent of fighter planes took off for Japan at 0245, 6th August. Most of the airbase knew something momentous was about to happen. Soldiers, sailors, and airmen waited and listened for the rest of the night as they crowded around civilian and military band radios.

At 0815 Japanese time, the atomic bomb known as "Little Boy" exploded over Hiroshima. Tibbets came up on the radio. He sounded relieved and was noticeably awed at the sight of the mushroom cloud that rose 45,000 feet into the air over the city and threatened to suck his bomber into the conflagration.

"Primary target bombed visually," Tibbets reported. "With good results."

Follow-up

After the war, Clinton Nesmith returned to Oklahoma and spent the rest of his productive years farming 10,000 acres in Greer County. Now retired, he and his wife Verna have four children.

Chapter 18

At the Bitter End

ENOLA GAY AND "LITTLE BOY" CAUGHT the people of Hiroshima on their way to work that historic morning of 6th August 1945. The 9,000-pound uranium bomb wiped out five square miles of city and immolated 120,000 people, about 40 percent of the population.

"The basic power of the universe" had been harnessed, declared President Harry Truman, who then warned Japan to surrender or face "a rain of ruin from the air, the likes of which has never been seen on this earth."

Government ministers in Tokyo were still not convinced that the Allies possessed such a devastating weapon. Some even thought that cooking fires had burned out of control in Hiroshima to cause a holocaust like that which destroyed Tokyo after the 1923 earthquake. Summoned to an emergency meeting on 8th August, Prime Minister Suzuki's cabinet opted to continue fighting.

The next day, 9th August, *Bock's Car* dropped the 10,100-pound plutonium bomb "Fat Man" on Nagasaki, this time killing 74,000 people and injuring another 74,000.

Emperor Hirohito, Prime Minister Suzuki, and the Japanese cabinet began having second thoughts.

* * *

Too Late to Fight

WHEN THE JAPANESE BOMBED PEARL HARBOR, Robert Williams was fourteen years old, a ninth grader among over 100 students in the freshman class at the Blanco, Oklahoma, High School. Blanco in 1942 was one of the most thriving little communities in the region. It had a drug store, several groceries, two gas stations, a big regional school . . . all supported by coal strip mining, the town's primary industry.

But something happened to Blanco after Pearl Harbor, something young Robert never understood. The coal mines shut down and people began abandoning the town. Especially the young men. Off to war, people said. Of the 100 students in his class in December 1941, only twelve remained to graduate in 1945. Williams joined the exodus by enlisting in the U.S. Navy as soon as he turned seventeen and finished school.

Rain was pouring down in April 1945 when the young boatswain's mate striker set sail from Astoria, Oregon, to Pearl Harbor on the U.S.S. *Clermont* (APA-143), an attack transport built to haul troops and cargo to and from combat zones.

The war was winding down in Europe. Hitler and his mistress would commit suicide in a Berlin bunker before the month was over. Old salts in the Navy were predicting a similar end for the Emperor of Japan.

Truly, the war wasn't what it had been only a few months previously when Japanese submarines still "lone-wolfed" the Pacific hunting for prey. Destroyer escorts for transports like *Clermont* had little to be concerned about. The closest *Clermont* came to an enemy submarine was when a dud Jap torpedo floated across its path as it neared Hawaii. A machinegunner from one of the destroyers got in a little target practice and disintegrated the dud. The depths closed around it.

Once, a Japanese reconnaissance plane buzzed the convoy. Destroyers filled the sky with tracers. The enemy aircraft fled back in the direction of Japan with its tail feathers properly singed. That and the dud torpedo were the only incidents to break shipboard tedium as the convoy sailed high seas that were not nearly as dangerous as they had been formerly.

Even Tokyo Rose didn't sound all that chipper. "Well, boys, wonder who's sleeping with your wife tonight?" she asked in perfect English radioese. But her voice had a fearful quality to it, like she might be contemplating which American division might soon be in *her* bed.

At Pearl, *Clermont* offloaded cargo and the 126th Navy Construction Battalion (SeaBees), which had caught a ride over. Then *Clermont* promptly set sail for Eniwetok and Okinawa with more men and supplies that were being assembled for the forthcoming invasion of Japan. Word on the ship, although not official, had it that *Clermont* and its crew would be part of the invasion fleet.

From Williams's perspective, it wasn't much of a war. He had been too young to get in on it at the beginning, and now not much was happening toward the end. Just a bunch of steaming around in the Pacific. As spring reached into the summer of 1945, *Clermont* sailed milk runs up and down the island chains transporting whatever needed transporting. You call, we haul. Most of the islands had been cleared of Japs and pacified. Only a few strays remained who attempted to make their presence felt now and then.

In July, *Clermont* anchored offshore of Okinawa after delivering more materiel for the invasion of Japan. A Jap still prowling the island sneaked down to the beach after dark, fired a few rounds at the transport in hopes of tagging someone, if only by accident, and then shagged back into the interior before the Americans had a chance to burn his sorry butt. "It's harassment," the crew was informed. "They only do it to save face. They know they'll be hunted down if they actually hit anybody."

In August 1945, *Clermont* was sailing from San Francisco to Pearl Harbor with more troops when the on-board PA system came to life. "All hands! Now hear this . . . Now hear this! It has been learned that the United States has dropped an atomic bomb on Japan with devastating results . . ."

Follow-up

That was Robert Williams's last wartime voyage. He returned to Oklahoma, where he still resides.

* * *

Final Plans

WHILE EMPEROR HIROHITO, PRIME MINISTER SUZUKI, and other government officials in a bomb shelter 100 feet below the Imperial Palace in Tokyo argued over what course the stricken nation should take after being bombed with atomic weapons, American bomber commanders in the Marianas were already preparing to follow up with additional conventional air attacks. The objective, according to General Curtis LeMay, commander of B-29 forces in the Marianas, was to "scorch and boil and bake to death" more Japanese.

On Friday, 10th August 1945, even as B-29s in the Marianas were loading for another raid, Suzuki's government decided to take the Emperor's advice to "bear the unbearable" and accept the terms of unconditional surrender outlined at the Potsdam Conference. The Japanese requested only one exception to the terms—that "his Majesty Hirohito must be retained as sovereign ruler."

However, hardliners in the United States, Australia, and especially in the Soviet Union, which had declared war on Japan on the 8th, insisted the Emperor must abdicate his throne. While the Tokyo ministry considered the humiliation of such a thought, General Henry "Hap" Arnold, Commanding General of U.S.A.A.F., went ahead with preparations for continued air raids.

His goal was to put 1,000 strategic bombers over Japan in a final effort to force unconditional capitulation.

"At the time these missions were planned," said the Tactical Mission Report, "peace negotiations were underway with Japan. The Commanding General [Arnold] gave orders for all Wings to be prepared to dispatch Maximum Effort forces on minimum time notice. Because it appeared the negotiations were being delayed by the enemy, these missions were ordered for 14th–15th August."

At 0400 on Tuesday, 14th August, while government officials in Tokyo continued to wrangle over the course they must follow, the first Superfort taxied onto Tinian's North Field and took off. Other B-29s followed at forty-second intervals for more than an hour. While General Arnold failed to assemble the 1,000 bombers he wanted, he did manage about 800, plus a large fighter escort. A portion of the bombers were held in reserve for a second wave.

The first wave made Japan landfall at 1131 hours. Twenty minutes later, the raiders released bomb clusters onto the railroad yards at Iwakuni, bombed the Navy arsenal at Wikari, and the Army arsenal at Osaka, killing over 1,000 people. Resistance was light over the first two targets, but heavy flak over Osaka damaged twenty-eight planes. None were shot down.

After this, Emperor Hirohito and most of the civilians of his cabinet wanted to quit on any terms. The military men dug in and wanted to fight on under the assumption that America would grant Japan softer terms if the expected U.S. invasion was made bloody enough.

The civilian side won the toss. A sobbing Hirohito volunteered to go on the radio and personally announce the surrender to people who, because of his being a god inaccessible to commoners, had never heard his voice. At 2200 hours, 14th August, he signed capitulation documents, making Japan's surrender effective at 2300 hours. At that same moment, the second wave of American bombers armed with white phosphorus bombs and incendiary clusters flew so low over the Imperial Palace that they set off air raid sirens.

The American night raiders reduced 45 percent of Kumagaya and 17 percent of Isesaki to ashes. The last B-29 dropped its load and turned back toward Iwo Jima and Tinian at 0221 hours, Wednesday, 15th August. Within the last fifteen hours, 10,000 U.S. airmen had flown over the Empire. Only one U.S. plane, a fighter shot down by flak, failed to return.

* * *

The Last Air Raid

THE ATOMIC BOMB, THE WEAPON THAT WAS SUPPOSED to finish the Japanese and end the war, was a big mystery to Lieutenant Warren Morris. He had only heard about it a few days ago. Two of the big bombs had been dropped on Japan so far. From what he understood, they wiped out Hiroshima and Nagasaki—their people, their dogs and cats, or at least those that hadn't already been eaten, and all the cockroaches. Those bombs had to be some mean boogers to kill cockroaches.

So why hadn't the Japs thrown in the towel? Criminy, it was the last round of the championship bout with seconds to go and Japan was on the ropes. So why were Superforts being sent back with conventional ordnance and incendiaries?

Captain Jack Payne looked over at Lieutenant Morris in the pilot's seat of their B-29, *Big Time Operator*, and shrugged. Today was Morris's turn at the helm. All either knew about the "Big Picture" was that this was the largest armada ever assembled in the Pacific for a single bombing run. Hap Arnold and Curtis LeMay were sending nearly 1,000 B-29s to pulverize the Japanese. That meant every airworthy plane available in the 313th, 58th, and the 73rd Wings.

"Maybe the Japs aren't giving up fast enough," Payne suggested. "Maybe we want to make sure they *don't* get back up."

In that pre-dawn of 14th August 1945, the sun was about to set on the Japanese Empire even though it had barely risen out of the eastern sky over Tinian. Superfortresses lined up nose-to-tail on the taxiways and ramps of the island's B-29 runways. A thunderstorm of engines shuddered tents and Quonsets as a constant stream of huge bombers lumbered into the air.

It was an awesome scene, all those magnificent Superforts leaping off the island one after the other, engines roaring and groaning under their heavy loads, coral dust whipping wildly about on the runway. As soon as one took off, another tailfin glided through the gray light into position.

Big Time Operator, its name generally reduced to the diminutive *BTO*, was one of the last to spring into the air. Feet on the brakes, Lieutenant Morris ran up the RPMs, then let it go. The ship rumbled down the runway in the half-light as it picked up speed. Just when it seemed the heavily laden plane with its crew of eleven was not going to make it, that it would surely go over the drop-off into the ocean at the end of the runway, Morris pulled back on the yoke with both hands.

Slowly, *BTO* lifted its wheels. It sank some toward the waves at the end of the runway, but then caught and began to climb into formation. Once in the air and at altitude, Morris, like most of the other pilots, turned on the autopilot. The crew settled back to eat, read, nap, write letters, or just bullshit for the fifteen-hour flight. The roundtrip from Tinian to Japan was equivalent to flying from New York to London. During their last six months with the 313th Bomber Wing, Morris and Payne had made thirty-three bombing sorties to Japan.

Their target today was the railroad yard at Iwakuni, a minor target compared to previous ones. *Real* targets seemed to be getting scarce. After all, B-29s had been pounding Japan for the past year, burning cities with firebombs and blowing up anything that might contribute to the Japanese war effort.

The Japanese were a hardy breed, Morris had to grant them that. They were starving on what was left of their streets—and still they fought on. Their country lay in rubble from coast to coast, entire cities torched to the ground. Morris could only wonder at what the atomic bombs must have done. They were many, many times more powerful than anything American bombers had dropped before. Take a thousand of the biggest bombs, he had been told, and you still didn't have one atomic bomb.

At mid-morning, the B-29s passed Iwo Jima. Mount Suribachi rose like a welcoming halfway beacon. It offered the crews' last sight of friendly territory on the way over and their first chance to make an emergency landing on the way out. The Marines had had one bloody fight for that piece of rock, all in order to provide an emergency airbase nearer Japan. Morris and Payne had nursed their flak-damaged plane back to Iwo on more than one occasion.

Lieutenant Morris turned his head and watched Suribachi's black volcanic cone until it faded from view to his rear.

Warren Morris was only twenty-one years old on this his thirty-fourth sortie over the enemy's homeland. Fresh off a farm near Eldorado, Kansas, he had enlisted in the Army Air Force in early 1944 to fly airplanes. Chronic airsickness almost washed him out of training, but he held onto his sick bag and made it through.

He had met twin-engine instructor Captain Jack Payne at the Rattlesnake Air Force Base in Texas. The two of them shipped off as a pilot and co-pilot team to Tinian in March 1945, where they were assigned to the 313th Wing. Between them at the time, they had had only sixty-five hours' in-type flying on the B-29. Both had trained in and previously flown B-17s. They had logged a lot more hours since then, what with going back and forth between Tinian and Japan.

On his third combat mission from Tinian, Morris lost an engine just at wheels-up on takeoff. The plane dropped off the cliff at the end and skimmed the surface of the sea, salt water washing over the windshield. Morris thought they were goners, but he fought on until he broke free of the ocean's suction and brought *BTO* back around for a landing. It took a lot of whiskey that night for the crew to recover.

It took even more whiskey after a dark night over Japan when the bomb bay door stuck and wouldn't open. While Payne flew the airplane, two crewmembers held on to Morris' arms and life jacket while he crawled down inside the bay with the bombs and jumped up and down on the door. It finally opened with a loud bang, leaving him dangling with his feet over a black abyss, his only lifeline the strength of the two airmen holding onto him. He was glad he owed them money. They jerked him to safety.

That one still made his heart pound. He wore a parachute, but the last thing an airman wanted to do was jump out over Japan. Most ended up dead. Even if they made it safely to the ground, they were often beheaded, used for bayonet and archery practice, or tied to posts on the streets for civilian passersby to torment. Everyone in the Pacific Theater knew how Imperial Japan worked and starved its captives to death. Some were burned alive, buried alive, dissected in weird medical experiments, tortured . . .

During one mission, the B-29 next to *BTO* in formation had its nose blown off by flak. It tumbled through the air all the way to the ground, where it exploded. Morris pitied crews whose planes were shot down and managed to bail out, knowing the treatment that awaited them on the ground. He wondered what he would do if he went down over enemy territory. He hoped he had the balls to kill himself before the Japs got hold of him.

Full daylight had arrived when the first wave of B-29s made landfall over Japan. There was surprisingly little resistance, compared to so short a time as a month ago when flak filled the air with dirty, exploding clouds. Planes then were always limping back to Iwo Jima on a wing and a prayer. Others simply vanished off communications nets and failed to make it back to Iwo or Tinian.

Recent light resistance was passed off as the Japanese conserving their depleted resources to be used in what they called *Ketsu-go*, the resistance to the expected American landing. In order to save fuel, Japanese pilots were ordered to ignore enemy fighters and small formations of bombers, which explained why *Enola Gay* and *Bock's Car* and their atomic cargoes penetrated Japanese airspace with hardly a challenge. And it explained today why the Japs weren't out trying to stop the B-29s. They were hoarding everything to drive the Americans back into the sea when they landed.

Twenty minutes after reaching dry land, through gaps in cumulus clouds, Morris and Payne spotted the railroad yards at Iwakuni, the target assigned to the 313th Wing. *BTO's* bombardier, Captain Jim Beck, took control of the aircraft to release its load of heavy ordnance. Even over target, the resistance offered only a couple of bursts of ack-ack. Then nothing more. No fighters intercepted them.

Clusters of bombs weighing 770 tons fell from the bombers of the 313th onto Iwakuni like heavy confetti, popping and growling and roaring up dust and debris and fire upon impact. A sudden impulse struck Morris when he resumed control of the B-29 and made his breakaway off-target.

"Plot a heading for Hiroshima," he instructed the navigator.

Hiroshima lay only about twenty-five miles northeast of their present positions. Morris, supported by the rest of his crew, had to see the results of the first atom bomb for themselves. No one on Tinian had even known it existed until after the fact. A cruiser had pulled in one day to deliver something, along with a small group of civilians. The *Enola Gay's* crew cranked out homemade ice cream while they were on Tinian. *BTO's* crew traded whiskey for ice cream, each side considering it got the best of the deal. And then *Enola Gay* left one morning to end the war.

And now Morris wanted to see what the *Enola* had wrought. He dropped down from 10,000 feet to 3,000 and barreled *Big Time Operator* toward the fallen city.

Only a week ago Hiroshima had been a city of more than a quarter-million people. Every crewmember in the bomber fell into complete silence as what was left of the city came into view. There seemed to be no people left. No movement at all down there among the square miles of nothing but rubble and smoldering debris. Here and there the partial wall of a building or a chimney stuck up out of nasty gray-green clouds of smoke and dust. Lieutenant Morris had never seen such utter desolation. There were no words to describe it or the emptiness and sense of dread it seemed to plant in his heart. It was like Armageddon, the end of the world, the end of time.

"My God!" someone breathed through the intercom. And, then, again, "Oh, my God!"

Follow-up

The two runs on Japan on 14th August 1945, one during the day, the other that night, were the last bombing raids of the Second World War. Japan capitulated that same day. Lieutenant Warren Morris returned to Eldorado, Kansas. Now a semi-retired lawyer, he lives in Tulsa, Oklahoma.

Chapter 19

Ending the War

PRESIDENT HARRY TRUMAN'S DECISION to use the atomic bomb was driven by his urge to "get this business over with." Only after the heavy destruction of Japanese cities did it become clear to the Japanese people that any hope they might retain for eventual victory was nothing more than cruel self-deception.

The Japanese envoy in neutral Switzerland delivered Tokyo's surrender message to the Allies at 0410 hours, 15th August 1945. Word reached Washington three hours later. At noon, Japan time, Emperor Hirohito's recorded surrender message was broadcast to the Japanese people, his high, metallic-sounding voice ringing from radios and public address systems all over the island nation.

The final process of surrender proved messy. There were some violent reactions. Japanese military policemen chopped off the heads of American prisoners at Osaka and Fukuoka; an admiral led eleven Navy aircraft in a suicide flight against Okinawa; soldiers tried to assassinate Prime Minister Suzuki; as many as 1,000 ranking officers committed suicide by ritual *seppuku* . . .

Many Japanese serving in distant outposts and garrisons could not be reached and continued the war for weeks. Even when reached, they refused to believe that the surrender was actually true and fought on in some areas into September. But the vast majority of Japanese simply dropped to their knees and wept. The Second World War was over, almost six years after Hitler invaded Poland and not quite four years after Japan attacked Pearl Harbor.

One of the major challenges now confronting American commanders was what to do with thousands of surrendering Japanese soldiers.

One of the first large-scale surrenders occurred on the Filipino island of Cebu. On 28th August 1945, the 35th Japanese Army with 10,000 surviving Japanese soldiers surrendered to General William H. Arnold of the Americal Division. Tears streamed down the faces of many of the Imperial soldiers as they gave up their arms and marched into captivity.

* * *

The Camp

U.S. ARMY CORPORAL LEONARD "SACK" OWCZARZAK, of the Americal Division's 746th Antiaircraft Gun Battalion, was in on the start of the Second World War and he was in on the end of it. He was eighteen years old and a member of an AA battery that returned fire when Pearl Harbor was attacked; three men in his battery were killed.

For the next three-and-a-half years, the tall young soldier from Detroit was all over the Pacific providing antiaircraft support for island landings and fighting entrenched enemy forces on Bougainville, Guadalcanal, and the Philippines. The 746th was on Cebu Island in the Philippines awaiting amphibious training for the invasion of Japan when American ships in the Cebu City harbor began firing guns and shooting rockets into the early evening sky. Bells in the local churches started ringing.

Japan had surrendered.

U.S. engineers hastily constructed prisoner of war camps to detain and process an influx estimated to exceed 10,000. "Base S" POW Camp located several miles south of Cebu City on the road to Tabunoc occupied one square mile of land enclosed by an eight-feet-tall barbed-wire fence. Guard towers rose on stilts at each corner of the compound.

Wire and guard towers were mostly for show and barely a deterrent since the strands of wire were one foot apart and the towers were often not manned. No one expected escape attempts. After all, the war was over, most of the prisoners would soon be sent home, and they were on an island. Where could they go?

Army GP tents arranged in "streets" inside the stockade housed detainees and served as showers, toilets, and dining facilities. Prisoners had their own cooks and their own diet. Officers were quartered separately in their own corner of the stockade.

A similar compound next door, separated from the Japanese by a single barbed-wire fence, billeted U.S. guards and administrators. The major difference between the two facilities was a large outdoor movie screen erected on the American side.

When the Americal Division pulled out for occupation duty in Japan, it left seventy-five soldiers from the 746th Battalion's Battery D to run Base S, Corporal Owczarzak being among them. The camp's commander assembled the guards and support staff before prisoners began arriving.

"We understand the animosity you guys might feel toward Japanese soldiers, considering the atrocities committed by them during hostilities," he began. "But we will not tolerate 'pay back' behavior. We expect you to treat prisoners fairly and humanely. That will make them goodwill ambassadors when they are repatriated, and it will make the occupation of Japan easier on U.S. forces."

Japanese soldiers on Cebu at first refused to believe their country had surrendered. U.S. units all over the island broadcast Emperor Hirohito's surrender message over loudspeakers to convince them. Finally, they began to straggle in to be picked up by military trucks and hauled into detention. They arrived tired, hungry, ragged, and filthy, a defeated and scrawny-looking bunch that wanted little more than to eat, take showers, and receive medical attention.

During processing, they were issued clean GI clothing, towels, blankets, and a cot in one of the tents. A major from the Criminal Investigations Division questioned each prisoner in order to positively identify him and his unit and to ferret out suspected war criminals. Sack was present when a tall, stern-faced Japanese wearing a common private's uniform caught the major's eye. He protested vehemently in Japanese when the CID officer ordered him to step aside for further questioning.

"Shut up!" the major snapped, having already been tipped off. "I know who you are. You are an officer of the Japanese Army, you speak English well, and you are a war criminal. Come with me."

Owczarzak later learned the tall private was actually a colonel attempting to pass through unnoticed. In March 1945, prior to the liberation of Cebu City, a U.S. B-24 bomber crashed on the island behind enemy lines. Although the American airmen survived the crash, they were captured and marched to the docks at Cebu City where the Japanese colonel forced them to kneel and bow to him in front of local civilians. He then personally beheaded each with a samurai sword.

Camp S quickly settled into a peaceful routine. Barring riot, escape attempts, or blatant violations of camp rules, the American staff allowed the impounded Japanese to police and govern themselves and refrained from interfering in petty disputes and domestic matters.

A guard shouted a warning one day during evening meal when a group of prisoners bolted out of the chow line and stampeded toward the nearest fence. "My God! They're trying to break out!"

Owczarzak and other guards snatched up rifles and rushed to head them off. They grinned in amusement when it turned out one of the prisoners had diarrhea and the others were chasing him away to keep him from fouling up the mess tent. He dropped his drawers and did his business when the barbed-wire fence stopped him.

One of the prisoners carried a shovel. He dug a cat hole and buried the mess before, nonchalantly, he turned and whacked the hapless miscreant over the head with his shovel. The guy lay on the ground for a few minutes moaning and rubbing his head before he got up and sneaked back into the chow line.

In contrast to the more agreeable enlisted men, Japanese officers were often proud and aloof and insisted on wearing their full military uniforms. One day, some officers collected a group of soldiers and forced them to conduct military drill. When the camp commander heard about what was going on, Corporal Sack drove him over in his Jeep. The CO lined up the Imperial officers and gave them a dressing down that would have peeled paint off a battleship, reminding them that the war was over and that prisoners were allowed to perform calisthenics but not to drill. The enlisted Japanese looked relieved and covered wide grins with the palms of their hands.

To while away time, prisoners read books passed among themselves, ate, talked, played a type of baseball with a stuffed rag for a ball, and kicked back to wait for repatriation. They looked forward to movie nights as much as the Americans did.

The open air movie screen was located next to the fence that separated the two compounds. Prisoners crowded against their side of the fence on show nights to watch John Wayne or Clark Gable single-handedly win the war. Owczarzak was surprised when a number of Japanese jumped to their feet and cheered during a newsreel that showed B-29s bombing Japan. Apparently, they understood that was what ended the war. They were happy that it was over, that they had survived, and that they would soon be going home.

Days and weeks at Base S for keepers and kept alike passed uneventfully for the most part. Americans were as relieved as the Japanese that the war was over and that they had lived through it. There were some, however, who harbored grudges.

While undergoing treatment for an old case of jungle rot at the nearby 21st Medical Evacuation Hospital, Corporal Sack became friendly with a Fijian who had fought with the Australian forces on Bougainville, infiltrating Jap positions, destroying artillery pieces, and harassing and frightening the sons of Nippon. "Joe" also had jungle rot all over his arms and upper torso.

Joe persuaded Sack to escort him to visit a hospital tent that housed sick and injured Japanese prisoners. He said he wanted to visit one of them. Pressed about why he would want to do that, and having been turned back by Army MPs, Joe finally confessed.

His cousin had been killed by Japanese while infiltrating enemy lines on Bougainville. Joe reached into his pajama bottoms and pulled out a highly honed mess kit knife with which he intended to kill as many of the hospitalized Japanese as he could.

Joe was promptly sent elsewhere, away from contact with prisoners.

After his release from the hospital, Sack was making his rounds as corporal of the guard when a Japanese officer hailed him from the fence.

"May I have a cigarette, Corporal?" he asked in perfect English.

"You speak better English than I do," Sack marveled.

"I should speak well," the Japanese said. "I attended university in your country."

Sack traded Lieutenant Tagawa a pack of cigarettes for his naval belt buckle to keep as a souvenir. The former enemies smoked and talked. Corporal Owczarzak learned how Tagawa had studied at UCLA in California until he returned home to Tokyo in early 1941 to see his parents. While he was at home, a pair of Imperial Army officers knocked on his parents' door and advised him that the Emperor required his services because of his studies in the U.S. and his knowledge of English. One of the intruders drew a knife-edge hand across his throat to emphasize what would happen if Tagawa refused induction.

During the course of their conversation, the two men explained their respective duties and where they had fought, as soldiers will. Turned out, Lieutenant Tagawa commanded a platoon working off a hill near a road where Sack and four other Battery D soldiers had set up a long-term roadblock as the war was winding down. To Sack's surprise, Tagawa described in detail the roadblock and the routine of Sack's men.

"We watched you," Tagawa explained with a mischievous smile. "You were next to a culvert where you set up a machinegun. You enjoyed teasing the pretty girls who walked down the road on their way to market." Sack and his men had thought they had it made. They had a nearby stream for water and bathing, a native hut for shelter, and as far as they knew there were no enemy in the area.

One of the guys, Schultz, made old-fashioned chicken soup in a five-gallon coffee can over an open fire. Tantalizing aromas wafted to another American roadblock a hill away. The portable telephone buzzed. "What the hell are you guys cooking over there? It's driving us wild over here."

Owczarzak volunteered for the humanitarian mission of delivering some of the soup across the hill. He rigged a handle to a smaller coffee can, filled it with chicken soup, put a clip in his rifle, and started through the bamboo thickets. An overwhelming sense of danger suddenly overtook him when he was halfway there. He aborted his mission and returned to his own roadblock, informing his buddies that he had a feeling that he shouldn't go on.

"We saw you with the soup," Lieutenant Tagawa now informed Sack. "We wanted it too."

"Why didn't you attack?"

"We did not want to give away our position, and we were afraid of your patrols. We had hopes that our navy would return to rescue us. But . . ." he added with a twinkle in his eyes, "we have never smelled anything more enticing than your soup that day."

They could chuckle about it now, whereas only a few weeks earlier they would have been at each other's throats. They smoked and they talked and they laughed. Peace had changed the equation between Americans and Japanese. They reached through the fence and shook hands.

Follow-up

By the end of November 1945, some 7,000 Japanese prisoners had been processed through Base S and released for transport back to their homeland. The camp closed down on 17th December. Not one Japanese attempted to escape from the POW stockade during its short history.

Corporal Leonard Owczarzak returned to Detroit. He later retired to California.

Chapter 20

Punishing the Guilty

THE NOTION THAT WARS SHOULD BE REGULATED by "civilized" rules extends back to classical antiquity at least. Among these "rules" were that innocents such as women and children not be harmed, that an unarmed and helpless enemy be spared, and that prisoners be treated with at least some compassion. It gradually evolved that rules were no good unless enforced. War crimes trials were not a creation of the Second World War and the twentieth century. The first recorded war crimes trial took place in Europe 500 years ago. Nearly every war since then has resulted in some sort of action against barbaric behavior as it was contemporarily defined.

The Allies reached a consensus early in the Second World War that belligerents of the Axis nations should be punished as war criminals after hostilities ceased. By 1943, Britain, Russia, and the United States were vested in the aim of turning accused war criminals over to governments that held jurisdiction over where their crimes were committed. Major war criminals such as Hitler, Tojo, Mussolini, and their closest henchmen would be tried by international tribunals.

Germany's war crimes have been well-documented in the aftermath of the Holocaust and the slaughter of nearly 6 million Jews in Hitler's torture camps, and in the regime's sanctioning of the mistreatment of individual human beings by the likes of "Doctor Death" Mengele and Adolf Eichmann. What is much less well-known are atrocities committed by the Japanese in Asia and the South Pacific.

Beginning as early as 1938, the Japanese were setting up biological warfare centers to experiment on captured prisoners, such as Unit 731 in Manchuria. The effects of biological agents like black plague, cholera, typhoid, malaria, and anthrax were tested by injecting pathogens into captured Chinese, Australians, Americans, and other enemy prisoners. As Nazi doctors did in the concentration camps of eastern Europe, particularly in Poland, so went the Japanese. They carried out innumerable medical experiments in frostbite, mustard gas, and anthrax exposure on victims they referred to as *maruta* ("logs"). Most of their human guinea pigs died.

In areas occupied by the Japanese, Imperial soldiers short of rations regarded local populations and captured POW as food sources. The Australian War Crimes Section reported that "the widespread practice of cannibalism by Japanese soldiers in the Asian-Pacific war was something more than merely random incidents perpetrated by individuals or small groups subject to extreme conditions. The testimonies indicate that cannibalism was a systematic and organized military strategy."

A Japanese soldier named Enomoto Masayo confessed to having raped, murdered, and butchered a young Chinese woman and sharing the meat with his comrades. "I just tried to choose those places where there was a lot of meat," he said. "It was nice and tender. I think it was tastier than pork."

Japanese troops attacking India kept locals and captured enemies alive so that they could be butchered and eaten when needed, like pigs and cattle.

To handle such atrocities, whether perpetrated institutionally or individually, the Allies formed an International Military Tribunal in August 1945 to try the most villainous of war criminals. International trials were held beginning in 1946 at Nuremberg, Germany, and by the Tokyo War Crimes Tribunal in Japan. Although overshadowed by the European trials, the War Crimes Tribunal in Tokyo actually sentenced more Japanese leaders to death or imprisonment than did the Nuremberg one. All told, twenty-five Japanese leaders were sentenced—eighteen to life imprisonment and seven to death, including former Prime Minister Hideki Tojo and General Tomoyuki Yamashita. The Tribunal even proposed trying Prince Konoye, but he poisoned himself first.

Cannibalism was never brought up during the Tokyo trials because Americans who conducted them thought the subject would be too upsetting for the families of soldiers who died in the Pacific Theater.

Of the twenty-three top-ranking Nazis charged at Nuremberg, eleven were sentenced to death and seven to terms in prison ranging from ten years to life. One committed suicide at the start of the trial. Three were acquitted. One, Martin Bormann, was tried *in absentia* and sentenced to be hung, but this judgment was never carried out. His body was recovered in Berlin years later; he is believed to have been shot when the Russians took the capital.

Lesser-known war crimes trials were held all over the rest of Europe as former Nazis from the SS, the armed services, and the civilian administrations faced charges of murder, plunder, and other offenses. These trials have continued up to recent times as fresh facts have surfaced and new war criminals have been uncovered or captured.

In Hong Kong, Singapore, Borneo, and elsewhere throughout the recent Japanese empire, over 900 war criminals were arrested and tried before lesser courts. Almost all of these were executed at a rate that exceeded by hundreds those executed in Europe.

* * *

Hangings at Nuremberg

ON THE NIGHT WHEN ADOLF HITLER'S MOST NOTORIOUS confederates were hung in Nuremberg Prison, U.S. Army Second Lieutenant George N. Garrett remained out of sight, preferring not to witness the executions of men with whom he had been in daily personal contact for the past months. As administrative officer for the defense team, Garrett, twenty-six, had acquired special insight into the lives of the Nazi war criminals who wrote the darkest pages of that era.

Allies began rounding up war crimes suspects as soon as Germany surrendered on 7th May 1945. By October, most of the top Nazis were in jail. Hitler, of course, had committed suicide with Eva Braun in a bunker of Berlin's Reich Chancellery, followed a few hours later by Josef Goebbels and his wife, who first murdered their six children. Heinrich Himmler took cyanide while being examined by British doctors soon after his capture.

The Allies conducted fourteen trials of accused Nazis over the next several years, the most important of which was the first one. The Trial of the Major War Criminals before the International Military Tribunal brought to justice twenty-two of the most notorious captured leaders of Nazi Germany. The initial count stood at twenty-three, but Robert Ley, the former Nazi treasurer, strangled himself to death in his cell with a towel while in custody awaiting trial.

The Palace of Justice at Further Strasse 110 in Nuremberg was selected as the site for the trail. Constructed in 1916, the palace complex was four stories tall with four wings straight across the front. Courtroom 600, the main court-room, was on the top floor of the third wing. The war criminals were allocated twenty-three tiny cells on the ground floor of the west wing, the Nuremberg Prison section of the complex.

The twenty-third cell, Lieutenant Garrett learned when he arrived in Nuremberg, was exactly like the other twenty-two but for one glaring exception: it was empty. This cell belonged to Martin Bormann, former deputy to the Führer, who had disappeared from the Chancellery bunker only hours before Hitler shot himself; he was to be tried *in absentia*. The hunt for Bormann or his body continued until his remains were conclusively identified in 1998. It is believed he was shot by Russian troops as he attempted to escape from Berlin.

One military guard was assigned to each of the twenty-two occupied cells, his single most important duty to keep his man alive to stand trial. Each tiny cell had one window at the back that was too high for a person to reach. A porthole in the solid door allowed the guard to keep watch on his charge at all times; a light shone through it into the cell at night. Prisoners were required to face sleeping away from the wall with their hands visible.

Furnishings were minimal: a table too flimsy to support a man's weight; a chair not quite as insubstantial; a cot in one corner; a toilet stool in another. Stairwells and landings leading to Courtroom 600 were fenced to prevent defendants from jumping either to freedom or to their deaths. A tank positioned in the prison grounds kept watch for escape attempts.

Lodged in the cells were the following former Nazis: Karl Dönitz, initiator of the U-boat campaigns and the man Hitler later designated to succeed him; Hans Frank, "Jew Butcher of Cracow"; Alfred Jodl, the Wehrmacht's Chief of Operations; Wilhelm Keitel, Wehrmacht Chief of Staff; Alfred Rosenberg, Minister of Eastern Occupied Territories; Albert Speer, Minister of Armaments and Hitler's architect; Reichsmarschall Hermann Göring; Julius Streicher, propagandist and publisher of Der Stürmer; Rudolf Hess, Hitler's deputy, who had been detained since 1941 when he parachuted into Scotland to try to convince Britain to make peace with Germany; Hjalmar Schacht, banker and economist; Wilhelm Frick, Hitler's Interior Minister; Hans Fritzsche, leading Nazi propagandist; Walther Funk, Minister of Economics; Ernst Kalten- brunner, highest surviving SS leader; Joachim von Ribbentrop, Foreign Minister; Konstantin von Neurath, whom Ribbentrop succeeded; Gustav Krupp von Bohlen und Halbach, a major Nazi industrialist; Franz von Papen, Vice-Chancellor; Erich Raeder, former commander of the Kriegsmarine; Fritz Sauckel, plenipotentiary of the Nazi slave labor program; Baldur von Schirach, head of Hitler Youth; and Arthur Seyss-Inquart, Reich Commissioner of the Occupied Netherlands.

Criminal counts against the prisoners were broad enough to cover almost any act and included: participation in a common plan or conspiracy for the accomplishment of crimes against peace; planning, initiating and waging wars of aggression and other crimes against peace; war crimes; and crimes against humanity.

Lieutenant George Garrett, born in Nebraska but reared in Muskogee, Oklahoma, had worked for DuPont in its uranium plant during the develop- ment of the atomic bomb before he enlisted in the Army in late 1943. Extremely high scores on his military specialty tests earned him an assignment to Officer

Candidate School. He missed the final months of the war and ended up postwar at Nuremberg Prison assigned as Administrative Lieutenant for the Defense Information Center.

As such, he was responsible for making sure defense teams received pay, clothing, a place to live, and that documents and witnesses were available to lawyers. He also saw to the prisoners' needs. He had two offices, one in the administrative section at the Palace of Justice, the other in the prison. Some 400 interpreters, translators, law clerks, lawyers, secretaries, and assistants worked directly or indirectly for or with him. He lived in a private apartment provided by the Army across the street from the palace.

British judge Sir Geoffrey Lawrence kicked off the trial by calling the court to order on 20th November 1945. "This trial which is now about to begin," he announced, "is unique in the annals of jurisprudence."

During the next year, the trial brought to light for the first time the atrocities committed by the Nazi regime—gory details of macabre medical experiments, heads chopped off and shrunk, soap made from human fat, wallets and purses fashioned from the skin of prisoners, gas chambers that consumed millions of Jews . . . The former commandant of Auschwitz, Rudolf Höss, gave evidence that he oversaw the gassing of two-and-a-half million Jews when he was commandant of the extermination camp there.

"Unless record was made [of the atrocities]," said Robert H. Jackson, chief U.S. prosecutor (on leave of absence as an associate justice of the U.S. Supreme Court), "future generations would not believe how horrible the truth was."

Garrett seldom occupied the permanent seat provided for him with the defense in the courtroom. He had no incentive to endure the long haggling between lawyers and witnesses. Even when he was present to produce documents or other materials for defense attorneys, he found it difficult to relate the horrendous crimes attributed to the defendants with the quite ordinary-looking men he came to know in their prison cells.

He often held long, first-name-basis conversations with Göring, Speer, Hess, Ribbentrop, and the others. He felt a certain human empathy for their plight aside from the great crimes they had committed. It seemed they considered him more their confidant than a keeper.

Hermann Göring was the most famous and undoubtedly the most fascinating of the lot. U.S. prosecutor Jackson referred to him as "half militarist, half gangster." Addicted to codeine pills, he had been brought to the prison in May 1945 weighing 264 pounds. He still had dark, wavy hair and the rock jaw of a Hollywood movie star. By the time Lieutenant Garrett arrived at Nuremberg, the former Reichsmarschall was free of his addiction, down to fighting weight, and prone to boasting about how it was his personal strength and willpower that freed him from the pills.

Garrett was introduced to him in the gymnasium that served as an exercise yard. Garrett nodded formally. Göring smiled and clicked his heels. Garrett found him personable and congenial, but a consummate braggart.

Like Göring, Garrett was a devout trout angler. Göring told the American the best spots on the Regnatz River. When Garrett returned from fishing and told Göring about it, the former Reichsmarschall would good-naturedly cuss him out.

In August 1946, Colonel John Amen from the Nuremberg prosecuting team was dispatched to Frankfurt to defend U.S. Army Major David Watson, who had been charged with two other officers with the theft of jewels from Kronberg Castle. When Göring heard about it, he pounded on the courtroom railing and shouted, "The SOB [Amen] can't do that. He is trying me for stealing art treasures. Now he's defending Major Watson."

Nearly every one of the prisoners arrived at Nuremberg with some sort of personal medical problem. Hans Frank was wheeled in on a stretcher after having attempted suicide by slitting his throat and wrists. After recovering, he offered to counsel Ribbentrop, whom he considered likewise suicidal. "It is the insane desiring to advise the insane," Ribbentrop told Garrett.

Although Lieutenant Garrett thought Ribbentrop neurotic and scared about his future, he was probably not insane. For months, Ribbentrop complained to Garrett and his guards that he had horrible nightmares and could not sleep. Garrett sometimes checked on Ribbentrop at two or three a.m. and found the balding, distinguished-looking ex-diplomat sitting on his bunk with his face in his hands. "I will go to hell with the others," he lamented.

Ribbentrop begged for sleeping pills. Doctors ruled against it on the grounds that the pills might impair his judgment in the courtroom. Instead, he was given a placebo capsule filled with high-strength compacted baking soda. Ribbentrop was delighted and commented to everyone how, "American medicine is much better than German. Not only am I sleeping nights, but my indigestion is much improved."

Garrett considered Rudolf Hess the most pathetic creature incarcerated at Nuremberg. He suffered from ulcers and may actually have been legally insane. Garrett obtained a photo of him sitting forlornly underneath a tree at the prison. He later found a note from Hess to one of the prison doctors that read: "Dr. Pflucker, may I ask for some white bread and some cheese. *Hess.*"

Albert Speer, Hitler's architect and friend, was Garrett's personal favorite of the Nuremberg defendants. Garrett thought him honest and sincerely sorry. They talked about architecture and what Speer would do when he got out of prison. "I got in over my head and made mistakes," Speer admitted. "I was a good architect and should have remained one."

Julius Streicher's pornography collection before the fall of Nazi Germany rivaled that of King Farouk. Garnett thought him a sleazy man with a bald head and a Hitler mustache.

President Franklin Roosevelt once described Hjalmar Schacht as "overbearing and haughty, slick and calculating."

Franz von Papen had served in many posts under Hitler, including that of vice-chancellor. Papen introduced Lieutenant Garrett to his son, who took him deer hunting on his father's estate and talked about the political history of Germany. At one point, Garrett had enough butchered deer stored in the prison's walk-in freezer to feed the entire palace.

Field Marshal Wilhelm Keitel was the only defendant who continued to wear swastikas on his uniform. Looking defiant and unrepentant, he sat in the courtroom chewing on a pencil with which he jotted down notes on a legal pad. He continued to insist throughout the trial that he was merely a soldier following orders.

Garrett thought Wilhelm Frick arrogant and standoffish. He suffered a bad reputation among prosecutors, defense attorneys, witnesses, and other prisoners.

Garrett saw former Economics Minister Walther Funk as a weasel pretending not to know anything. He maintained throughout the trial that he had not known about all the gold teeth he kept in his bank from people killed in the concentration camps.

Most of the other prisoners were introverted and sometimes hostile, expressing little interest in conversation with their captors.

The trial ended on 1st October 1946 with eleven of the twenty-two handed the death sentence. They were: Göring, Ribbentrop, Keitel, Kaltenbrunner; Rosenberg, Frank, Frick, Streicher, Seyss-Inquart, Sauckel, and Jodl, with Bormann sentenced *in absentia* to die. They would be hung like criminals rather than face the firing squad like soldiers.

Hess, Funk, and Raeder were each sentenced to life imprisonment; Speer and Schirach each received twenty years' imprisonment; Neurath fifteen, and Dönitz ten. Fritzsche, Papen, Krupp, and Schacht were all acquitted.

Justice in regard to the major war criminals moved swiftly. Within two weeks, the prison gym/exercise area was converted into an execution chamber with three black wooden gallows occupying one end of the large arena.

An air of depression and suspense seemed to hang over the prison during the day of 15th October 1946. Executions were to begin immediately after midnight. The slightest sound echoed within the rock walls of the prison. The cells of the condemned were exceptionally quiet as each prisoner considered his fate and counted down the remaining hours of his life. The atmosphere only deepened as night drew near and tension mounted.

Lieutenant Garrett took one look into the gym, saw the black gallows and did not return again. He spoke to none of the prisoners that day. He thought he heard a single sob from one of the cells as he passed down the dimly lighted hallway between them. There was no other sound, not even of movement. Guards standing outside the cell doors seemed frozen in place.

The official hangman, U.S. Army Master Sergeant John C. Woods and his assistants, Sergeant John Malta and a former Nazi executioner named Johann Reichhart, arrived shortly after nightfall. Garrett admitted them to the prison and escorted them only to the door of the gym before he turned back.

Woods was a short, chunky, nondescript NCO who appeared rather cheerful about the macabre event. "It's just a job," he remarked to Garrett. "Somebody has to do it." He had hung 347 men during his career, most of them Americans.

Reichhart was credited with hanging over 3,000 people, the majority of them during his Nazi years. Perhaps without intent of irony, Allied occupation authorities employed him to execute German war criminals following VE-Day. He had a reputation for being a thorough professional who openly considered Woods to be a crude amateur.

Two hours before the event kicked off, a guard came running to fetch Garrett and other prison authorities to the cells.

"I saw him put his hand in his mouth. I heard him choking," the shaken guard explained.

Garrett was one of the first to reach Hermann Göring's cell. The former Reichsmarschall lay on his back on his cot, one arm draped over onto the floor. He had committed suicide rather than appear as one of the main attractions at the gym. Remnants of potassium cyanide were later discovered in his mouth. He left two hand-scribbled notes behind, the first insisting that none of the guards was to blame, that he had arrived at the prison with the poison concealed in a jar of hair cream.

The second note was addressed to the Allied occupation authorities. It read: "I would have had no objection to being shot. However, I will not facilitate execution of Germany's Reichsmarschall by hanging. For the sake of Germany, I cannot permit this. Moreover, I feel no moral obligation to submit to my enemies' punishment. For this reason, I have chosen to die like the great Hannibal."

Controversy over how Göring obtained poison to cheat the hangman was never resolved, although a former Nuremberg guard, Herbert Lee Stivers, confessed in 2005 to having delivered it hidden in a fountain pen.

With Göring prematurely dead, ten Nazis remained to mount the gallows. The night was gloomy and overcast, perfectly suitable for such a grim event. As the clock ticked past midnight into 16th October, Garrett helped admit a handful of military officers, a few dignitaries, and eight journalists into the prison to witness the hangings. Again, he did not enter the gym.

At 0111 hours, 16th October 1946, Joachim von Ribbentrop was the first to make the long silent walk to the black gallows. *Time* magazine reported the scene: "[H]e entered the gymnasium and all officers, official witnesses and correspondents rose to attention. Ribbentrop's manacles were removed and he mounted the steps (there were 13) to the gallows. With the noose around his neck, he said, 'My last wish . . . is an understanding between East and West.'"

Master Sergeant Woods tightened the noose around the neck of the black-hooded man. A chaplain on the gallows prayed. Woods's assistant, Sergeant Malta, dropped the trap door. Ribbentrop disappeared into the closed-in area below.

His was the first death in a series of macabre blunders. Woods had apparently miscalculated the length of rope needed to ensure the condemned man's neck vertebrae were severed on the "jerk" to cause instant death. In addition, the trap door did not retain in its rubber bungs when opened. The heavy rebounding door slapped Ribbentrop in the face as he fell into the darkness below. Rather than his neck being broken, Ribbentrop choked to death. He took fourteen agonizing minutes to die.

The executions that followed were almost a repeat of the first. Sauckel also took fourteen minutes to die.

Julius Streicher cried out "Heil Hitler" as he mounted the thirteen steps. He delivered his final declaration in a ringing voice: "The Bolsheviks will hang you one day!" Woods slipped the hood over his head.

Streicher's groaning underneath the gallows chilled the souls of witnesses. Sergeant Woods slipped out of sight to help Streicher die more quickly.

Wilhelm Keitel's last words were: "I call upon the Almighty to have mercy on the German people. More than 2 million Germans went to their deaths for the fatherland before me. I now follow my sons. Everything for Germany!" His death was the most painful. He struggled for twenty-four minutes at the end of his rope before succumbing.

It was a ghoulish affair later criticized by Johann Reichhart. "One can wonder why the Allies let such a butcher accomplish this crucial job in such a disgusting manner. Was it sheer and ill-conceived retribution?"

"I hanged those ten Nazis," Woods came back in his own defense. "And I'm proud of it . . . Ten in 103 minutes. That's fast work . . . I wasn't nervous. A fellow can't afford to have nerves in this business . . ."

"It was a grim, pitiless scene," wrote Robert E. Conot, author of *Justice at Nuremberg*. "But for those who sat through the horror and torture of the trial, who had learned of men dangled from butcher hooks, of women mutilated and children jammed into gas chambers, of men subjected to degradation, destruction, and terror, the scene conjured a vision of stark, almost Biblical justice."

Lieutenant George Garrett left the prison after the hangings were over. He went to his apartment and to bed. He was unable to sleep.

Follow-up

The verdicts at Nuremberg established new international law to govern "civilized" warfare. Legally, reprisals could no longer be taken against POW or hostages; forced labor was outlawed; captured partisans were given equal status with regular POW; soldiers were required to disobey orders to commit war crimes. Out of the trials and executions also came the United Nations Genocide Commission and its Declaration of Human Rights, established primarily to make sure there was never again another Holocaust in the world.

Lieutenant George Garrett remained in the U.S. Army as a thirty-year man, although he resigned his commission in favor of returning to enlisted status. He retired from the U.S. Army as a Command Sergeant Major and lived in Muskogee, Oklahoma, until his death in 2009.

Afterword

THE SECOND WORLD WAR WAS CERTAINLY the greatest man-made disaster of all times. It took more than fifty years to arrive at any reasonable estimate of the war's death toll. Tens of millions, both military and civilian, were killed, often without records of their names, how they died, or where they fell. Death numbers lie somewhere between 60 and 100 million people—approaching one out of every twenty living on the planet at the time.

While the malignant cancer that was anti-rational authoritarianism may have been defeated in 1945, it was only a reprieve. Neither authoritarianism nor the fighting ended with the defeat of Germany, Japan, and their satellites. Unfortunately, war is an inescapable part of the human condition. Having come unglued, the world has never been put back together. Quite reasonably, many historians agree that the Second World War has still not ended, that it continues into the twenty-first century.

If it hadn't been for the war and China's conflict with Japan, Chiang Kai-Shek may have been able to contain the Chinese communists, resulting in a far more stable world. The enmity between India and Pakistan may not have been so fierce if the world war had not happened. But for WWII and the resulting Zionist surge, Israel would probably not have chopped into Arab real estate to cause continuing unrest in the Middle East. But for the war, the unpleasant Nazi regime may not have been replaced by the even more unpleasant and dangerous Soviet one. But for WWII, the Arab–Russian alliance and the burgeoning Islamic terrorist movement might not have erupted . . .

The dropping of the atomic bomb on Japan followed by the Soviet Union's acquiring it a few years later ushered in a nuclear age that makes the world an even more dangerous place to live than before the war. Even while the horrors of the Second World War are still in our memory, "the Bomb" has infected the globe. Tyrants and despots and rogue nations like North Korea and Pakistan, and, most assuredly sooner rather than later, Iran, have it or will do. This undoubtedly increases the possibility of all-encompassing and perhaps fatal-to-mankind wars at some point in the future.

Accompanied by the underlying threat of nuclear Armageddon, the un-intended consequences of the war have precipitated further continuing conflicts all over the globe. The Cold War, an extension of the Second World War, and perhaps even of the First World War, pitted the West, led by the United States, against the Soviet Union. It continued for over fifty years and was the source of "brush fire" wars that persist into the present era: Malaya, Korea, Vietnam, Cuba, Central America, Iraq, Afghanistan, Pakistan, Syria, Libya, Israel . . .

Even as the world grows more dangerous, the status of the United States as "Leader of the Free World," the world's policeman, the greatest force for stability on the planet, is rapidly devolving economically and militarily. The West is actually disarming itself while it submits to political correctness and a "New World Order" that makes war not only more likely but more probable as much of the rest of the world rearms.

The United Nations, created to make the world more stable, is not only ineffective, it is an actual threat to world stability as it increasingly defers to despots and dictators. Madmen like those at the helms of North Korea and Iran rattle their nukes and promise to rain death and destruction upon the world while the West and the UN issue countless resolutions and wring their collective hands. Terrorists are rapidly approaching the likelihood of being able to attack any city anywhere on any continent with "suitcase nukes" while the West and the UN refuse even to give the enemy a name.

Theodore Roosevelt warned a century ago that the only way to safety and security was to "speak softly and carry a big stick." What the world sees now is that everyone has a big stick and no one is speaking softly. No one is at the helm. The planet is out of control, like an engine that, drained of lubricant, keeps banging until it explodes.

The ways in which the Second World War changed the lives of not only its generation but all the generations that have followed are too numerous to contemplate. Today, there are somewhere around 7 billion people clinging to the crust of this ball we call Earth as it hurtles through space. All of these have their own lives and futures, dreams and desires, and are directly affected by the "Big Picture" of events and history. Few of them desire war, yet war has become a constant in their lives.

The First and Second World Wars introduced the era of constant world war; over 100 wars are being fought at any one time on the planet. The world wars, in effect, have never ended. They will not likely end in the lifetime of anyone alive today.

Bibliography

Interviews

Barber, George R. (D-Day, Ch. 8)

Bates, Taffy (Europe, Ch. 16)

Billey, Rayson (Italy, Ch. 4)

Boehm, Roy (Guadalcanal, Ch. 5)

Brown, Charlie (Germany, Ch. 5; interviewed by Michael Sasser)

Carl, Jim (France, Ch. 11)

Cole, Arles (Pearl Harbor, Ch. 1)

Cottick, John (son of Tom Cottick, Ch. 9)

Dade, Floyd (Black Panthers, Ch. 10)

Fulcher, John (Italy, Ch. 4)

Garrett, George N. (Nuremberg, Ch. 20)

Gautier, James Jr. (Bataan, Ch. 1)

Gordon, Charles (Wereth, Ch. 13)

Hill, Robert K. (Iwo Jima, Ch. 14)

Holmes, Johnny (Black Panthers, Ch. 10)

Kittleson, Galen (Cabanatuan, Ch. 15)

Koobatian, Haig (Italy, Ch. 7)

Lantz, Jack (Holland, Ch. 5, 6)

Latimer, Philip (Black Panthers, Ch. 10)

Mauldin, Bill (Italy, Ch. 4)

McNiece, Jake (D-Day, Ch. 8)

Morris, Warren (Japan, Ch. 18)

Naverre, Chris (Black Panthers, Ch. 10)

Nellist, Bill (Cabanatuan, Ch. 15)

Nesmith, Clinton (Tinian, Ch. 17)

Owczarzak, Leonard (Philippines, Ch. 19)

Peniche, Ed (Bulge, Ch. 13)

Powell, Robert W. (Holland, Ch. 12)

Shaw, Dale (Guadalcanal, Ch. 17)

Stevens, Johnnie (Black Panthers, Ch. 10)

Williams, Robert (Pacific, Ch. 18)

References

Beevor, Antony, *Berlin: The Downfall 1945* (Viking Penguin, 2002)

_____, *The Second World War* (Little Brown, 2012)

Bell, Raymond E. Jr., *Black Gunners at Bastogne* (Unpublished, 1995)

Breuer, William B., *The Great Raid on Cabanatuan* (Wiley, 1994)

Calvocoressi, Peter, and Guy Wint, *Total War* (Macmillan, 1972)

Cole, Arles, *A Brief Story About My Life* (Unpublished , 1998)

_____, Notes and Diaries from WWII

Cook, Charles, *The Battle of Cape Esperance* (Naval Institute Press, 1992)

Corrigan, Gordon, *The Second World War: A Military History* (Thomas Dunne, 2010)

Cottick, Tom, *Hello Tomorrow* (Unpublished manuscript)

Crookenden, Napier, *Drop Zone Normandy* (Scribner's, 1976)

Curtis, Gene, "Artist bucked Patton to Amuse WWII Soldiers", *Tulsa World*, 1st Apr. 2007

Flanagan, General E. M. Jr., *Corregidor* (Presidio, 1995)

Folsom, Burton W. Jr., and Anita Folsom, *FDR Goes To War* (Threshold, 2011)

Frese, Janelle, *O Chaplain! My Chaplain! Man of Service* (Trafford, 2005)

Gautier, James Donovan, *I Came Back From Bataan* (Blue Ridge, 1997)

Gilbert, Martin, *The Second World War* (Henry Holt, 1989)

Hargrove, Thomas, "Massacre of Blacks in WWII . . .", *Sun Herald*, 25th Dec. 2002

Hoyt, Edwin P., *Pearl Harbor* (G. K. Hall, 2000)

Johnson, Gerald K., "Black Soldiers of The Ardennes", *Soldiers*, June 2004

Judgments of The International Military Tribunal (1946)

Killblane, Richard, with Jake McNiece, *The Filthy Thirteen* (Casemate, 2003)

Koobatian, Haig, correspondence with the author, Aug. 2006—Feb. 2007

Lantz, Jack, Flight Journal, 1944

Lichtenfeld, Norman S., *The Wereth 11* (Unpublished)

McEntee, Marni, "Town Memorializes Massacred Soldiers", *Stars & Stripes*, 20th Nov. 2002

McNutt, Michael, "Soldier Behind 'Dirty Dozen . . .", *The Oklahoman*, 27th Sept. 2012

Naval Institute Press, *The Messman Chronicles: African-Americans in U.S. Navy* (2004)

Overy, Richard, *War in The Pacific* (Osprey, 2010)

Owczarzak, Leonard, "Remembrances of V-J Day . . .", *The Exponent*, 8th Aug. 1995

Nuremberg News, "The Execution of Nazi War Criminals" (16th Nov. 1946)

Peniche, Ed, "The Cross and The Crucifix at Longchamps . . ." (Unpublished)

Reader's Digest, *The World at War 1939–1945* (Reader's Digest Books, 1998)

Roberts, Craig, "B-17 Story" (e-mails, 2nd Dec. 2006)

Ryan, Cornelius, *A Bridge Too Far* (Popular Library, 1974)

Sasser, Charles W., with Roy Boehm, *First SEAL* (Pocket, 1997)

_____, *God in The Foxhole* (Simon & Schuster, 2008)

_____, with Craig Roberts, *One Shot-One Kill* (Pocket, 1990)

_____, *Patton's Panthers* (Pocket, 2004)

_____, *Raider* (St Martin's, 2002)

Smith, Howard Kingsburg, "The Execution of Nazi War Criminals", *Eyewitness*, 16th Oct. 1946

Sun-Herald, "Chivalry in The Sky During WWII" (4th July 2005)

Tilles, Stanley, with Jeffrey Denhart, *By The Neck Until Dead . . .* (Zona Books, 1948)

Time/Life, *The Battle of The Bulge* (Time/Life Books, 1979)

_____, *The Air War in Europe* (Time/Life Books, 1979)

Time Magazine (28th Oct. 1946)

U.S. Army Headquarters 333rd Field Artillery, After Action Reports, 5th Jan. 1945)

U.S. Naval Historical Center: "Ship's Cook Third Class Doris Miller"

Utley, Freda, *The Nuremberg Judgments* (Regnery, 1948)

Wilson, Joe Jr., *The "Black Panther" Battalion in WWII* (McFarland, 1995)

Wilmot, Chester, *The Struggle for Europe* (Konecky & Konecky, 1952)

Index